MUSLIM YOUTH

MUSLIM YOUTH

Tensions and Transitions
in Tajikistan

COLETTE HARRIS

Institute of Development Studies, Sussex

Westview
PRESS

A Member of the Perseus Books Group

I dedicate this book to the young men and women of Tajikistan.

May you find your way to fulfillment and happiness.

~

Westview Case Studies in Anthropology

Copyright © 2006 by Westview Press, a Member of the Perseus Books Group.

Published in the United States of America by Westview Press, a Member of the Perseus Books Group, 5500 Central Avenue, Boulder, Colorado 80301-2877, and in the United Kingdom by Westview Press, 12 Hid's Copse Road, Cumnor Hill, Oxford OX2 9JJ.

Find us on the world wide web at www.westviewpress.com.

Westview Press books are available at special discounts for bulk purchases in the United States by corporations, institutions, and other organizations. For more information, please contact the Special Markets Department at the Perseus Books Group, 11 Cambridge Center, Cambridge, MA 02142, or call (617) 252-5298, (800) 255-1514, or email special.markets@perseusbooks.com.

Library of Congress Cataloging-in-Publication data

Harris, Colette, 1948–
    Muslim youth : tensions and transitions in Tajikistan / Colette Harris.
        p. cm. — (Westview case studies in anthropology)
    Includes bibliographical references and index.
    ISBN-13: 978-0-8133-4294-8 (pbk. : alk. paper)
    ISBN-10: 0-8133-4294-5
    1. Muslim youth—Tajikistan—Social conditions. I. Title. II. Series.

HQ799.T3H37 2006
305.23509586'09045—dc22

2005029004

The paper used in this publication meets the requirements of the American National Standard for Permanence of Paper for Printed Library Materials Z39.48–1984.

10   9   8   7   6   5   4   3   2   1

Contents

List of Illustrations

Series Editor Preface

Nestled between Afghanistan, Uzbekistan, Kyrgyzstan, and China, the land that is today called Tajikistan has long stood at the crossroads of different cultural traditions, absorbing outside influences into vibrant local and regional traditions through the various reigns of Persians, Mongols, and Russians.

The country's modern boundaries were established in 1929 by Stalin, part of his strategy to attract other Muslim states into the socialist fold, and were maintained after the country's 1991 independence from the Soviet Union. Civil war broke out soon after independence, pitting a coalition of democrats and Islamists from regions that had been excluded from power-sharing for seventy years against the neocommunist, Russian-supported government and killing more than 50,000 people. Nonetheless, following a formal peace agreement in 1997, Tajikistan has emerged as a relatively stable, apparently pluralistic state that is at least nominally democratic (President Emomali Rakhmonov has ruled continuously since independence).

In *Muslin Youth*, Colette Harris presents us with a compelling ethnography of the changes Tajikistan faces at the turn of the twenty-first century as seen through the eyes of its youth. Based on years of fieldwork in Dushanbe, the capital city, and the southern province of Khatlon, Harris takes us behind the scenes of youth culture and vividly shows the ways that gender identities are being renegotiated. We go with her to a high school sex education class and discover how boys and girls may be at cross-purposes on the subject of dating—in some ways not that different from U.S. adolescents but in other ways a world apart.

Despite the fiercely atheistic Soviet rule, traditionalistic Tajik culture maintained a typically Muslim segregation of postpuberty boys and girls. Parents arranged their offspring's marriages, and for the most part young people learned to live with their chosen partner. As Harris shows, since independence this system has been slowly breaking down. Gradually a small number of Tajik youth in the capital have adopted a self-consciously "modern" identity, as opposed to the more traditionally inclined lifestyles of their parents. This is most visible in the tight jeans and short blouses favored by the most modern young women.

In tracing changes in the job market, in education, and in family structure, Harris weaves her narrative with gripping life stories. We meet young women such as Bahorgul, who describes herself as modern and chafes at the difficulties she faces in getting an education and finding a good job. We also meet young men such as Umed, a student who observes his fellow students' casual dating with great interest, although he has decided to wait until he meets a girl with whom he can really fall in love. He is lucky; unlike many of his classmates, his progressive parents will let him choose his own wife.

From these narratives, Harris teases out the complexities of modernity versus tradition and individualism versus collectivism, showing that these are not mere binaries but rather that people take up multiple positions in relation to one or another side. Traditional Tajik collectivism creates strong social networks, often romanticized from afar. Harris shows the material and affective benefits of such networks, but she also shows how they can be oppressive, supporting androcentric and gerontocratic hierarchies. Although men are generally expected to control women, Harris reveals the tremendous power mothers have over even adult sons. They are able, for instance, to force them into such actions as marrying against their will.

Harris shows the difficult decisions parents and children face as they adapt to an increasingly globalized world. She shares with us the heart-wrenching stories of girls' ambitions cruelly thwarted by gender expectations and boys torn between competing obligations. Ultimately, however, Harris imparts an optimism born of the courage and determination of her interlocutors, young and old.

Muslim Youth turns the ethnographic gaze on the tremendous cultural changes being played out in post-Soviet Tajikistan. With compelling life stories of young Tajik women and men, Harris manages a fine balance between humanizing ethnographic particulars and social analysis of broader trends. *Muslim Youth* makes an important contribution to the Westview Case Studies in Anthropology series and to the discipline as a whole. This series presents works that recognize the peoples we study as active agents enmeshed in global as well as local systems of politics, economics, and cultural flows. There is a focus on contemporary ways of life, forces of social change, and creative responses to novel situations as well as to the more traditional concerns of classic ethnography. In presenting rich humanistic and social scientific data born of the dialectic engagement of fieldwork, the books in this series move toward realizing the full pedagogical potential of anthropology: imparting to the reader an empathetic understanding of alternative ways of viewing and acting in the world as well as a solid basis for critical thought regarding the historically contingent nature of ethnic boundaries and cultural knowledge.

Edward F. Fischer
Hannover, Germany

Acknowledgments

It is a truism to say that any author is supported by a large number of people in many different ways, not always directly connected with the writing of the book. In the present case, so many people helped me that it is impossible to name them all. I will do the best I can, but please forgive me if your name is not here.

First of all I want to thank my friends for putting up with my lack of sociability while I was working on this book. Since the only way to get it done was to spend virtually every evening and weekend on it, I accepted almost no invitations for the entire eighteen-month period I was writing it.

A couple of months before I was due to submit the manuscript, I accepted a job offer in the United Kingdom, which entailed fixing up and selling my house and moving my possessions from central Virginia to the south of England. This not only took up a great deal of time but left me homeless for the last weeks of writing. I give very special thanks to those who gave me somewhere to live during that time while I was completing this book—to Ozzie Abaye and most particularly to Margaret Merrill, whose wonderful hospitality allowed me to finish this book in peace.

Many thanks to Angela Mendes, whose support went far beyond her duties as my research assistant, and who made my life considerably easier for the last few months of writing. Thanks to her also for reading and commenting on parts of the manuscript and for discussions that helped sharpen my ideas on some aspects of this book.

Thanks to Martin Marine for drawing the Kenyatta book to my attention.

I want further to thank both the anonymous readers, whose comments greatly helped me strengthen the book, and those whose positive evaluations of my proposal persuaded Westview to publish it in the first place. You know who you are even if I don't!

In addition, I wish especially to thank Bernice Hausman, Lorraine Nencel, and Aslı Baykal for their comments on earlier drafts.

The funding for my work in Tajikistan came from various sources. I did not receive any for my ethnographic research per se and the costs of my first trip to Tajikistan were paid out of my own pocket. The following year I was able to make another trip thanks to a planning grant from the University of Amsterdam that allowed me to write a proposal for our first health project. My subsequent trips were financed first by the grant from Christian Aid of London that enabled me to set up the Bokhtar Health Project and later by the European Union's TACIS-LIEN fund. My last two visits were the result of invitations by CARE International/Tajikistan and ACT Central Asia to run workshops and/or evaluate the work of local organizations. I wish to thank all of these organizations for their support, as also the other organizations that provided funding for Ghamkhori's projects.

The people I most have to thank of course are all of those men, women, and children in Tajikistan who welcomed me and allowed me into their lives, especially those whose stories are told here. Without them there would not have been a book at all. I want to single out here Karomat Isaeva, who gave me wonderful insights into her culture and helped me greatly with my Tajik; Mouazama Jamalova for her help with arranging interviews for the book; the staff of ACCELS and of IREX for providing me with contacts with scholarship students; the faculty of the Pedagogical Institute in Dushanbe, the university in Qurghonteppa, and the high schools in both Dushanbe and Qurghonteppa, whose students I interviewed; the staff of the Open Society Institute for providing me with copies of their literature; and Tat'yana Bozrikova for her book.

I further wish to thank the staff of NGO Ghamkhori, whose collaboration in our development projects taught me so much about their country.

Finally, I give my thanks to the editors of this series—Karl Yambert and Ted Fischer—for their help and support from the time we first started tossing the idea around right through production.

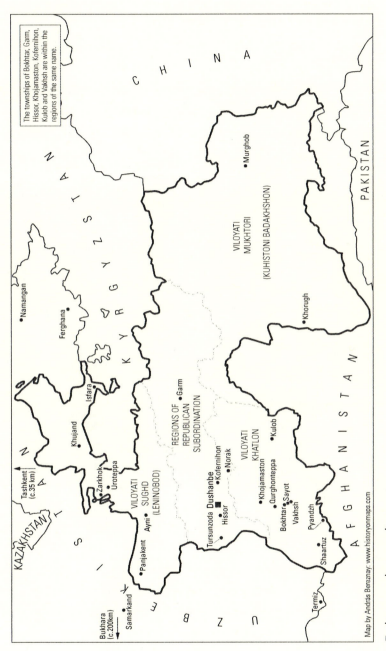

C H I N A

K A Z A K H S T A N

U Z B E K I S T A N

K Y R G Y Z S T A N

A F G H A N I S T A N

PAKISTAN

• Murghob

VILOYATI
MUKHTORI

(KUHISTONI BADAKHSHON)

• Khorugh

• Namangan

Ferghana
•

Isfara
•

Khujand
•

Zarkhok•
Uroteppa•

VILOYATI
SUGHD
(LENINOBOD)

Ayni •

Panjakent •

Tursunzoda
•

REGIONS OF
REPUBLICAN
SUBORDINATION

Garm
•

Dushanbe
Kofernihon •
Hissor • Norak •

VILOYATI
KHATLON

Khojamaston •
Qurghonteppa •
Bokhtar• Sayot •
Vakhsh •
Pyandzh
•

Kulob •

Shaartuz
•

Termiz
•

Tashkent
(c.35 km)

N

Bukhara
(c.200km)

Samarkand
•

Map by Andras Bereznay: www.historyonmaps.com

Tajikistan and surrounding region

INTRODUCTION: MUSLIM YOUTH

*I*n December 2003 I visited one of the better Dushanbe high schools located not far from the center of town, where I had been granted permission to talk to students in the top class.

About twenty students, ten of each sex, assembled in the head teacher's office. We started to discuss their lives and aspirations. One of the girls said something about modernity (sovremennost'). Intrigued, I asked them what they meant by this. Several girls said they thought it was great but they found it difficult to define. Nevertheless, they considered themselves modern. I asked them how one could tell who was modern. They started to discuss this among themselves. Finally, one of them said, "Look at my clothes. This is how you know I am modern." That day she was wearing an ankle-length jean skirt and a tight sweater with puffed sleeves. Another girl was wearing an even tighter sweater with jeans, and a third a knee-length skirt and long boots. The consensus among the girls was that all three were modern but that the utmost in modern dress could only be seen when the weather was warmer—tight jeans with short midriff-baring tops. That was the coolest of cool and super daring.

A simple skirt and blouse of the kind that in Soviet times had been worn as a school uniform was not to be thought of as a marker of modernity, it appeared, although it was better than national dress. Everyone agreed that it was completely nonmodern, practically beneath contempt, to wear Tajik national dress, and not a single girl wanted to be seen doing so. They all solemnly expressed pity for those forced to wear this in public, although they said it was fine to do so at home where no one could see.

When I wanted to know if clothes were the only marker of modernity, the girls said that this was the main way of distinguishing modern females. It was different for males. They didn't have any special clothes that could be thought of as modern. You could tell a modern boy by his manners. Modern boys are not rough (gruby) *but refined, civilized, and intellectual* (intelligentny).

The boys agreed about the way to distinguish modern girls. However, they were not so convinced about boys. They couldn't specify what made them modern. Only a few agreed with the girls that manners were part of it, but they all said there was no obvious way to distinguish modern boys by their clothes.[1]

Dushanbe, the home of these students, is the capital of Tajikistan, a former Soviet Central Asian republic. The students were of Tajik nationality and almost certainly would all consider themselves Muslims. Their parents and older siblings had been raised in the Soviet Union, and they themselves were the first generation to be exposed to clothes as markers of fashion. In the past there had been little choice. Now that Western goods were available, a whole range of different styles could be purchased in the shops and markets of Dushanbe.

It was certainly noticeable in 2003 that a huge change in women's clothing had occurred, even since my previous visit two years earlier. I had spent a great deal of time in Tajikistan over the previous decade, but I had never before seen girls dressed like this.

Looking back, I could understand why girls found dress to be such an important indicator of modernity.[2] Under the Soviet regime, women in Tajikistan had been persuaded to abandon their former regional costumes in favor of a generic national one—a loose-fitting dress, with either short or long sleeves and varying as to length, worn over a type of loose trousers known as *ezor* (see Figure I.1). A small kerchief (*rumol*) is tied at the back of the head, only partially hiding the hair and too small to reach neck or shoulders, as can be seen on the cover photo. Although Tajiks consider the wearing of the kerchief a mark of religious respect, it bears little resemblance to the head covering of religious Muslims elsewhere, which conceals head, neck, and shoulders (see Figure I.2).

In 1994, when I first arrived in Dushanbe, it was common to see women wearing national dress in the streets. Many were recent rural immigrants who had never worn anything else. Others were longtime urban inhabitants, who might wear national dress for their leisure activities but would dress in serviceable European dress at school or work. There was a scarcity of most goods in the shops, including clothes, and those that were available tended to be conservative, drab garments typical of the Soviet period.[3]

Over the following years, as fashionable clothing became common in Moscow, traders began to import it into Dushanbe. Youngsters in Tajikistan could finally buy a somewhat conservative version of the clothes they saw their contemporaries wearing on foreign television.[4]

Figure I.1 The author with girls from rural Khatlon

Figure I.2 Canadian woman wearing *hijab*

By 2003 very few women in central Dushanbe were wearing national dress, and for the first time I saw girls and young women dressed in tight jeans and leather jackets. It was not just the students from this high school; all the young people I interviewed told me they considered such clothes to be the ultimate in modernity and chic.

Most interesting of all was the fact that these youngsters claimed to be in favor of modernity, which the older generation considered alien to Tajik culture. Their forebears had struggled to prevent the culture from being destroyed by modernization, and yet these teenagers were all in favor of it. What was going on? Were these youngsters using the term *modern* in the same way their parents did? How far would their interest in modernity take them on a trajectory away from the traditions and what did all this mean for family relations? These are some of the questions I asked myself after my conversation with the students. I kept them in mind as I wrote this book.

My Research in Tajikistan

I first became involved in Tajikistan in the mid-1990s, while looking for a setting in which to study the effects of socialism on Muslim women. I had been considering Muslim communities in Western China but knew it would be difficult to do research there because of the language barrier and the reluctance of the government to allow foreigners into the area. Tajikistan was just over the Chinese border. It was no longer under Soviet control and was relatively open. Moreover, I had connections there, so it seemed a logical setting for my work. Between 1994 and 2001, I spent an average of six months a year in Tajikistan, and I have been back several times since.

Soon after my arrival in Tajikistan, my interactions with locals, especially with girls and young women, convinced me to change the topic of my study to social control. This was the subject of my first book on Tajikistan.

While working on this I began to realize that the children of my friends, particularly the girls, some of whom were the elder siblings of the students introduced above, existed in an ongoing state of tension between their own desires and the traditions espoused by their parents and society at large. Research showed this process had started with the Tsarist conquest and continued throughout the Soviet period, but its pace had accelerated sharply with Tajikistan's exposure to globalization after the end of the Soviet Union.

As outside influences began to permeate the republic, young people were the first to be affected. Films and soap operas from many parts of the world, pornographic videos, advertisements of Western products, television broadcasts of pop concerts, and scenes of youth culture shown on Moscow television were introducing new ideas into Central Asia.

Scholarships from the United States and to a lesser extent other Western countries, as well as mass labor migration to more Europeanized parts of the former Soviet Union, have given some young Tajiks the chance to experience other lifestyles firsthand. Novel commodities in the stores, including fashionable clothing, have allowed youngsters back home to experiment with new concepts and styles.

The resulting changes in dress, attitudes, and aspirations have produced clashes with the traditional ideas of the older generations. These are particularly notable in the capital and to a lesser extent in other urban areas. However, television, videos, and labor migration have also brought new ideas into rural areas.

While listening to the stories and observing the problems of these young people, I could not help sympathizing, especially with the women, who were often faced with much more complex and difficult problems than the men. Their struggles seemed daunting, and so much personal happiness seemed to depend on the outcomes. As a result, I frequently found myself taking sides with them.

LANGUAGE IN TAJIKISTAN

Tajikistan differs from countries of the South[5] in having been part of one of the two great superpowers for many decades. This gave them access to a fairly well-developed infrastructure, including universal primary and secondary education and relatively easy access to tertiary education, especially for those living in urban areas.

An important issue in this respect was language. Most of the best urban schools taught in Russian, as did institutions of higher education. Students who studied in Russian from primary school on tended to think easily in that language and to prefer it to Tajik, which some of them virtually never spoke and others did only on visits to rural areas. It was notable that they had an edge at university over students who had studied in Tajik-language schools. As a result, many parents did their best to enroll their children in Russian schools. The best-educated of the people in this book had all attended Russian-language schools.

When I first arrived in Tajikistan, my Russian was fluent but I spoke only very elementary Tajik. Over the years, my Tajik has improved and now it too is fluent, stimulated by my work with rural women. As a result I sometimes rather bizarrely found myself translating for locals who had never bothered to learn the language. A few of these were Tajik, but mostly they were Russians, Tatars, or members of other Russian-speaking ethnic groups.

The interviews in this book were carried out in a mixture of languages but mostly in Russian. With families whom I have known for many years I started out speaking Russian, but as my Tajik became fluent I began to use this with those who felt comfortable with it. With those who did not, I continued to speak Russian. The result is that the language of my discussions varied. It was not uncommon to switch back and forth during the course of a conversation or change language when someone else joined in.

In the group interviews with students, I allowed them to choose the language. In both cases we ended up in Russian, which appeared to be the language they felt most at home in, although I offered to speak with them in Tajik. This is probably because, although there are now Tajik-language streams in some universities, the best education is still given in Russian.

THE SUBJECTS OF THE STUDY

This book deals mainly with inhabitants of the Tajik capital, Dushanbe. However, I also introduce people from the southern province of Khatlon.

Tajikistan is not a culturally united republic. In fact, not all of its citizens are comfortable identifying themselves with the label *Tajik* (Edgar 2001). Nevertheless, for want of any other designation, I have used this term for people belonging to what the Soviets termed the titular nationality of Tajikistan. I feel justified in so doing since the particular elements of identity I deal with here are common to all the cultural groups to which the people in this book belong. So too are those aspects of local traditions that formed the basis of Tajik resistance to colonialism, as I explain in the following chapters.

In order to preserve their privacy, I have taken steps to disguise the identity of the people whose stories I tell here, including giving them different names. The one exception is Karomat Isaeva, with whom I had a close relationship from our meeting in 1994 until her death in November 1997 at age seventy-two. I visited her almost every day I was in Dushanbe, sometimes spending hours listening to tales of her youth, and much of my knowledge of life in Tajikistan comes from her.

As I have explained elsewhere, Karomat was anxious to be remembered after her death because she did not leave any children to keep her name alive. She therefore specifically asked me to make her name known. I have done my best to honor her request by using her real name in this book, as in my other writings about her (Harris 1998, 2004).

Most people in Tajikistan love having their photos taken, provided they get copies afterwards. However, it would clearly be an invasion of privacy to publish these in a book where their stories are presented. For this reason there are no photos in this book of any of the people who appear in it. The one exception is Karomat, who welcomed having her photos published and indeed provided me with pictures of her when younger so I could publish a greater range than I was able to take of her myself.

A number of the people presented here also appeared in my previous monograph on gender relations (Harris 2004). It is not necessary to read that in order to understand this book, but the two together give a much broader picture of life in Tajikistan and of the gender-related constraints on youth.

GENDER AND FEMINISM

The word *gender* refers to the types of behavior expected of males and females.[6] For instance, women are supposed to be caretakers while men serve as breadwinners. As a result, issues pertaining to daycare, family leave, health care, services for the mentally ill and the elderly, and so on, affect women differently from men, and thus their interests are often different. Without gender-sensitive analysis, this difference tends to be skated over or hidden from view.

My own use of gender analysis is inseparable from my identity as a European feminist ethnographer. This means that I see the whole of society as gendered and all issues as affecting the sexes differentially. It also means that I consider it my scholarly obligation to use my work to stand up for the most oppressed people in the societies I work in, whoever they may be (cf. Schrijvers 1993).

Feminism started out as a movement to address the oppression of women as a group, and for many feminists this is still its sole function. However, along with many others today, I believe that feminism must move beyond dealing with a monolithic set of women's issues to address ways in which women are implicated in other kinds of social oppression on such grounds as race, religion, class, economic position, age, and skin color.

Moreover, it is clear that men are under strong pressure to conform to acceptable gendered behavior. This is not only detrimental to them but is also a major cause of their oppression of women, as will be shown in this book. Therefore, it is my contention that masculinity is an important women's issue and that we need to work with men to help them renegotiate the way they define this, both personally and at community level.

Finally, we should consider how the social construction of young people as subordinate to their parents and as lacking the ability to make rational decisions regarding their own lives has led to the oppression of this group by adults of both sexes.

Feminism is not generally supported in Tajikistan, even by members of the women's movement.[7] From early on, the Bolsheviks took the stance that the introduction of socialism benefited the women of the Soviet working classes along with the men and that feminism was a middle-class movement deleterious to working-class interests (Lenin 1972). Consequently, feminism was banned from the former Soviet Union. In the 1970s, when women in Russia started a feminist movement, it was outlawed and many of the leaders expelled from the country (Mamonova 1984).

People in the Soviet Union had little information about the civil rights movements of the mid-twentieth century. As a result, even among women's organizations there is little awareness of issues regularly debated in the United States, including racism as well as sexism. Moreover, while women from the Tajik women's movement today may be invited to meetings of Western feminists, it is much rarer for them to have contact with feminists from over their southern border in countries like Afghanistan, Pakistan, or India.

The result is that many people still endorse the Soviet ideology that considered Islam detrimental to women, since they do not understand that it is not Islam itself but the way it is reflected through local cultures that is constraining for women. Therefore, the concept of Muslim feminism is unintelligible to most women I have spoken to in Tajikistan.

DATA COLLECTION

The data I present in this book are the result of many visits to Tajikistan. Some of those whose stories I relate are friends of long standing; others I met only once or twice. These stories were collected using ethnographic methodologies. A few came out of group discussions, but most came from participant observation and life histories.

Two group discussions were held with students. I presented part of the first one at the beginning of this Introduction; the second was with students of the Pedagogical Institute and is included in Chapter 5. For the rest, I lived and worked among the people whose stories are narrated here and interacted with them frequently, in some cases over months or even years.

Karomat's story resulted from this type of contact, as did also the story of Sadbarg and her family. The discussion with Umed took place on one day in 2003, although I had known him for some time, since I am friendly with his family. Zebi and her family told me her story over a couple of weeks in that same year. I have known Ruzikhol since 2000, and this story came out over the course of that year. Both student discussions took place in December 2003.

I lived next door to Nahdiya and her family for almost six months on my first visit to Tajikistan and have continued to visit them since. Thus, I have met all their family members many times, although I saw relatively little of the men, who were hardly ever home. Over the years I became close first to one and then another of the women. They were thrilled on my last visit to hear that the first book they were in, the one on gender relations, was finally to materialize and that I was including them in another one.

All my research subjects were aware I was writing about life in Tajikistan, and they agreed to my including their stories in my publications. Nevertheless, our interactions were informal. I never announced we were going to do an interview. Rather I simply became part of their lives. Sometimes we did things together; at others I sat quietly at gatherings, observing what went on. Much of my information was gained during one-on-one discussions, but these occurred spontaneously rather than being formally arranged. During these times, I would ask some questions but mainly would simply allow conversations to flow.

Almost none of these conversations was taped, since this would have changed the nature of the interactions. Instead, I would find a private place to write up detailed notes as soon after each encounter as possible, usually immediately.

METHODOLOGY OF PRESENTATION

Ethnographers use multiple strategies for the presentation of their materials. Very commonly they do this in the form of stories—narratives in which they describe their own personal interactions with their research settings. In this way they explicitly move their ethnographic selves onto the stage (cf. Abu-Lughod 1993; Kondo 1990). In this book I do not do this to any great extent because the narratives I present here were woven together out of material gathered during multiple interactions. Most of them concern not individuals but families. In some cases only one person's viewpoint is represented; in others multiple viewpoints appear, as first one then another person is highlighted. In order to avoid confusion, therefore, I have reported the stories in the third person, with myself as the first person narrator, where applicable.

In most chapters, the basis for the theoretical discussion is provided by a lengthy story. My aim in presenting such extensive material is to bring an unfamiliar society alive for my readers (cf. Personal Narratives Group 1989: 4). The details serve to enrich the context and make it more vivid.

Because the stories come out of particular historical moments, they also provide insights into how material circumstances intersect with cultural influences on such issues as the upbringing of young people, the kinds of personal aspirations they develop, and how these change over time (cf. Personal Narratives Group 1989: 21). This is important in a book dealing with transitions.

REPRESENTATIONAL ISSUES

An issue that confronts all ethnographers is that of representation. Questions arise such as: Who has the right to represent whom and within what parameters? Was it justifiable for me to take sides with one group, or as a scholar should I remain neutral? Was it even valid for me as an outsider to study this society in the first place? What were the implications of the fact that the majority of my research subjects were educationally and socially in a lower position than I (cf. Schrijvers 1991; Wolf 1996b: 217ff)?

It is my belief that there is no such thing as value-neutral science and that all research is ultimately subjective (Bell 1993). A scholar should take into consideration the power relations between the ethnographer and the subjects of her research, such as those resulting from the respective backgrounds of researcher and researched, those that come into play during fieldwork, and those that derive from writing about and representing others (Wolf 1996a: 2).

This is closely related to the issue of authority, in particular to that of who has the authority to speak for whom and how, and the issue of "othering" (Lal 1996). As I previously stated, it seems to me that the important point here is for the researcher to be aware of her responsibility for the knowledge she produces and to take a standpoint of support for the least powerful, such as women or youth.

In regard to studying a society other than my own, I came to the conclusion that the important point was to acknowledge that each type of relationship has something to recommend it, and it is likely that each will reveal different facets of research subjects. The truth of this was interestingly demonstrated by an experiment carried out by a Chicana, Tixier y Vigil, and an Anglo-American, Elsasser, during a research project in the United States. When each put the same questions to a group of Chicana women, they received very different answers. In this case the women were able to be more open on intimate subjects, such as sex, with the outsider (Wolf 1996a: 15). In fact, I was able to take advantage of this phenomenon in my own fieldwork. I found that people would tell me things that they would never have disclosed to someone from their own culture (cf. Harris 2004).

In the end I decided it was important to be aware of the power relations inherent in this type of work and to use them to understand the dynamic involved, rather than feeling guilty about the fact that I was a middle-class Western academic studying people largely from a lower social group in Eurasia.

Researchers such as ethnographers, who represent others, run the danger of presenting themselves rather than their subjects. I am sure my protagonists would have said quite different things to another researcher and that their perceptions of me as well as our personal interactions inevitably influenced the outcome of my interviews. In my writing, I have tried to respect the viewpoints and ideas of those whose stories I recount.

I also work from the premise that I have a responsibility to ensure that no one is hurt by my work, and if possible to see that the lives of people in Tajikistan are actually improved by my presence. However, this has occurred less through my scholarly work than through my participation in development, although my book on gender relations in Tajikistan has been used as a text at the Slovyansky University in Dushanbe.

NGO Ghamkhori

Most of the development work I have carried out in Tajikistan has been in conjunction with the local nongovernmental organization Ghamkhori. This organization started as the Bokhtar Women's Health Project, which I helped establish in 1997 in the Bokhtar district of Khatlon province with funding from Christian Aid of London. The project provided gynecological services, including contraceptives, and health education and was developed in response to requests from women in Bokhtar for birth control.

The initial success of this project (cf. Harris 1999) helped us win more funding both from Christian Aid and the European Union's TACIS-LIEN fund. In early 1999 we extended the Bokhtar project to other districts, calling it the Khatlon Women's Health Project (KWHP). At the same time, Ghamkhori, which means "care" in Tajik, formally incorporated as a nongovernmental organization.

In 2000 we were given a grant by the Swiss Development Corporation (SDC) to open a Women's Center in Qurghonteppa intended primarily to support women living in situations of violence. The Center provides educational, medical, psychological, sexological, and legal services.

Ghamkhori is still funded by Christian Aid through its membership in ACT Central Asia and has a second TACIS grant. Its projects focus mainly on health and social issues, including gender relations, sex education, and domestic violence. The NGO currently has an office in Qurghonteppa from which its more than thirty full-time employees carry out community development work in the surrounding villages.

My chief role in the organization was to carry out training, although I was also project advisor and managed the grants. As the staff learned to deal with the administration themselves, I slowly withdrew from the management side until by 2001 the organization was working independently. I draw on experiences gained while working with Ghamkhori in a number of places in the present text.

Theoretical Concepts

Discourse

The use of the term *discourse* in the social sciences today has been greatly influenced by the work of the French philosopher Michel Foucault. For Foucault, discourse refers to sets of statements that combine to produce a

Figure I.3 The staff of Ghamkhori in 2003

regulatory effect. They are similar to ideologies but more complex, owing to the fact that they are embedded in power relations, which simultaneously support and resist them (Mills 2003: 53ff).

Gender, for instance, is discursive. This means that gender norms—those characteristics attributed to masculinity and femininity within a particular society—are made known through discourse that suggests to community members the importance of demonstrating conformity. Of course, not everyone concurs. While the more powerful community members may define public discourse, they cannot prevent others from resisting, reformulating, or subverting it, since power circulates and is not only applied from the top downwards (Foucault 1980: 96–102).

Which discourses are dominant at any one time depends on power positions. The Soviet regime developed a discourse regarding Central Asian traditions that on the one hand was powerful since it had the might of the state behind it and on the other hand was ineffective due to being subverted by the Central Asians, as we shall see.

Identity

Discourse is fundamental to the construction of identity. Our ideas of what it means to be a woman, a Tajik, a Soviet citizen, or a Muslim are formed by discourse and affected by changes in it. They are also context specific. Thus, for instance, while U.S. discourse today associates Islam with terrorism, most Muslim communities conceptualize Islam as a peaceful religion.

Identities exist at the intersection of multiple indicators. Thus, words like *woman, Tajik, Soviet,* and *Muslim* are only partial descriptors. It is necessary to combine these in order to arrive at a description of a real person, such as Karomat.

At the same time, their meaning is neither fixed nor static. As we shall see in this book, in Tajikistan what it means to be a woman has changed over the past century. The meaning of Islam also continues to be renegotiated. In Soviet Tajikistan, for instance, Islam was banned in the public (Soviet) context, since all religion was considered to be against the interests of the "people," while in the private (Central Asian) context it was venerated. Again, Tajik as a marker of identity has historically had quite different meanings; its current meaning has been constructed in an effort to legitimize the Republic of Tajikistan as a nation state (Edgar 2001).

People's personal sense of identity depends both on their internal references and on other people's views of them. For instance, in July 2005, during a discussion with a group of Muslim women students in the United States, two white American women, who had converted to Islam and wore *hijab*, stated that they thought of themselves in the first place as Muslims and secondly as Americans. However, after their conversion to Islam they found themselves practically excluded from the latter group. Fellow Americans would hesitate to speak English to them, thinking they might not understand. Nevertheless, when in their husbands' home countries in the Middle East, these women were always immediately spotted as Western and probably American, even though they dressed as Muslims.

In other words, when these women changed their religion, and especially when they started wearing *hijab*, fellow Americans ceased to identify them as belonging to their own cultural group. This made them feel like outlaws in their own country. They felt as if they were being covertly informed that to be American one must be Christian, or at least part of the Judeo-Christian tradition, and that there was no space for others, despite the rapidly expanding community of American Muslims. As a result, upon changing their religion these women experienced drastic shifts not only in self-identity but also in the way others related to them.

Dualistic Models

There has been a great deal of discussion in feminist literature about the narrowness of working with dualistic models, which tend greatly to oversimplify social issues as well as to exclude potential variations (Kane 1995).

The theoretical basis for this book consists of two sets of what are conventionally seen as binaries—modernity and traditionalism, collectivism and individualism. My use of these terms moves beyond a simplistic set of oppositional pairs. As I explain in Chapters 2 and 3, I see them not as occupying fixed points but as being represented by a set of continua[8] that have at one end the traditional, collectivist lifestyles of Central Asians prior to the Russian conquest of the late nineteenth century and at the other the modern individualism displayed in Western television shows broadcast in Tajikistan.

Virtually everyone in the republic is positioned somewhere between these two extremes. People move along the continua at differing rates and not always in the same direction, and they shift position depending on context and audience. Nevertheless, most people exhibit a reasonably clear tendency towards one side or other. I indicate this by using terms such as "traditionally inclined" and "modernistic" rather than "traditional" and "modern," as the latter suggest fixed points.

In this way I have tried to make it clear that there are many varieties of the traditional and the collective as also of the modern and the individualistic, acknowledging, as Kane suggests for sportspersons (1995), that differences among those with the same overall inclination may be as large or larger than between those who come down on opposite sides of the divide.

These theories have been derived from the dominant discourse in Tajikistan, whereby people on both sides see a large gulf between the cultures of Central Asia—characterized as traditional and collective—and that of the Russians—said to be modern and individualistic. People were always explaining that *they* were different from *us*. For instance—"We Tajiks really care about our families. We revere our elders and acknowledge their rights in family decision-making. Those Russians are hard. They do not care about their families. Look how their children emigrate to Russia, abandoning their parents here to starve." Or—"Those Tajiks always obey their elders. They have to suffer arranged marriages and have no freedom to make their own decisions, while we Russians decide our own lives. We love our families but we don't see why our parents should order us around once we are grown up."

In this book I explore these issues through the two sets of concepts presented above.

Social Control

In scholarly literature social control is usually seen as control imposed from above by the state (Edwards 1988). In my earlier book on Tajikistan, I show social control to be imposed at multiple levels, by multiple actors, and not just from above. The state has a role to play, but communities also impose their own types of control. All community members, irrespective of power position, can use practices such as spying on and gossiping about others in such a way as to exert a measure of control over them (Harris 2004). In other words, social control is not one-sided but is exerted at multiple points and in various directions, and discourse plays a very significant role in its functioning (Foucault 1990: 94–96).

ISLAM IN TAJIKISTAN

There are two main branches of Islam—Sunni and Shi'a. Worldwide, about 90 percent of believers are Sunni, but Iran is largely Shi'a, and so is Iraq.

Virtually all Central Asians are Muslims. The vast majority are Sunni. However, the Pamiris, who come from Tajikistan's Gorno Badakhshon Autonomous Oblast', belong to the Shi'a Ismaili, whose leader, or *imam,* is the Agha Khan.

The rupture within Islam came about through a quarrel about who should become ruler of Arabia after Mohammed's death. The group that came to be known as Sunni, who were in the majority, elected Abu Bakr, while the group that came to be known as Shi'a supported the Prophet's son-in-law, Ali. The subsequent rift has continued to this day. Theologically, the main difference between the groups centers around interpretations of the *hadith.* There are also differences in style of worship (BBC n.d.).

Another important difference is the fact that Shi'a Muslims acknowledge the right of their religious leaders to interpolate themselves between the community and Allah. Although the Sunnis also have religious leaders, who in Tajikistan are called *mullahs,* they do not hold the same level of authority as the Shi'ite *imams.* According to religious law, each Sunni Muslim has the right to make his or her own religious decisions.

Being born into a Muslim household bears implications that go far beyond religion to encompass a whole range of cultural concepts. In theory, it is possible to be a nonbeliever and still feel and act like a Muslim, just as it is for a Jew. Indeed, in Tajikistan, the population makes little distinction between being Central Asian and being Muslim. The important thing is that they are culturally as well as religiously distinct from the atheistic[9] Russians and other non-Muslim ethnic groups.

It is for this reason that, despite decades of antireligious pressure under the Soviet regime, most Central Asians have quietly continued to consider themselves Muslims, even though few have ever read the Qur'an. Even many local religious leaders have not read the Qur'an, or at least not in any language they understand, since they can read the Arabic writing and recite the text while not necessarily knowing the meaning of the words.

Since the breakup of the Soviet Union, Islam has once again assumed an important role in Central Asian public life; organizations from other Muslim countries have helped to build mosques and open religious schools (*medressas*). Small groups of very religious Muslims exist, particularly in Uzbekistan and Tajikistan. However, they remain very much in the minority.

Islam is nevertheless important for the inhabitants of Tajikistan, who are now increasingly fasting during Ramadan, the Muslim holy month, and attending Friday prayers. A beautiful new mosque has now been built in central Dushanbe.

President Emomali Rakhmonov calls himself a Muslim, but he leads an updated version of the Communist Party in an entirely secular government. Freedom of worship exists, but the government is vigilant to suppress any suggestion of extremism. Instead, it has continued Soviet practices by promoting an official, watered-down version of Islam that has little to offer young people.

Together with President Karimov of Uzbekistan, Rakhmonov has long supported the Russian government's suppression of Islamists.[10] As an extension, he also supports the United States' war on terror.

Tajikistan is in a particularly vulnerable position, since it is immediately to the north of Afghanistan, and before the defeat of the Taliban in 2001, there were fears that the war there might spill over the border. These have now quieted down, and indeed in 2003 the threat of Islamization in Tajikistan seemed very distant, despite continued pressures from Islamist groups such as *Hizbi ut Tahrir* and others from the northern Ferghana Valley region. Only a very few of the most religious have joined the radical Islamists. Recently teachers at the Islamic University in Dushanbe complained that they had far fewer applicants than in the 1990s, despite the low cost of education there compared with secular establishments (ICG 2003: 22ff).

In fact, in Dushanbe, on the surface at least, modernization appeared to be a far stronger force than religion. Almost none of the locals I saw dressed in a conspicuously Islamic fashion. In fact, there seems to be little support for any kind of Islamization among Dushanbe's population—"I don't think people will ever support the Islamists again. When we got independence, we were told we lived for 70 years in a Soviet prison. Now we realise we lived for 70 years in paradise[11] compared to our life today," commented one young man (ICG 2003: 22).

A NOTE ON CLASS

I use the term *class* in this book to refer to a social stratification or grouping that has arisen through capitalist development. Marx defines class according to people's relations with economic production. The upper class, or aristocracy, have historically been landowners. The middle classes have been owners of the means of production—the upper middle class owning factories and large enterprises, and the lower middle class being small shopkeepers. At the bottom come the urban proletariat, or working class, whose labor provides the profits for the middle classes, and the rural peasantry, whose labor enables aristocrats to live without producing (Marx 1867).

Figure I.4 The new central mosque in Dushanbe

The economic positioning of each class is accompanied by specific educational levels and lifestyles. As Marx suggests, the ruling class—that is, the class that controls the dominant means of material production—also controls the production of ideas, since these are simply the material turned into ideology (Marx 1846: 64). In other words, it is the ruling class that produces public discourse.

Marx proposed that the best way for the working classes to flourish would be to take over the means of production communally in order to apportion the profits from these fairly among those who actually did the work (Marx 1867). After the Russian Revolution of October 1917, Lenin and his Bolshevik Party attempted to put this proposition into practice. The Soviet Union was ruled in the name of the proletariat, and the state owned all means of production.

The class system was formally abolished. This did not completely equalize all social groups. Nevertheless, by the end of the Soviet period the kind of class system found in capitalist settings had ceased to exist.

For this reason, people in Tajikistan do not generally think in terms of class. They feel that people are, or should be, equal. However, most people do accept the existence of an elite that is set apart from the rest. This consists of socially prominent, well-educated families who have usually spent considerable time outside Tajikistan, in former Soviet republics and/or abroad. Often they have a non-Tajik mother or grandmother, dating from the times that Central Asian men seeking a high-level political career were encouraged to marry European women.

During Soviet times there was little in the way of class differentiation among the rest of the populace. Since many urban families were only one or two generations away from the village, close ties were often kept between them and intermarriage was common, thus leveling out potential class differences.

The result was that urban Tajik culture remained very similar to rural culture. A high educational level was not an acceptable excuse for contravening the most important of the traditions, particularly those to do with gender identities.[12] So the families of university professors and senior researchers at the Academy of Sciences seem to live by very much the same rules as everyone else.

A newly emerging social group is known as the "new Tajiks." They are essentially the *nouveaux riches* who have made their money through trading. They splash money around, build enormous houses in Dushanbe and elsewhere, and are starting to live very differently from other Tajiks. I do not know any of them personally and this book does not deal with them.

Families that have lived in Dushanbe or other urban areas for several generations and whose members have typically gone on to higher education will be likely to speak excellent Russian, have good connections, and send their children to the Slovyansky[13] rather than the Tajik State University. Some of them may even speak English and work for an international organization. This gives them a certain resemblance to the elite. Such families tend to have modernistic leanings and to be flexible regarding their offspring's aspirations.

Although distinct social classes do not exist, there is somewhat of a social distance between the more educated families described above and the less educated majority. Despite all this, the traditions all these families live by are remarkably similar.

TENSIONS AND TRADITIONS

The tensions this book deals with arise mainly from pressures towards one side or other of the above-mentioned continua. I define traditionalism and modernity in Chapter 2, where I explain how people from the area that came to be known as Tajikistan were confronted with new worldviews that challenged their previous customs and stimulated the development of intercultural tensions. After analyzing the pressures towards modernity initiated by the Soviet regime, I consider how similar pressures are being experienced today upon contact with globalization.

In Chapter 3, I define collectivism and individualism and show how these affect family relations in Tajikistan. I further look at how young people feel constrained by collectivism, even though they are deeply and inescapably embedded in their family relationships and appreciative of the protection these afford them in a society with no social safety net.

Chapter 4 continues the theme of tensions, this time examining how they arise through contradictions between Tajik culture and a modernistic education system and job market. Chapter 5 looks at how the burgeoning desire of young people in Dushanbe to make their own life choices finds expression within romantic friendships, and investigates the intergenerational and intersexual tensions this causes.

Finally, Chapter 6 analyzes the characteristics of modernistic and traditionalist family types. It explores how families can move between the two types and how this affects family relationships. It examines current trends and estimates numbers of modernistic and traditionally inclined families in the republic.

The book ends by demonstrating how levels of intergenerational tensions are dependent on rates of social change. It describes ways in which traditionalism and collectivism have served to protect society from the worst of the post-Soviet chaos. It also points out that there is much more ambiguity in Tajikistan than appears at first glance as regards both Islam and the so-called binaries.

In relation to all these topics, the issue over which people struggle the most is that of gender identities (Chapters 2 and 3). It is this that so often pits young men and women against each other rather than uniting them against parental authoritarianism (Chapters 5 and 6).

Since the people this book deals with live in a region about which very little is generally known, in Chapter 1 I present a brief social and political history of Tajikistan. Finally, it should be noted that in order to explain the more obscure terminology, and especially the Soviet and Tajik words, there is a glossary at the end of the book.

CHAPTER ONE

HISTORY OF TAJIKISTAN

Each nation has its own unique history that plays a significant part in its subsequent development and which therefore must be grasped in order to comprehend its current situation. In the case of Tajikistan, its people are particularly proud of their long and illustrious history, which they trace back beyond Alexander the Great, and which at one time put them at the center of world civilization.

Tajikistan became a nation state in 1991, having started out as a Soviet republic in the 1920s under Stalin's leadership. Before this, the area was part of a large amorphous mass of land in the central part of Asia. By the eleventh century it had been so dominated by Turkic tribes that it came to be called Turkestan (Glenn 1999: 51). More recently, this region was split between Russian or Western Turkestan, which was incorporated into the Soviet state, and Chinese or Eastern Turkestan, currently the province of Xinjiang in the People's Republic of China. Unless otherwise indicated, the history that follows is common to all the peoples of Western Turkestan.

EARLY HISTORY TO THE RUSSIAN REVOLUTION

Central Asia is part of Inner Asia, an area stretching east-west from the Carpathians to Korea, and north-south from the Arctic Ocean to the Himalayas.[1] The Central Asian segment consists of the central steppes and part of the southern desert rim, as well as reaching south to the foot of the Himalayas in the Hindu Kush and Tien Sen mountains. It contains two major rivers, the Oxus (Amu-darya) and the Jaxartes (Syr-darya), both originally flowing into the Aral Sea.

As early as 7000 BC, the main inhabitants of Central Asia were probably nomadic pastoralists. A few millennia later Central Asia became the seat of Zoroastrianism, which can be considered in some sense to be the first world religion (Adshead 1993: 33). After 500 BC, it formed a significant part of the first interregional world empire, that of the Achaemenids, which stretched from China into Africa. Shortly thereafter the region was absorbed into the empire of Alexander the Great.

By the seventh century AD, much of Central Asia was Buddhist. However, less than two centuries later, the region had largely converted to Islam, leading to a great flowering of philosophy, science, and the arts that made the region one of the foremost centers of world civilization. The founder of algebra and of arabic numerals, Al-Khwarazmi (780–850), came from Central Asia. The poet Firdausi (d. 1020), author of the Shah-nâma, and Ibn Sînâ (980–1037; known in Europe as Avicenna), the foremost medieval philosopher best known for his *Qânûn*, were both born in Central Asia and spent most of their lives there.

In 1206 Chinggis Khan was elected Great Khan. A few years later along with his Mongol hordes he conquered most of Central Asia. By the end of the century, the Mongols had conquered China. They occupied parts of southern and southeastern Asia, and penetrated as far into Europe as Kiev and the Adriatic Sea. From 1300 to 1370 Central Asia was ruled by the Chaghatai Khanate, led by descendents of Chinggis Khan's second son. Between 1370 and 1405, the great Tamerlane, or Timur, became the most powerful conqueror Central Asia had ever seen. He built stronger and better-equipped armies than ever before and at the same time strengthened Turkestan as a trade route. Tamerlane's successors were the Timurids, who reigned until 1510.

The trade route espoused by Tamerlane was known as the silk route, along which merchants brought silk, spices, and other exotic goods from China to Europe. This was the route that had gained fame in Europe in the early fourteenth century as a result of Marco Polo's published descriptions of his travels.

After 1510 a number of lesser powers ruled Central Asia, among them the Uzbeks. In the late eighteenth century, the latter divided their polity into the three city-states of Khiva, Bukhara, and Kokand.

In the early nineteenth century, Central Asia was experiencing an economic renaissance. It was hampered in its growth, however, by its low population, apparently due to the use of birth control (Adshead 1993: 201). The low population rates continued until after World War II largely due to epidemics of measles and other contagious diseases, many of which resulted from contact with the Russians. These caused extremely high rates of infant and child mortality. Only from around 1960 did living standards improve enough to encourage rapid population growth (Harris 2002).

In the mid-eighteenth century Russia started its advance into Central Asia. In 1865 it conquered Tashkent,[2] one of the most important cities in the region. In 1868 the area that now encompasses Tajikistan came under a Russian protectorate, and by the end of the century the entire sweep of Western Turkestan was under its control.

This vast region was inhabited by many different peoples. Among them were nomadic tribes, who wandered over it with their large herds of cattle, living in enormous felt tents called yurts. Their descendants are the Kazakhs and Kyrgyz of today. Sedentary tribes who lived by cultivating the land had settled in the fertile oases, which had been divided into small fiefdoms, each ruled by a khan or emir. Among them were the peoples known today as Uzbeks and Tajiks.

By the time of the Russian conquest, these sedentary peoples had become devout Muslims, living according to *sharia*. Female seclusion was practiced, especially in urban areas. According to Muslim law, men's responsibility was to serve as breadwinners, while women carried out domestic labor. They were not forbidden to carry out income-generating activities, however. They could sew, produce silk, or make handicrafts, always provided their menfolk procured the necessary raw materials and sold their goods for them.

Only in the most desperate cases did women head households or support their families financially. However, wealthy men with far-flung business interests might take a wife in each place and entrust to her the running of their estates in that location (Harris 1996).

Married women could leave home only with the explicit permission of their husbands and/or mothers-in-law. Upper-class women might pride themselves on never leaving the house from the time of their marriage to their death (Meakin 1903: 193). However, most women did leave home on occasion, whether to visit the local bathhouses or their parents (Donish 1960). When they did so they would be escorted by relatives and bear on their bodies the "curtain" (*purdah*) that hid them from the view of strangers.

In what is now northern Tajikistan and in much of Uzbekistan this curtain consisted of the *chachvan* and *faranja*. The former was a thick veil made of black horsehair. This covered the face uniformly without finer mesh or holes at eye level. Over it was worn the *faranja*, a cloak that hung over the head and reached down to the ground, concealing the entire body (Harris 1996).

Before the Russian conquest, almost the only educational establishments in Turkestan were religious schools, which largely taught rote repetition of the Qur'an. Women religious leaders—known as *bibiotuns or bibikhalifas*—

Figure 1.1 Turkestani women spinning, circa 1900 (Meakin 1903: 38)

taught girls and led female prayer groups (Fathi 1997; Kamp 1998). *Medressas* provided more sophisticated, but still largely religious, education for young men. In the late nineteenth century Russians set up schools, mainly for their own people, and a progressive group of Tatars known as Jadidists started "new method" schools with a secular curriculum (Kamp 1998: 26–63; Tokhtakhodjaeva 1995: 26).

Turkestan grew a number of crops that could not be cultivated in Russia. The most important was cotton. One of the chief purposes of the Russian conquest had been to fill the gap left by the fallout from the American civil war that had deprived Russia of its main source of this material.

Because of this the Russians strongly promoted cotton cultivation. In order to increase it, they intervened in both the land system and the modes of production. At that time, land in Central Asia was not individually owned but rather allotted by either the secular overlords or the religious authorities. This state of affairs did not suit the Russians, who introduced the capitalist system of land as private property. Together with pressures on farmers to produce ever larger quantities of cotton, this ended up bankrupting many peasants, who were forced to sell their land, and ended up as impoverished agricultural laborers (Vaidyanath 1967: 45n51).

Figure 1.2 The *faranja* and *chachvan* at the end of the nineteenth century (Schwarz 1900: 268)

HISTORY OF THE SOVIET PERIOD

The continuation of these trends might have produced significant social change by forcing large masses of peasants off the land (cf. Marx 1867: 876), but the process was interrupted by World War I. Turkestan almost slipped out of Russian hands when in 1916 the government tried to conscript local men. Their wives sparked off a revolt in their determination not to allow the Russians to deprive their families of their breadwinners (Kamp 1998: 98–104). In the midst of the ensuing chaos came the Revolution; the Tsar was deposed and the Bolshevik Party assumed power under Lenin's leadership. By 1920 the whole of what is now Tajikistan had come under Soviet rule (Robertson 2000: 327).

The immediate post-Revolution years were difficult and chaotic. Problems intensified because of a lack of food. The Tsarist government had induced local farmers to plant cotton rather than grain, assuring them this could easily be imported. During World War I the train lines were cut. This prevented grain arriving from the north. The result was a serious famine, estimated to have killed almost a million people, which took years to recover from (Etherton 1925: 154).

Despite Lenin's reassurances, the Central Asians were highly suspicious of the Bolsheviks. This was particularly true of the region that now forms the southern part of Tajikistan. Until the 1920s this had been in the Emirate of Bukhara, not under direct Russian rule like most of Western Turkestan. Its inhabitants had therefore had little contact with Russians. They were extremely religious, having followed a very strict form of *sharia* law, and therefore especially difficult to convince of the benefits of joining a regime that was preaching atheism. They formed a resistance group known as the Basmachis, which in the mid-1920s mounted an unsuccessful military campaign against the Red Army (Rakowska-Harmstone 1970). After the Basmachi defeat, the Central Asians were forced to accept the inevitability of Soviet rule. This was especially galling, since the new regime was not content with military victory alone but was determined also to impose itself culturally on its subject peoples.

The impact of this policy was very strongly felt in Central Asia, where the Soviet regime made great efforts to produce cultural transformation. A major issue of contention was the attempt to change social organization from reliance on local elites to adherence to Party politics and cooperation with local Party cells.

Even more contentious was the issue of religion. Atheism was one of the lynchpins of the socialist regime. While it had been possible to disestablish the Orthodox Christian Church and shut down most public worship in Russia, the situation in Central Asia was very different.

The population was mainly Sunni Muslim, which had neither a central governing body nor even official clergy. Moreover, while Russians were able to separate their religious from their cultural identity, Central Asians were not. This made it virtually impossible to persuade the population to accept atheism as a ruling principle, since this would have been tantamount to denying their own cultural identity. As a result, Central Asians continued to identify as Muslims throughout the Soviet period.

Gender identities proved to be another particularly conflictive issue. In the 1920s the Bolsheviks used multiple strategies to gain the support of Central Asian women, conceptualizing them as a surrogate for the proletariat they had been unable to find in rural Turkestan (Massell 1974). These were strongly opposed and in the end only partially successful.

Therefore, the Bolsheviks decided that the best long-term tactic would be to convert the younger generation of Central Asians to its ideologies. One of the chief instruments for achieving this was the school, and Soviet ideology became an important part of school curricula.

A further tactic was to try to put an end to the institution of the extended family whereby married sons lived in their parents' homes (Rakowska-Harmstone 1970). The Bolsheviks reasoned that physically separating young people from their parents would result in psychological separation. When parents and their married offspring lived apart, it was thought, each unit would behave like a separate nuclear family. The result was supposed to be that young people would become increasingly open to outside influences, which would facilitate their acceptance of the new ideas introduced by the Party (Bacon 1966: 168).

The government tried to achieve this aim by building apartments too small for the cohabitation of extended families. However, in Tajikistan at least, physical separation appeared to make little difference. Parents still kept a tight rein over their children. Young people who attempted to move outside their parents' sphere of control were sharply brought to heel or else cast out of the family circle. Moreover, irrespective of place of residence, decision-making continued to take place in the extended family council, where older men had the most say. As a result of the firm control each generation kept over the next, the pace of social change was considerably slower than the government had hoped for (Rakowska-Harmstone 1970: 62, 275).

In the early 1930s, the Bolsheviks collectivized agriculture. Farmland and animals were pooled and made the general property either of the state (*sovkhoz*) or the collective (*kolkhoz*). In what are now Kazakhstan and Kyrgyzstan, this was accompanied by the forced settlement of the nomadic tribes. Collectivization was not achieved without enormous resistance and tremendous suffering. Among the resistance tactics was the killing by the nomads of tens of thousands of animals to prevent them falling into the hands of the Bolsheviks (Conquest 1986: 189–98).

Another strategy the regime used to control Central Asia was to divide it up into separate republics. In 1924 Tajikistan had been made into an autonomous republic under the Union Republic of Uzbekistan. In 1929, with the addition of the northern region, including Hujant, it became a union republic in its own right. By 1940, all five Central Asian republics had been created.

The Bolsheviks made Dushanbe[3] the Tajik capital. In 1924 it was an overgrown village, far from any cultural center. The Bolsheviks built schools and accommodation for workers. After World War II, monumental buildings were constructed in the center, including the parliament, the Academy of Sciences, and the university.

Figure 1.3 The Academy of Sciences in central Dushanbe

Over the following decades, the Soviet regime built roads; put in electricity, a telephone system, and a network of railways; and organized bus services. They constructed factories and workshops, stores and apartment blocks. They also established hospitals, clinics, village medical centers, schools, colleges, and universities; opened public libraries in towns and large villages; and trained the professionals necessary to work in these. Radio and television stations were established, and newspapers, magazines, and books were published in Russian and Tajik. Cinemas and theatres opened, as well as concert halls and the Dushanbe opera house. They developed a bureaucratic governing system, including police, army, the KGB, civil servants, ministries, and a parliament.

A system of universal education was set up. First primary and later secondary education became compulsory, and after the war increasing numbers of students went on to tertiary education. The standard of Dushanbe's universities was high, especially because of the presence of large numbers of intellectuals from the European regions of the USSR, who had sought refuge there during World War II.

After the war immigrants from the European republics started to arrive in Central Asia in large numbers. Many of them came to work in industry and other enterprises where there were insufficient locals willing or able to take the jobs. People of local ethnicities preferred the humanities or social sciences

Figure 1.4 Aerial view of Dushanbe

to engineering, or else remained in rural areas working in agriculture. There were not many economic incentives to be gained from factory work compared with more traditional sources of employment (Lubin 1984: 206–11).

Few women entered the formal workforce. The majority of those working outside the home were part-time agricultural laborers (World Bank 1994).

From the late 1950s, improved nutrition levels produced better health. Combined with local cultural ideals and material rewards for having children, this resulted in some of the largest family sizes anywhere in the world. It was not uncommon to find fifteen or more children born to one set of parents (Harris 2002).

By the late 1980s, the average family had 7.1 members, rural families being on the whole considerably larger than urban ones (UNDP 1996: 82). These high birth rates, combined with the refusal of the population either to leave rural regions for urban industrial jobs or to migrate to underpopulated regions to the north, led to significant underemployment (Lubin 1984: 133–134). Together with the worsening economy of the late 1980s, this left many young Tajik men without occupation and eventually led to unrest and rioting, starting in February 1991 (Tadjbakhsh 1998).

The Soviet Union had been occupying Afghanistan since 1979. This had a significant impact on Tajikistan because of both its proximity and its cultural and linguistic similarities. Many Tajiks worked there as interpreters, which brought them into contact with strongly religious influences. In 1989, the year the wall between East and West Germany was demolished, the Soviet Union lost most of its influence in Eastern Europe and was forced to pull out of Afghanistan.

In 1985 Mikhail Gorbachev had been appointed secretary general, the Soviet equivalent of president, and had set into motion a movement called *perestroika,* or reconstruction, accompanied by *glasnost',* or openness. The result was to open up the Soviet Union to new ideas and make public some of the worst social problems, hitherto hidden under a cloak of silence.

Accompanied by the serious deterioration of the economy, this openness allowed opposition to flourish for the first time in many decades. The result was that Boris Yeltsin was elected president of the Russian Federation; in mid-1991, the Soviet Union imploded. One by one the separate union republics declared independence. So started the era of the Commonwealth of Independent States, of which Tajikistan is a member.

INDEPENDENCE

Tajikistan declared its independence on September 9, 1991. Once it became a separate state it could no longer depend on support from Moscow, and its economic situation drastically worsened. It had always been the poorest of the union republics, but independence left it in a particularly vulnerable position.

Tajikistan is a tiny country whose territory covers a mere 55,240 square miles, of which only 7 percent is as arable land, almost 80 percent of it irrigated. The rest of the terrain is too mountainous for cultivation. The country is at the foothills of the Hindu Kush and is the highest part of the former Soviet Union, with mountain peaks rising almost to 25,000 feet. The plains area has hot summers and mild winters, while the high mountains have a polar-type climate (Robertson 2000: 327; World Bank 1994: 95).

Its main agricultural product is cotton. It has only one large industrial enterprise—the Tursunzoda aluminum plant. During Soviet times the republic was dependent on other parts of the Soviet Union for grain, gas, and other vital products. This has made independence extraordinarily difficult (Islamov 1994).

By the beginning of 1992 the country was in turmoil, ending up in civil war (1992–1997). This was chiefly a struggle over access to political leadership. During the Soviet period most leaders had been from the Leninobod region, now known as Soghd. They wanted to hold on to power, while the newly formed political parties with leaders from other regions wanted a chance to share in it. The poor state of the economy facilitated the fomenting

Figure 1.5 The Fan Mountains, Tajikistan

of discontent, and the high unemployment rates provided a large contingent of unoccupied young men to co-opt into fighting forces.

The warring sides were composed of the former Communist Party on the one hand and a coalition of democratic and Islamic parties[4] together with the main party of the Pamir region, La'li Badakhshon, on the other. Owing to the fragmented nature of the Tajik nation, the two sides divided up along regional lines. Effectively this meant that the Leninobodis and Kulobis, who supported the Communist Party, banded together against the Gharmis and the Pamiris. The latter group was first known as the Islamic Democratic Opposition and later as the United Tajik Opposition (UTO) (Glenn 1999: 110–111, 125–130).

In 1992 the Opposition briefly came to power but was soon forced out in favor of the present government, under the leadership of the Kulobi, Emomali Rakhmonov. In late 1992 war broke out, most severely in the southern region of Qurghonteppa, and to a lesser extent in Dushanbe. Some 50,000 were killed, 600,000 were internally displaced, and over 500,000 left the country, many fleeing across the border into Afghanistan (Abdullaev and Akbarzadeh 2002: 39; WHO 2000: 5n6). In their absence, their cattle were stolen, their houses sacked and burned (Akiner 2001).

In late 1994, when I first arrived in Tajikistan, the worst of the fighting was over. Large numbers of exiles had returned to their villages and were busy rebuilding them. It was far from peaceful, however. Over the next few years, there were sporadic outbursts of violence. I soon became accustomed to hearing tanks rumbling past my windows at night and seeing men carrying Kalashnikovs in the streets.

During the civil war and in its immediate aftermath, the importation of grain and other food products largely stopped. Since most arable land was still sown with cotton, there was little food available. During the first winter I was in Tajikistan it was almost impossible to buy bread, the local staple food. My diaries from that period show that I mainly subsisted on potatoes and other vegetables, along with cheese, on those occasions when I could find any. The triumph with which I recorded each purchase of this last commodity points to the difficulties of living under such conditions.

Indeed, the diaries of my first couple of years in Tajikistan make somber reading. It was so hard just to survive. If this was difficult for me, living alone and with sufficient money to buy whatever food I could find, it must have been very much harder for the impoverished locals with their large families.

In a near repeat of the famine of the early part of the century, the population was this time kept alive by food supplied by the United Nations and other international agencies. These organizations also helped with the repatriation of refugees, the reconstruction of their homes, and the recovery of stolen land and houses.

In June 1997, the government of Rakhmonov signed a peace agreement with the UTO (Akiner 2001). By the end of the 1990s, almost all the refugees had returned home and the country was on its way to peace. By December 2003 it was again possible to walk safely around the streets at night.

There have been many negative consequences of the war besides a legacy of everyday violence (cf. Schrijvers 1993). One of these is the deepening of the economic woes that helped push the country into war in the first place. This was exacerbated by the emigration of the majority of the non–Central Asian population, which left the republic essentially without engineers and other skilled industrial workers. The large numbers of men killed in the war resulted in many female-headed households, which further increased poverty.

By the late 1990s, the economy had deteriorated to the extent that it was impossible for most people to survive on their official source of income. The average monthly wage at the end of 1998 was 8,590 Tajik rubles[5] (TR), or $7.20,[6] and the average monthly pension was 3,019 TR ($2.78). The minimum student grant was 330 TR a month ($0.24). Meanwhile, inflation in 1999 was at 25 percent, and the price of a very modest basket of the basic foodstuffs consumed by the average Tajik was 18,940 TR per month ($13.20)[7] (Robertson 2000: 347–50). While in 1991 families spent on average half their income on food, by 2000 they were spending 86.5 percent (Bozrikova 2003: 85).

As these figures suggest, poverty rates were very high; to purchase even the smallest amount of food necessary for survival cost several times the average income. Everyone who could find a way to do so started growing their own vegetables and even grains, as well as keeping chickens and small ruminants. Apartment dwellers would fence off the land around the buildings to plant food.

As I stated above, during Soviet times Tajikistan had been dependent on imports from the neighboring republics. Now that they are separate states this has become problematic. Tajikistan has good water sources and a number of hydroelectric plants, but despite this there are frequent electricity cuts, especially in the winter when it is needed to heat homes.

Almost half of Tajikistan's export income comes from the aluminum factory in Tursunzade. Cotton accounts for about 10 percent of exports, while tobacco, fruits, vegetables, textiles, and carpets are also exported (Robertson 2000: 329, 356).

In the last few years, the international agencies in Tajikistan have turned from relief to development aid. This is insufficient, however, to provide employment for the majority of its population. The result has been that large numbers of men and, to a lesser extent, women have begun seasonal migration to the Russian Federation for labor purposes. It is estimated that some 800,000 people, around a third of the Tajik work force, are regularly employed in Russia, often under extremely bad conditions (ICG 2003: 32). Recently, whole families have started settling there.

In 1999 the population of Tajikistan was around 6.5 million, of whom some 62 percent were Tajik. The largest other groups were Uzbek, Russian, Tatar, and Kyrgyz. However, owing to emigration, the numbers of Russians and other European ethnic groups have fallen significantly since Soviet times.

The adult literacy rate is around 97 percent. However, this is dropping in the younger generation. In the mid-1990s Tajikistan had the lowest percentage of

Figure 1.6 Barakat Market in Dushanbe

young people in primary and secondary school of any former Soviet republic (ICG 2003: 6; Robertson 2000: 327–330).

Crime is growing and many young people are involved with drugs. Neighboring Afghanistan supplies a high proportion of the world's heroin, and most of it passes through Central Asia on its way west. In Tajikistan, as of 2003, 61 percent of drug users were under thirty and over 95 percent were male. However, females are increasingly using drugs also (Drug Control Agency 2003). Among the consequences of addiction have been a rapidly growing HIV-positive population, large numbers of birth defects, and a dramatic rise in both the extent and the brutality of domestic violence, including femicide (Harris 2005b). Together with poverty, malnourishment, and poor health, this has resulted in a dramatic fall in life expectancy—from seventy-five years in the 1980s to between sixty and sixty-four today (ICG 2003: 1).

The population of Dushanbe has gone from some 500,000 inhabitants in 1991 to over a million, but without any new buildings. Large Tajik families take over apartments formerly inhabited by much smaller Russian ones. The city center is small but there are a number of suburbs (*mikrorayony*). It has a cheap but crowded public bus system and a network of more expensive minibuses, along with increasing numbers of private vehicles. Cafés, restaurants, nightclubs, bars, and stores selling a wide variety of merchandise can be found in the central area. A number of small and several large markets provide a venue for the cheaper food products, as well as an outlet for clothes and household goods.

Meanwhile, the Tajik government is working to develop a viable new state (Akbarzadeh 1999). It is hampered in this effort both by economic and political problems inherited from Soviet times and by tremendous levels of corruption.

It is difficult to tell how much support the government actually has, since the official numbers of votes are unlikely to reflect this. In view of the way Rakhmonov and his successive administrations have systematically excluded non-Kulobis from positions of power at all levels, it would seem likely that there is little support for him by those from other regions. However, there has not been a candidate sufficiently strong to challenge him successfully. This is particularly difficult since Rakhmonov controls the army, police, and most media, and the civil war has made people fearful of being drawn into further conflict. For this reason, there is little overt opposition.

In any case, the inhabitants of Tajikistan are too busy trying to survive to organize any concerted opposition. Moreover, the high levels of migration referred to above have greatly reduced the numbers of young men in the republic. Thus, what the Soviet government had been unable to accomplish when they tried to persuade Tajiks to migrate to more prosperous northern regions, poverty has now achieved. Moreover, in spending large amounts of time outside the republic young men are systematically separating themselves from their parents, and thus from their cultural influence.

It remains to be seen whether Tajikistan will continue its modernizing trend or whether its people will react to the increasing social chaos by returning to more traditional lifestyles dating from the times before the Revolution.

Figure 1.7 Cult of personality. President Emomali Rakhmonov's portrait on the Qurghonteppa town hall below a bust of Lenin

CHAPTER TWO

TRADITIONALISM
VERSUS MODERNITY

While the Tsarist regime had produced social change in Turkestan mainly as a by-product of the introduction of capitalist relations of production, the Soviet government made a conscious effort to change cultural practices in the region. At first, the fierce resistance of the locals made this very difficult. Nevertheless, by the end of the 1920s the Bolsheviks had started to make some headway. They did this by making laws that declared many local customs illegal and pressuring veiled women, found mostly in Uzbekistan and Tajikistan, to show their faces in public.

The following story narrates what happened when one Tajik family joined the Communist Party and went to work for the Bolsheviks. It shows how its members were torn between two lifestyles and how they coped with this, at times following more modernistic, at others more traditional, practices.

Karomat Isaeva was born in her mother's native village of Zarkhok in 1925. Her father was from the nearby town. He was a religious man, who had studied in a medressa, unlike her uneducated mother.

In the late 1920s Karomat's father was conscripted into the Red Army and did so well that afterwards he was invited to join the Communist Party. By that time their region had been incorporated into the newly formed Republic of Tajikistan. He and his wife went to the recently established capital, Dushanbe, to study. Afterwards he became a Party official, his wife a teacher.

Previously, Karomat's mother had worn the faranja and chachvan. In 1930 the Bolsheviks had come to their village and ordered the women to burn their veils. They started a big fire, lined up the women, and forced them to throw their veils on it. Although Karomat was only five, the memory of what she saw that day was so vivid it remained with her all her life. Some of the women, she said, were too scared to obey the officials. They had never imagined going out in public, exposing their faces to men. The very thought was horrifying. Others were scared of what their husbands might do to them afterwards. The officials had to tear the veils out of these women's hands. This caused some of them almost to fall over, so tightly were they clutching them. For a long time afterwards, Karomat said, most of the women would put some sort of cloth on their heads and pull it around their faces whenever they saw a strange man. She thought that without their covering they looked like plucked chickens, but gradually they got used to going around unveiled and stopped trying to cover themselves.

Karomat's mother voluntarily threw her veil on the fire. Her husband had told her he would support this. He was already planning on attending Party school and knew he would be in trouble there if his wife were veiled. In any case, despite his religious education, he was pretty liberal, Karomat said, and did not mind his wife's face being seen in public.

Karomat had her first encounters with Russian culture through the teachers in her Dushanbe kindergarten, which she attended while her parents were studying there. They taught the children how to live like Russians, dressing them in European-style trousers in winter and shorts or short skirts in summer, and teaching them how to sit on chairs,[1] draw pictures, and play games. They also taught them good manners, Russian-style.

Party officials kept a watchful eye on local cadres, who knew it was dangerous to be seen following religious rituals such as praying or fasting, which were frowned upon. Therefore, after they left the Party school, Karomat's family continued to follow many Russian norms while simultaneously observing many local traditions. Thus, they neither prayed nor fasted. They cut their daughters' hair short,[2] dressed in European clothes, and even drank alcohol[3] on occasion. Nevertheless, Karomat's mother had to ask her husband's permission to leave the house, as did the daughters. Whenever he was at home, her father expected instant attention to his needs, demanding that his womenfolk wait on him hand and foot.

Karomat attended Russian schools, which gave her a good grasp of the language. However, she had many negative experiences there because of her lack of understanding of Russian culture. For instance, in Tajik it is customary to address schoolteachers as muallim *(teacher). Russians, however, call teachers by their first name plus patronymic. Karomat had not understood this, and after she once addressed her Russian teacher incorrectly, the other children started to*

jeer at her, and in the playground at breaks they would mimic her way of talk-
ing. Karomat was very upset by this. She was the only Tajik in her class and had
no defense against this racist bullying. At times it got so bad it made her hate
school. However, she hid this from her parents, so as not to upset them. Both as a
child and as an adult Karomat experienced similar episodes. She said that Rus-
sians often treated locals badly, pushing in front of them in queues and saying
derogatory things about them in the street. This made her furious.

Karomat's childhood was disrupted in 1941 when the Soviet Union entered
World War II. Her father was conscripted into the army and sent to the war
front. As the eldest child, Karomat became her mother's mainstay since her par-
ents had no family in Dushanbe to help out.

The government closed the schools and commanded older students to enter
employment. At first only boys did so because females rarely worked outside the
home. When rationing was introduced, however, families had to have a member
in the official workforce in order to be eligible; this obliged many of them to allow
their daughters to go out to work. Karomat had no brothers old enough, so at age
fifteen she started in her first job.

During the war everyone was made to work very hard and for long hours.
They worked seven days a week without any holidays or vacation time.⁴ The
only days on which Karomat didn't have to go to her place of employment were
when she was needed for other types of war efforts. One important seasonal task
was harvesting cotton.⁵ Everyone who could be spared would be sent into the
fields and made to pick from dawn to dusk.⁶

Karomat's first job was in a printer's workshop. She really loved it; seeing how
materials were printed fascinated her. She worked as a typesetter, using a ma-
chine a little like a typewriter. Later she worked as an assistant in a scientific lab-
oratory. There were only two Tajiks working there; the rest were European
women, mainly Russians. The laboratory didn't pay very well so Karomat was
eventually forced to take less interesting but higher paid jobs, such as cleaning or
carrying water, since with her mother and four younger brothers and sisters to
feed they needed all the money they could get. Her father's army pay was too low
for them all to live on.

Despite the stresses of wartime, Karomat managed to enjoy herself. She loved
going to the cinema, for instance. She went whenever she could, and saw all the
latest films, many of them stories of life on a collective farm, with romances be-
tween rosy-cheeked young farm laborers and tractor drivers.

Not long after she started her war work, Karomat met seventeen-year-old
Khudoydod, a young man who had been kept out of the army by a bronchial ail-
ment. The two soon become good friends. However, in those days boys and girls
could not mix openly. That would have been shameful. Dushanbe was very
small, and there was no way for them to go anywhere together without being

seen, so they got round this by arranging to go to the cinema or theater at a particular time.

Karomat would go with a group of about four or five girlfriends, while Khudoydod would go with the same number of boyfriends, each of whom was interested in one of the girls. The boys would walk in front and the girls behind, because in Tajikistan women don't walk in front of men. In the theater also, the boys would sit in front and the girls in the row behind so it wouldn't be obvious they were together. By the time the show finished, it would already be dark. As they walked home, the boys would go very slowly, and the girls would tread hard on their heels so they would practically trip over each other. Thus, they would begin to talk. There would be few people on the street and little light. In this way, the two groups were able fleetingly to split into couples, each of whom was able to snatch a few precious minutes of private conversation without anyone else knowing. In this way Karomat and Khudoydod secretly courted for two years.

Shortly after Karomat turned seventeen, the government issued a decree calling all single women to the front for war work. Her mother was in despair. How would they survive with no one to support them or even get them a ration card? She was needed at home to look after the children. The next child after Karomat was still too young to work. In any case, there was no way she was going to let her unmarried teenaged daughter go to the front. Who knew what might happen to her there? Afterwards nobody would marry her. Karomat and her mother pondered the question over and over. Finally, they decided there was only one way out—she must get married as soon as possible.

Once it was known she was interested, Karomat's mother received a number of offers for her daughter's hand, including one from Khudoydod's family. Without revealing that she knew him, Karomat was able to persuade her mother to pick her friend. In this way they were able to marry. When Karomat's father returned from the war, he was furious to find his daughter had married without waiting for him to make the arrangements. He believed that a child had no right to marry without her father's approval.

After the wedding, Karomat moved in with her husband and mother-in-law. Their family had had much less contact with Russian culture than Karomat's (Harris 1998) and so lived more traditionally. Her mother-in-law wore Tajik dress. Within a few months she had persuaded her kelin[7] to do likewise (Harris 2004: 86).

As soon as Karomat's father returned from the war and started to support the family once more, Khudoydod ordered his wife to give up working and stay at home like a good Tajik wife. She was not happy about this but felt obliged to obey. However, later on she managed to persuade him to allow her to go out to work again. She was bored at home, especially as Khudoydod was a long-distance truck driver and therefore absent much of the time.

Karomat had an excellent relationship with her mother-in-law, who soon became as dear to her as her own mother. She was devastated when she died when Karomat was thirty-eight. Karomat had borne three children, but all of them had died in infancy, and by this time it was clear she was not going to be able to have any more. Her mother-in-law had protected her from Khudoydod's other family members, but after her death Karomat found herself constantly under attack by them. They would tell her she was bad and selfish because she had no children yet occupied such a huge havli, while they all had smaller and more crowded homes. Eventually, she became so annoyed at their constant whining she decided to divorce her husband so he could marry again and have children. Khudoydod did not want her to leave him but she insisted.

After her divorce, Karomat moved back with her parents, with whom she lived until their deaths, and went to work in the Dushanbe Textile Factory, where she made many Russian friends. Nevertheless, she resented the way Russians would put on airs of superiority. For instance, one of her acquaintances used to mock Tajiks for sleeping on kurpachas *on the floor. Civilized people, she maintained, slept in beds. After the end of the Soviet Union this woman became so poor that she was forced to sell much of her furniture. She shamefacedly admitted to Karomat that after all it wasn't so bad sleeping on the floor. Karomat told me scornfully, "You see. This is what comes of their snooty attitudes! In the end pride comes before a fall. These people are really horrible. She is poor because*

Figure 2.1 Karomat as a young woman after resuming national dress

her children emigrated to Russia and abandoned her here. We Tajiks would never do such a thing. We respect our parents too much. Only Russians are so inhuman as to behave in this way."

Figure 2.2 Karomat in old age poised between the traditional and the modern. She is seated on a *kurpacha* in front of a *dastarkhon;* behind her are two chairs and a table.

After Karomat's father retired he resumed many of the customs of his youth. He wore local attire, stopped drinking alcohol, prayed, and fasted. As she grew older, Karomat also began to turn to the old customs. During the last few years of her life, she even tried to stop her family members from speaking Russian in her presence, insisting on their using Tajik instead. She also strongly encouraged them to maintain the traditions, and was adamant that Tajiks must continue to live by them. "We are not like Russians," she would say, "They have no traditions. We Tajiks have strong traditions. They made us what we are. We are nothing without them."

Karomat's story shows how it is possible to embrace some aspects of modernity while simultaneously retaining many local traditions. She felt ambivalent about the Russian lifestyle. Nevertheless, as a girl she had welcomed the freedom to meet with Khudoydod and thereby to be able to choose her own husband, even if she did not seek to date in the Western sense of the word. She did not try to break with the traditions over this, instead managing to manipulate them while outwardly appearing to conform. In this way, she managed to have the best of both worlds—she chose her own husband and simultaneously allowed her mother to think she had had a purely arranged marriage.

Similarly, Karomat's parents made a public show of practices that suggested they had adopted modernity, while their behavior in private essentially negated this. Thus, Karomat and her sisters never wore veils, and her mother did not resume hers after the official unveiling in her village. They even cut their hair short. At the same time they retained traditionalistic patterns of social interaction, especially the local sets of gender identities that emphasized female submission and young people's obligations to obey parental authority.

In old age nothing could sway Karomat from her firm belief that for Tajiks the local customs were the best. She conceded that the Russian lifestyle worked well for Slavs but insisted that this had nothing to do with her. It was a matter of culture. Each community had evolved its own best possible lifestyle and should not change it.

These ideas are very similar to the opinions of Muslims in Western Europe, who reject most of the modern features they see there in favor of their own culture (Vertovec and Rogers 1998). This contradicts the Western belief that all societies will eventually reject their own traditions in favor of modernity. Both in Tajikistan and Western Europe, people who felt under attack by pressures towards modernization were able to turn their traditions into a structure in the Lévi-Straussian sense (Hénaff 1998), in order to protect their cultures. That is to say, through repeatedly referencing their customs, they turned them into a "formal" structure, as I describe below.

THE MEANING OF TRADITION

It was not only Karomat and other Tajiks who talked frequently of Tajik traditions, but also Russians. "Those are their traditions," they would tell me. "That is how they live." When I tried to find out what exactly they meant by this, they would explain that Tajiks were "different from us Europeans." The implication was that, despite the benefit of contact with Soviet culture, Tajiks had stubbornly maintained their (backward) traditional lifestyles.

Karomat and her compatriots suggested the same thing. They told me they lived according to ancient customs that had originated in the mists of the historical past and subsequently been followed by generation upon generation of Tajiks (Akbarzadeh 1999: 157).

The question is whether customs can really stay the same over so many years and in spite of the many significant material changes that have taken place. Was it really possible that women's abandonment of seclusion and the veil, their education, and their entrance into formal employment had had no effect on their lifestyles? Some changes had to have taken place (Northrop 2004: 27). It certainly did not *look* as if the Tajiks were living in a truly traditional society (cf. Kandiyoti 1996).

A traditional society is one in which traditions function as an organizing principle, where people honor the past and value its symbols, which reflect the experiences of their ancestors (Giddens 1990: 37–38). Such traditions also organize time, since they connect the past and the future. They are normative and moralistic, and as such binding on group behavior. At the same time, the continuity provides a feeling of safety (Giddens 1994: 62–66).

Hobsbawm (1983) points out that such traditions are unselfconscious repetitions of practices that, as Butler suggests, eventually produce seemingly solid residues, which then seem to be a force of nature. We call these residues traditions or customs (Butler 1995: 135). They may appear to be static, but this is only because each repetition is varied so slightly that it is barely noticeable. This gives traditional societies their air of continuity, while simultaneously providing space for change (Harris 2004: 15), and enables them to respond to new circumstances by adapting current customs or producing new ones as necessary (Vansina 1990 in Ranger 1993: 75–77).

What distinguishes such customs from what Karomat was talking about is the fact of their being an *unselfconscious* organizing principle. The very fact that people in Tajikistan were able to make explicit reference to their traditions suggests that they were consciously following them.

Hobsbawm calls the unselfconscious kind of tradition *customs*, employing the term *tradition* to designate a set of practices "invented" in the recent past, often with the intent of producing symbolic normative power—for instance, for the purpose of legitimizing authority. It may also be used to give an air of continuity and coherence to practices connected with new political formations. In this case, there is a conscious attempt to preserve social cohesion within a specific social group.

This type of tradition is produced deliberately, with the aim of influencing the community at large, and so enters public discourse. The result is that it becomes relatively fixed and difficult to vary (Hobsbawm 1983: 1–9), in part because this is a kind of (oral) codification (Foucault 1990: 101–102).

I suggest that what occurred in Tajikistan was the use of Hobsbawm's concept of tradition as an anticolonialist strategy to preserve local culture and power structures and simultaneously resist cultural penetration (cf. Nandy

1983, 2004: 17–23). In order for this to have legitimacy, the sets of traditions in question had to look as similar as possible to the previous customs for them to appear a seamless continuity of them.

In Tajikistan this occurred not as the carefully planned strategy of a political party, as in Hobsbawm's example, but rather as an attempt to preserve an earlier way of life despite alterations in material circumstances. This attempt was led by religious and other community leaders[8] and was not identical across the republic. In each region the "new" traditions copied local customs. As a result, countrywide they differed in regard to many aspects of daily life. However, as far as gender was concerned there was relatively little differentiation, at least among the Sunni Muslim group to which Karomat and her family belonged.

COLONIAL HISTORY AND TRADITIONALISM

In the late nineteenth century, the arrival of Russian settlers in the wake of the conquest had brought Central Asians into contact with a group of people whose way of life was qualitatively distinct from theirs, most especially as regards the behavior of their women. Russian women worked alongside men and walked around openly in the streets with their legs and faces exposed. The women of the sedentary peoples of Central Asia on the other hand never appeared in public unless covered from head to toe, most of the time remaining secluded in their homes. For both groups the sight of the other's women produced a deep culture shock (Harris 1996).

During the late nineteenth century these two cultural groups coexisted without much interaction. The Tsarist government was not intent on creating social change and did little to interfere with Central Asian customs (Kamp 1998). This was not the case for the Tatars who had accompanied them to the region. They were Muslims and as such felt a strong cultural connection to the Central Asians. However, their longer contact with the outside world had exposed them to new ideas that brought them to question the current organization of Muslim societies. Among the most important issues under discussion were the introduction of secular education and the emancipation of women.

The Tatars derived these ideas from other Muslim countries, such as Egypt, Turkey, and Iran, where the intellectuals were trying to develop ways of improving living standards. This was a time when the question of whether the adoption of Western-style modernity would prove a successful route to prosperity was hotly debated in the Muslim world[9] (Ahmed 1992; Kamp 1998). Tatar intellectuals were in favor. As a result, their most progressive social groups had accepted secular education, as well as women's right to mobility.

Many of the Tatar women who came to Central Asia were professionals—schoolteachers or doctors. They were as upset as the Russians at seeing the veiled Turkestani women and the customs that seemed to oppress them so strongly (Kamp 1998).

The new ideas Tatars brought with them to Central Asia set off fierce debates there. These created tensions for Central Asian women, especially for those few who welcomed the idea of change (Kamp 1998: 27–28), since they were unable to prevail against existing customs. A Western traveler observed that Turkestani women, together with some of the younger men, were annoyed with the Russians for not making it possible to end female seclusion. The older men were not in favor of this, and since they held the dominant power position their views prevailed (Bourdon 1880: 151). Apparently, however, once introduced to the idea that they could live a different kind of life, some women preferred to leave their husbands and become prostitutes rather than put up with the harsh control of their marital households (Schuyler 1876: I, 124).

From the Russian conquest on, numerous debates occurred over these issues. Some Central Asians were very much in favor of adopting a modernistic worldview; others insisted that the old ways were all that stood between them and the social chaos that would result if people persisted in sinning against the will of Allah (Kamp 1998: 26–63).

These debates introduced Central Asians to the concept of questioning their own customs. Once this had happened they could no longer so easily take them for granted. They had entered public discourse and thus become visible. Moreover, the very fact that there were debates around the possibility of changing them meant that they were not after all part of the natural order but man-made, despite claims that they had come directly from Allah.

BOLSHEVIK INTERVENTION IN LOCAL TRADITIONS

These local debates were interrupted by the Revolution. After 1917 the Bolshevik-led government was determined to impose its own ideology on the peoples of the new state. Its members wanted both to set the goals and to control the pace of change.

The 1917 Russian Revolution had been carried out in the name of the proletariat. On November 15, 1917, Lenin declared all the peoples of the Russian Empire to be equal and to have a right to sovereignty, self-determination, and secession from the union (Caroe 1967: 105). However, soon afterwards, the Fourth Regional Congress of Soviets declared that the principle of self-determination of peoples was to be subordinated to socialism and defined this solely as the self-determination of the "toiling classes" (Park 1957: 19).

Lenin saw Central Asia as barbaric, savage, and completely alien. He was baffled by the question of how to tackle such a backward region so as to incorporate it into socialism. He was also troubled by the chauvinistic tendencies of many of the Russian revolutionary leaders, who openly talked about Turkestan as fit only to be a source of cotton and other raw materials, rather than as an integral part of the new state (Lenin 1960: 504). He was particularly concerned since he saw Central Asia as the place that other Asian and African peoples would look to when deciding whether or not to fight for socialism in their own countries, and he therefore believed that the future of world socialism might hinge on developments there (Massell 1974 : 41–55).

One of the problems the Bolsheviks faced in Central Asia was that they had conceived of the Revolution as being spearheaded by an urban proletariat, not by a rural peasantry. In Russia, they never accepted the peasants as capable of forming a revolutionary force in the way that the proletariat did, instead treating them as reactionaries (Marcuse 1961: 33–43; Massell 1974). This was made possible by the fact that in Russia the Bolsheviks had a large enough proletariat to support them. However, there was no discernible proletariat in nonindustrialized Central Asia. The vast majority of the population were peasants even less inclined to accept revolutionary ideas than their Russian counterparts.

This put the Bolsheviks in a difficult position. By the mid-1920s, they had already managed to conquer the Central Asians physically in their defeat of the Basmachi revolt. However, in order to bring them into the Revolution they needed to conquer them mentally as well. To this end, they looked to the least powerful groups for support.

They started with the poorest peasants. When they could not persuade them to embrace socialism, they courted the young men, whom they saw as occupying a subordinate position, but this did not work either. In a last attempt to penetrate this cultural fortress, the Bolsheviks went after what they saw as the most oppressed and vulnerable group of all—the women (Massell 1974).

The sight of women in what are now Uzbekistan and Tajikistan wearing the *faranja* and *chachvan* appeared to provide conclusive evidence of deep discrimination. These women seemed so much more subordinated than the most deprived Russian peasant women.[10] When other local customs were added to the mix, this made women's position seem even more horrendous. The concept of the arranged marriage appeared monstrous, and bride-price was seen as purchasing women and therefore making them into objects, possessions little different from cattle[11] (Massell 1974; Northrop 2004).

As a result of their conceptualization of women as oppressed, the Bolsheviks were able to justify trying to free them. They drew up a code of laws to proscribe what were termed "crimes of daily life"—polygyny, underage or child marriage, forced marriage, and the payment of bride-price (Northrop 2004: 243). Officials were expected to be vigilant, take offenders to court, and see they were sentenced to prison. However, this rarely happened since both offenders and officials were usually locals who followed the same traditions (Northrop 2001).

The Bolsheviks also decided to try to rescue women from the "monstrous" custom of seclusion. Their main tactic was to persuade women to remove their veils, which were presented as thoroughly dehumanizing. One of the regime's Western supporters, who visited Central Asia in the 1930s, declared that a "woman dressed in a *paranja*. . . looks like a ghost, a walking darkroom, . . . [a] formless, repulsive silhouette" (Halle 1938: 104). Another claimed that veiled women looked like "silhouetted upright coffins" (Maillart 1935: 150). Still another maintained that the costume they wore was "monstrous and degrading," the women resembling "living corpses" (Kunitz 1936: 274).[12] This was typical of Bolshevik discourse on the subject also (cf. Raskreposhchenie 1971).

In 1927 the Bolsheviks started their attack (*hujum*) on this custom, hoping to force large numbers of women to abandon their *faranjas*. Most mass unveilings took place in large towns (Massell 1974), but sometimes they were organized in smaller places, such as Karomat's village. In reality, the numbers of women who unveiled were very small. Moreover, most of the women who did so in the early days, such as during the ceremony for International Women's Day on March 8, 1927, in Tashkent (Pal'vanova 1982), quickly resumed their veils afterwards (Halle 1938: 174; Strong 1930: 273).

The Bolsheviks had assumed that the chance to leave seclusion and receive equal treatment with men would be attractive to Central Asian women, who would come out en masse in favor of Soviet rule and Soviet ideology. Unfortunately, they sadly miscalculated. Some women, it is true, took advantage of the Bolsheviks' offer. However, it appears that this may have been because they had little to lose. They were largely women who had become alienated from their families and who were only too happy to become part of the Soviet family instead. The Bolsheviks took these women, educated them, placed them in high positions, and used them to promote their ideology (Massell 1974).

Most Central Asian women, however, were reluctant to adopt Soviet ideology. Some had practical reasons for wearing the veil, such as for protection against harassment. Others simply clung to the lifestyles they were used to.

They may not have seen the Bolshevik alternative as preferable. Karomat's mother, who told her daughter many stories of her life before the Revolution, seemed largely to have enjoyed her childhood and youth. Her accounts of life in her native village in what is now northern Tajikistan portray it as hard but generally pleasant. Women had to work a great deal, but on holidays they could go out and enjoy themselves. Itinerant performers would come around and play music, and everyone would have fun with games and feasting. These women were content with their way of life, and it took force to get them to abandon it.

Apart from life histories collected by contemporary scholars, there is little evidence of how Central Asian women felt about the Bolshevik pressures. The historian Marianne Kamp quotes Tajie, a Turkestani woman who published a letter in 1906 in the earliest Muslim women's periodical in Tsarist Russia. According to Tajie, Central Asian women were among the most oppressed in the world. They were badly treated by their husbands or abandoned without resources, so that they were forced to turn to prostitution to survive. Tajie welcomed the newly established Tatar schools, where children could learn about the liberating influence of the Qur'an and thereby realize that many Central Asian customs that oppressed women had nothing to do with Islam. She thought that this would open the door to change (Kamp 1998: 26–30).

Like this letter, other published accounts of women from both the pre- and postrevolutionary periods mostly present highly negative stories of women's oppression at the hands of parents, in-laws, and/or husbands. Clearly much of this was propaganda against the Central Asian lifestyle first by Tatars and later by Bolsheviks (Kamp 1998).

When Kamp interviewed older Tajik and Uzbek women about their youth and asked about their experiences of veiling as well as about their reactions to unveiling, she received highly varied answers. Some women had felt oppressed in prerevolutionary times, others had not. Some had disliked wearing the veil and abandoned it as soon as possible, while others had felt comfortable wearing it and left it off with reluctance. Eventually, all the women unveiled, but they did this at their own pace, often over a long period during which they wore the veil at some times but not at others. Some women felt so uncomfortable after unveiling that they would try to hide their faces in the street (Kamp 1998: 269ff).

Materials from other sources suggest similar reactions. One woman said she would walk just behind her husband so he would shield her from sight (Kisch 1932: 355). Another carried a newspaper in front of her face when walking through town. Some women resumed the veil because they were jeered at or even attacked for being without it. Others removed the veil but were then too frightened to leave home and remained inside for months or even years afterwards (Northrop 2004).

Moreover, men did not simply allow their womenfolk to make up their own minds. Most of them actively opposed unveiling, even at times to the point of killing any close relative who did so. They justified this by the fact that such behavior dishonored them and the only way to redeem their honor was to kill the offender (Kamp 1998; Massell 1974; Northrop 2004).

In the end, it took several decades for most women to unveil, and some women continued to veil throughout the Soviet period, mainly in Uzbekistan (Northrop 2004). In Tajikistan the change was less strongly resisted. This was in part because the wearing of the *faranja* had been largely restricted to the north, where Karomat's village was. Women in the rural southern and eastern parts of the republic had never used this kind of veil. There women would cover themselves with long-sleeved flowing dresses worn over wide pants, their heads and necks shrouded in a white headscarf.

Gradually most rural women in southern Tajikistan adopted a Sovietized form of national dress, which exposed part of their hair, neck, and arms, as the cover photo shows. However, a few, including the Gharmi women of the Qurghonteppa region, continued to wear long-sleeved dresses and white headscarves covering hair and neck, which could be pulled across the face, leaving only their eyes visible.

TAJIK TRADITIONS REINVENTED

As I suggested above, the Bolshevik attacks on Central Asian lifestyles had the result of making the population resolve not to abandon their traditions. They were forced to change the form of some of them when women came out of seclusion, and girls as well as boys were made to attend school. However, they managed by subterfuge to continue the practice of polygyny, child marriage, and the payment of bride-price, although to a much smaller extent (Northrop 2004).

The practices that came most strongly under attack were those relating to the status of women. What the Bolsheviks were effectively trying to do was to change what are known as gender identities.

Gender is a difficult concept to define. There is no universally accepted definition of it, not even by those scholars who use it as an analytical category. However, it is generally agreed that the term concerns the norms of male and female behavior within a particular social setting (Weedon 1999). I take this slightly further and suggest that gender identities comprise "a culture-specific ideal, varying over time, that males and females are supposed to live up to in order to become intelligible to, and accepted members of, their own communities" (Harris 2004: 14).

In Uzbekistan and Tajikistan veiling was central to the culture. Forcing women to abandon their veils rendered them unacceptable within their own communities since it made them appear sexually available (Mernissi 1987). This amounted to making them socially unintelligible as decent women.

Moreover, masculinity depended on men's ability to ensure women's compliance with the norms. Therefore, unveiling also caused men to lose

Figure 2.3 Gharmi women with their white headscarves. Note that the scarves can be pulled over the face if a strange man comes along.

their social intelligibility and with this their acceptance in the community.[13] Thus, both sexes had much to lose through unveiling.

The Bolsheviks saw the veil largely as a physical impediment that kept women from equal participation in the community. They thought that with its removal the barriers to female integration into Central Asian society would fall, and unveiled women would emerge as the social equals of their male peers. What the Bolsheviks had not counted on, however, was that the material function of the veil—that is, the physical concealment of women from the gaze of strange men—was only part of its role. The veil was also an important symbol of female acquiescence to the public portrayal of obedience to their menfolk.

Wearing the veil was therefore the equivalent to women's announcing both their willingness to keep their bodies inviolate for their (future) husbands and their agreement to demonstrate public submission. This does not mean that women were necessarily subservient in private. Each household had its own dynamic in which the relative position of the members was not only and always dependent on their sex and within which mothers tended to dominate[14] (cf. Donish 1960).

Because the veil was a symbol, it was possible to reinvent it nonmaterially. That is to say, it was possible for women to declare their sexual inviolability and their submission by other means than veiling. It was also possible to keep men and women socially separated without physical seclusion, just as it had previously been possible for them to meet despite it.[15] In the post-*hujum* period, therefore, in much of Tajikistan a symbolic veil was incorporated into the "invented" traditions.

In the mid-1990s, when I first visited Tajikistan, local women were constantly telling me that they must at all costs obey their husbands. This appeared to be more discursive than real—a case of informing me about what they were *supposed* to do rather than describing actual behavior, since their speech rarely matched their actions. Certainly, the requirement of obedience did not stop them arguing with their husbands or even shouting at them. In other words, it appeared to be a symbolic agreement. Men held the superior power position and were generally able to enforce their commands if they really insisted, but the Tajik women I knew were not simply submissive, any more than their grandmothers and great-grandmothers had been when they veiled. In a recent survey, 57 percent of Tajik women said they did not believe that women had to be submissive towards their husbands (WHO 2000: 23).

Thus, this public discourse was a *symbol* of women's acceptance of their obligation to be obedient, not *proof* that they actually were obedient. It was a way of preserving traditional gender identities and keeping men and women intelligible in their communities. The corollary has been that it has also kept alive the concept of male control over women as an essential element of masculinity together with the underlying understanding that veiling and seclusion are valid elements of feminine identity. In other words, despite decades without it, the material veil is still a legitimate concept in Tajikistan and as such hangs over the heads of women in the post-Soviet period as something that could easily be reinstated as a general practice given the appropriate political climate.

In the early days after women stopped veiling, they were faced with the most stringent restrictions on their mobility. It was important to demonstrate publicly that females did not have the smallest chance of meeting a person of the opposite sex in any even remotely compromising situation. This was especially vital for unmarried girls, who had to preserve their virginity not only physically but also in regard to their reputation. The slightest gossip could shame their families and reduce their chances of making a good marriage. It was equally important for girls' reputation that they demonstrate willing obedience to their parents' demands.

Since there were no restrictions on young men's sexuality, they were freed from constraints on their mobility. However, they also were expected to acknowledge their duty to obey their parents.

Such obligations had their origins in material circumstances.[16] Before the Revolution, young men had been economically dependent on their fathers, just as women were dependent first on their parents and later on their husbands. Families were patrilocal, and three or even four generations might live in the same large house and work the land together, the head of household controlling all finances (Kislyakov 1935, 1959).

In the 1930s, the collectivization of farmland removed economic resources from family control. Both men and women supposedly had access to salaried employment, which in theory would make them financially independent. In Tajikistan, however, everyone was expected to put their wages into the family pot, thus losing individual control over their spending. Moreover, few women were permitted to enter employment, and when they did their wages were often paid directly to the head of household. In this way, they lost most of the advantage of having their own incomes (Kislyakov and Pisarchik 1976: 17; Monogarova 1982, I, 91–92). It was also very difficult to gain access to separate housing. The Soviet state never managed to build enough for everyone's needs.

The result was that young people remained almost as materially dependent on their families as before (Rakowska-Harmstone 1970: 62). The most powerful family members continued to enforce highly traditional gender-appropriate behavior, choosing their children's spouses so as to keep the young people under control even after marriage.

Thus, the Bolsheviks failed in their attempt to move young people away from parental influence in great part because of their inability to provide the material conditions to do so. Moreover, young people could not break away, because of both the fear of losing their families and the threat of being ostracized from their communities.

It was considered a betrayal of national honor to adopt Russian customs. In the early days, even something so apparently trivial as a woman wearing Russian-style shoes was construed as a sign of abandonment of her culture and therefore carried negative connotations[17] (Northrop 2004: 57). Community pressures made it very difficult to persist in such betrayals. In this way, the Tajik people banded together to resist cultural assimilation and make the penalties of deviance high enough to be a serious deterrent. By doing so they doubly defeated the Bolsheviks' pressures towards modernization.

The idea that Central Asian lifestyles were based on so-called traditions had been introduced by the Bolsheviks themselves. They used this as a way of discrediting Central Asian culture through defining it as backwards and barbaric, as opposed to Soviet modernity.

The Bolsheviks were not the first to employ this sort of discourse. It had been done earlier by Western European powers—for instance, by the British in reference to what they termed the inferior lifestyles of the Indian peoples. Intimately associated with this was the concept of ahistoric stagnation[18] that supposedly characterized Asian states (Marx 1858: 486–487).

The West prided itself on the driving force of the capitalistic market, which privileged the concept of rapid change as a good, terming it *progress*. This made it possible to characterize as inferior those societies that did not prize change, and thus permitted Western states to assert the legitimacy of their colonial rule. They could claim that it benefited the colonized, since the result would be to civilize the "savages." This discourse even succeeded in convincing many Indians, producing what Nandy has termed "internal colonialism," a situation in which the politically colonized also became psychologically colonized into accepting the colonizers' pejorative judgment of them (Nandy 1983: ix–xvii).

In other words, Europeans used the concept of modernity in a normative manner. They employed the term to imply "a process of differentiation, an act of separation from the past. . . a rejection of the dead weight of history and tradition. Increasingly, 'modern' was to become synonymous with the repudiation of the past and a commitment to change and the values of the future" (Felski 1995: 13). The future here included economic development as well as the political and administrative structures that accompany the building of a nation-state (Lewis, Rowland, and Clem 1976: 4).

Following the same logic, the Bolsheviks conceptualized Central Asian customs as static and unchanging, stretching back into ancient times. They associated veiling with the Middle Ages, for instance (Massell 1974). In fact, there is evidence to suggest it was far more recent. In other Muslim countries—for instance, Egypt and Algeria—women may have adopted the veil much later than is often thought, possibly even as a protective mechanism against Western men's harassment of local women (Keddie 1992: 47ff). It has been suggested that the same may have been true for Central Asia (Kamp 1998: 254–255; Northrop 2004: 44). Local men were taught to keep their eyes away from other men's womenfolk as laid down in the Qur'an; it was only the impious Europeans who boldly dared to gaze at local women (Bourdon 1880: 262). Certainly, Western men who visited the region in the nineteenth century seemed to have taken great delight in staring at the local women (Meyendorff 1870: 63). Thus, in Turkestan the custom of veiling may well have started within the century before the Russian occupation.

Conceptualizing Central Asian customs as originating in the Middle Ages gave them negative connotations, which the colonial rulers then contrasted with their own "superior" modernity. Lenin's concept of socialism was strongly influenced by Western ideas of material progress. He admired such institutions as the postal service, which he thought would make an excellent model for a socialist government (Lenin 1933: 59–61). To these ideas of progress the Bolsheviks added their belief that they had a mandate to represent the proletariat, which they insisted legitimized significant levels of cultural and social intervention in the lives of Soviet citizens, far greater than had ever been attempted by Western colonialists.

In Central Asia as a whole, the Soviet regime's construction of the material infrastructure mentioned in Chapter 1 produced fewer lifestyle changes than had been expected, as locals continued to prefer traditional houses and other material appurtenances of their pre-Soviet lives that suited their lifestyle and religion. Tajikistan, where even most educated people continued to follow the traditions, was the most conservative of these republics (Rakowska-Harmstone 1970: 274ff).

For both the Bolsheviks and the peoples of Central Asia, therefore, the terms *modern* and *traditional* came to stand for two opposing worldviews. For the Bolsheviks, *modern* implied everything that was beneficial in the newly developing Soviet socialism. For the Central Asians, their traditions were all that stood between them and losing intelligibility as men and women in their own communities. Relinquishing these traditions would amount to the destruction of their culture, and they were determined this should not happen, especially because their customs were virtually inseparable in their minds from Islam, which stood at the center of their personal identities (Akbarzadeh 1999).

Therefore, resistance to the Bolsheviks' decrees took the form of determined and conscious maintenance of local traditions. It was irrelevant that these traditions had undergone modification and therefore did not seamlessly derive from the distant past. The point was that they took on the legitimizing force of unbroken custom and in so doing gained sufficient might to serve as a shield from Bolshevik cultural encroachment, as well as to support the preservation of traditional power positions.

Since the Bolshevik attacks of the 1920s on customs the traditions have been passed down from generation to generation, inculcated into children by parents from birth. Along the way adaptations have been made to take into account material changes. Despite this, there was little essential difference between the traditions followed by Karomat and those of the younger generations.

Compared with the changes that have taken place in the customs of other Muslim peoples over the last century, those that occurred in Tajikistan seem remarkably small. One has only to think of Iran, for instance, and the immense changes that took place there.

After the Shah tried to bring the country into modernity in the middle of the twentieth century, many urban women, particularly among the upper and upper-middle classes, abandoned veils and even headscarves in favor of modern dress. They were highly educated, and many studied abroad. The 1979 Revolution put a stop to such practices, and the Islamic Republic has enforced compulsory dress codes for women and separated the sexes at all levels, including education and employment. Today, while supposedly the compulsory wearing of the *chador* gives women a uniform appearance, a significant contingent of young people seeks to emulate youth from other countries in their dress as in other aspects of life. They are challenging the dress codes and other restrictions, such as that on popular music. For instance, girls have found ways to get away with wearing miniskirts and makeup under their *chadors*[19] (Adelkhah 2000; Keddie 1981; Naficy 1981; Najmabadi 1991).

In Syria, Lebanon, Turkey, Tunisia, and Egypt, many women have been educated and incorporated into the workforce; such women often wear modern clothes, although over the last couple of decades more and more of them are wearing *hijab* (Duben and Behar 1991; Hoodfar 1997; Kandiyoti and Saktanber 2002; Macleod 1991; White 2002).

In these countries, pressures towards modernity were initiated by governments from the same backgrounds as the general population. This was not the case in Tajikistan, where the Soviet regime was run by an alien cultural group trying to impose their lifestyle on their colonial subjects. The way the population of Tajikistan used their *invented* traditions to resist this can be construed as a use of what James Scott (1985) has termed "weapons of the weak." That is to say, the fact that control over the state, the army, and the legal system was in the hands of the colonial overlords did not prevent the peoples of Tajikistan from resisting, despite their lesser power positions. They used whatever means they had to shield themselves from Russification.

The use of traditions as an everyday form of resistance occurred in all Central Asian republics. This frustrated the Soviet regime, which could never quite come to grips with it or force its abandonment. The effect of the traditions, as with Scott's "weapons," was to foil the intentions of the authorities without direct confrontation. Thus, while on the surface the population appeared to accept Soviet rule, underneath they were subverting it and preventing its transformatory aims from succeeding.

But this was not the only way change was hindered. At the same time as the state was applying pressures on the peoples of Central Asia to abandon their local customs, its very organization was putting significant obstacles in the way of social change. For instance, for decades after collectivization, strict laws prevented the rural population from migrating and even made short-term travel to urban areas difficult (Humphrey 1983: 14). This slowed the pace of change by keeping the majority of the Tajik population from contact with anything outside their own small area. Further barriers to the development of new ideas were the tight controls on scholarship and the mass media. Exposure to media from beyond the borders of the USSR was almost nonexistent (Mickiewicz 1980).

Furthermore, Tajik determination to preserve their own culture was reinforced by constant friction between Russians living in Central Asia and the locals. According to Karomat, the Russians in Dushanbe behaved extremely arrogantly. They treated Tajiks as inferiors on a daily basis. They would shout at them in the streets. They would even try to cheat them, believing they were too ignorant to realize what was going on. For instance, Karomat said the bookkeeper in the Dushanbe Textile Factory would take more taxes out of her wages than she was legally obliged to pay, expecting her to be too ignorant to notice. This infuriated Karomat, who knew her rights very well.

Karomat had a few Russian friends, but even they did not always treat her well, and she believed that most of them looked down on the locals. This belief has been backed by research (Wixman 1991). According to Russian ethnographer Natalya Kosmarskaya, who interviewed Russians who had returned to the Russian Federation from Central Asia after the breakup of the Soviet Union, most displayed a chauvinistic feeling of superiority towards the local population. In their opinion they had been doing the locals a favor by taking over Central Asia and "civilizing" it.[20]

The fact that the majority of the inhabitants of Dushanbe and most other Tajik towns were Russians produced the impression that the Tajik people living in their own native land were in effect living in a diaspora. This was enhanced by the fact that although they formed the majority of the inhabitants of the republic, they were a tiny minority within the Soviet Union as a whole.[21] This produced further pressure on the Tajik people to preserve their cultural identity.

CULTURAL IDENTITY IN TAJIKISTAN

The great complexity of societies today and the diverse influences to which they are subjected has given rise to the concept of identities as dislocated and fragmented. There is no longer any certainty about what constitutes an individual, nor about the processes that cause identities to be formed and re-formed. Even the relationship of individuals to national cultures is unsettled (Hall 1992: 282–292). In fact, today little in life appears to remain the same for very long. As a result, contemporary scholarship on identity focuses on the discontinuities, fragmentation, shifting, and malleable nature of identities in the globalizing world (Appadurai 1996; Giddens 1990; Hall 1990; Vertovec and Rogers 1998).

It is hard for people to retain a unified identity when immense changes are occurring around them. It is particularly difficult for those who have either moved away from their place of origin or who have to share space with persons with a very different sense of identity. Increasingly, people all over the world are being drawn into such positions through economic, environmental, and/or politically generated diasporas.

As I have suggested, the immigration into Tajikistan of people of other nationalities, the majority of whom were Russians, produced the effect of a diaspora, even while the Tajik people remained within their own republic. Karomat's story demonstrates how this produced a shifting relationship with many elements of identity. For instance, from the time her parents started Party school in about 1930, the family sometimes lived in a more Sovietized manner and at others in a more Tajik style, depending on the pressures they were subjected to at the time. I observed the same phenomenon among many other acquaintances of mine in Tajikistan.

As I explained in the Introduction, the inhabitants of Tajikistan usually identify more strongly with their region of origin than with their nationality. As a result, they usually start by saying they are Gharmis, Leninobodis, Hissoris, or Kulobis. However, as soon as the subject of gender is broached, people immediately scale up their identity, claiming to be Tajiks, Central Asians, or even Muslims. No doubt this happens because this is the most sensitive component of their identity and the one where the shield of the invented traditions is most needed for protection and preservation. This brings people to place the largest possible mass behind it. It also implies a belief that there is a great similarity among gender identities over these large areas.[22]

It is this that justifies my use of the term *Tajik* in this book to designate people from different regions of the republic, since I am using it precisely in this context: to distinguish them from Russians and other non–Central Asians in relation to issues around gender identities.

A Transitional Lifestyle

By now it should be clear that those who claim to live by Tajik traditions are not actually following a traditional lifestyle. But neither have they embraced modernity, not even the somewhat limited Soviet version. The story of Karomat shows us an outlook that is neither one nor the other.

Karomat was ambivalent about the Soviet Union and modern practices. She had been happy under socialism. People had been relatively equal. There had always been enough to eat. Everyone had had a roof over their heads and there was very little obvious unemployment. The slow rate of change produced social stability and inflation was almost nonexistent. In other words, Karomat did not believe the Soviet period had on the whole been negative for Tajikistan. Moreover, she had been proud of living in one of the world's most powerful nations.

This did not mean she viewed the accompanying cultural pressures as positive. To her, modernizing influences were part of the forced Russification that had gone hand-in-hand with Soviet cultural encroachment. Thus, she saw them not only as alien but also as an integral part of colonial rule, to be resisted and opposed.

For Karomat, therefore, Soviet rule had had both positive and negative aspects. In fact, she changed her mind frequently regarding which was which. Karomat had been strongly influenced by Soviet ideas she had gained through school, personal contacts, and the media, but local concepts had left their mark also. The result was that often she did not seem to have one constant position but would vacillate between Tajik and Sovietized views. For instance, she would frequently change her opinion as to whether it was good to plan ahead (the Soviet way) or whether it was a sin to do so because it contravened the tenet that true believers should leave the future to Allah.

In fact, Karomat never definitively resolved for herself which concepts were positive and which negative. It all depended on her mood and what she was thinking about. For instance, when she considered how happy she had been with Khudoydod, she rejoiced in the fact that she had managed to manipulate her mother into allowing her to marry him. On the other hand, when she thought about her childlessness and the way she had been manipulated by her husband's family into divorcing him, she would be upset with herself for having married him in the first place. She would insist that she would have been much better off had she followed the "clean Tajik way" and had an arranged marriage.

When she had problems with her fertility, Karomat had consulted *mullahs* and made pilgrimages to holy shrines. This was the traditional way. Only as a very last resort did she turn to biomedicine, which had actually caused her infertility by mistreatment after a miscarriage. She said to me sadly that she wondered whether had she started with biomedicine she might have been cured.

Karomat was glad she had worked outside the home, she said, because women who had never done so were completely ignorant. They could not stand up for their rights or face down an official. They did not know how to demand the appropriate piece of paper from bureaucrats in order to get their pensions or other entitlements. However, she also thought life was hard on women who had jobs because they still had to do all the housework when they came home, since men never contributed to this, even if their wives worked outside the home.

Despite having been happy during the Soviet period and deeply regretting its passing, Karomat maintained that in many ways it had been negative for women. She said that in her childhood women had not been in employment and that this had allowed them to live in a more relaxed manner than during the Soviet period, when women had done nothing but work from morning to night. Nevertheless, she was not in favor of returning to a prerevolutionary lifestyle. For instance, she opposed bringing back the *faranja* and *chachvan* because, she said, this would encourage licentiousness. Women could hide behind them and get up to all sorts of mischief.

Thus, Karomat's personal identity was both fragmented and shifting. She was constantly changing her points of reference and with them the way she thought about herself. Such fragmented and unstable identities, containing unresolved or contradictory elements, have become commonplace today as so many people are confronted with multiple cultural positions. They have become so common that they are said to characterize postmodern societies (Hall 1992: 276–277).

In Karomat's case, the fragmentation was produced by her encounters with the alien cultural values of the Russians. From an early age she was subjected to contradictory influences. Her kindergarten teachers would tell her one thing, while at home she would learn something different, often diametrically opposed. Moreover, the Russians would insist *their* lifestyle was superior while her parents would tell her that as a Tajik she had to keep certain traditions, which her Russian teachers would tell her were bad.

The majority of the Russians with whom I spoke firmly believed there was an immutable difference between their modern outlook and Tajik traditions, and that the former was unfailingly positive, the latter negative. Most Tajiks also believed in the gulf between the two but reversed the good and bad. Indeed, Karomat never wavered in her basic belief that Tajik values were good. Her ambivalence showed itself in specific ideas and practices.

Similar dichotomies have been expressed by Western theorists analyzing differences between colonized and colonizing cultures. During the 1960s

Inkeles and his colleagues carried out a massive inquiry into the elements that brought men out of traditionalism into modernity.[23] In so doing they intimated that the two were mutually contradictory positions and that once a person modernized "he" never returned to traditionalism[24] (Inkeles and Smith 1974; Inkeles, Smith, et al. 1983).

However, the idea that people move only in one direction and that once traditionalism has been renounced it has vanished forever seems to contradict actual lived experiences, such as those of Karomat and her family. Their exposure to modernity produced neither total acceptance nor total rejection, but rather partial acceptance that changed over time. Karomat would even vacillate between traditionalistic and modernistic positions during the course of one short conversation.

As we have seen, the fragmented and shifting identities of Karomat and her family are neither completely traditional nor totally modern. Attempts to return to traditionalism do not actually work, since the original state of unselfconsciousness has been lost. To this extent Inkeles and his colleagues are correct. Once people become self-conscious about their customs, they can no longer return to the previous stage of simply taking them for granted, considering them natural and God-given (Inkeles, Smith, et al. 1983).

Tajik culture started on a trajectory of change at the time of the Bolshevik attacks on it in the mid-1920s, if not before. By now the element of unselfconsciousness characteristic of traditional societies has long since vanished, making it impossible to return to this state. However, the wish to retain traditionalism keeps people from reaching out to modernity other than in a very limited way, such as I described in the case of the high school students in the Introduction.

Tajikistan, in fact, remains a long way from modernity. One mark of this is that Tajik gender norms continue to privilege strict male control over female sexuality above all other masculine attributes and thereby legitimize constraints on female mobility that often keep girls from studying and women from entering employment.

Interestingly, in other Muslim societies where women have been faced with constraints on studying and employment, they have employed the *hijab* to overcome them (Macleod 1991) by creating "a kind of mobile honor zone" (White 2002: 52, 220). This is currently unavailable to Tajiks, many of whom regard any kind of veiling with suspicion, as does the government (Glenn 1999; Harris 2004a). This keeps them stuck in a kind of limbo. Maintaining the traditions in the face of ever-increasing poverty is getting harder and harder, but so far this has not stopped people from trying.

Stuart Hall suggests that a consequence of exposure to hybrid influences is that people find themselves in a state of nonfixed identities, where they hover among different positions. He calls this a state of being *in transition* (Hall

1992: 310). The same term has been applied by Minai to lifestyles in Algeria, where similar changes away from traditional society have taken place to those in Tajikistan. Minai uses the term *transitional* to denote social changes that brought women out of the traditional female realm of domesticity into education and the workforce, and in so doing produced cultural changes that have affected gender identities (Minai 1981).

This term has also been applied to post-Soviet societies, with the somewhat different connotation of states in transition between Soviet socialism and a putative capitalism. Although this usage is somewhat further away from mine, it is not totally unrelated, because the post-Soviet transition goes beyond the economic. It is impossible to develop capitalism in the absence of corresponding social and political institutions, and a certain level of modernization is also required. However, I date the start of the transition much further back, to the 1920s, when the Bolsheviks started their campaign of cultural penetration, or even to the nineteenth-century Russian conquest. In other words, in my opinion the transition started once people in what is now Tajikistan were forced to face different lifestyles. At that point Central Asia began to be pushed by its Russian colonial masters in the general direction of a state of modernity that may well never be reached.[25]

The idea of a transition implies movement and change. In the case of Tajik society, I suggest, as I explained in the Introduction, that its people are moving at very different points along what might be visualized as a continuum of transition, and that they travel along it at different rates and not always in a straight line or in the same direction. At any given time, some are nearer to the traditionalist end, others nearer modernity. When parents and children occupy significantly different positions along this continuum, intergenerational tensions are likely to arise, as we will see in the following chapters.

CHAPTER THREE

FAMILY RELATIONS

The modern versus traditional dichotomy discussed in Chapter 2 represents only part of the difference in outlook between Slavs and Central Asians. Differences in the relative strength of family relationships and types of parenting styles also play an important role.

Tajiks tend to develop close relationships between family members, while they hold the rest of the world at a distance, and parents retain considerable power over their children, even when the latter are legally adults. This derives in part from the gender norms that give adult males control over the whole family and in part from the Muslim ideology that states that parents, especially mothers, deserve high levels of respect. This is interpreted to mean they are also owed unquestioning obedience (Altorki 1986).

The following narration relates the story of a contemporary family and shows the dynamics that keep young people, especially girls, from being able to express their desires in front of their parents. The father, Jumabek, strongly upholds Tajik traditions, but he also has contradictory attitudes about the influence he thinks Russians should have on his children. On the one hand he does not want any interference in the way he is bringing them up, but on the other he wants the schools, established according to Russian principles, to teach his children the discipline he is unwilling to impart himself.

Kutfi and her husband live on the outskirts of Dushanbe, where they have a havli with cows and sheep, as well as a vegetable plot and orchard. When I first met her in early 1995, Kutfi was a thin, tired-looking woman in her late thirties.

Figure 3.1 Kutfi and her family in their *havli*

She told me she had borne ten children spaced roughly one and a half years apart, three of whom had died in infancy. She had not enjoyed having children at such short intervals and in fact had wanted no more than four, but her husband had insisted on having as many as possible and had refused to permit her to use contraception. Now that the toughest period is over and Kutfi no longer has to deal with pregnancy and babies, she is happy to have a large family. They need all their children to help them with labor, she maintains.

Kutfi's younger sister has only two children because she used an IUD. Kutfi thinks this is bad. It is very important to have more than one son to say prayers properly when one dies.

As a child Kutfi had loved school, where she got high grades in every subject except geometry. However, after she finished eighth grade at age seventeen and a half, her parents decided it was time for her to marry. Her younger sisters were permitted to finish high school, but they were not allowed to continue their education beyond that. Their brothers all have university degrees.

Kutfi's husband, Jumabek, grew up in the mountains north of Dushanbe and is some twenty years older than his wife. As a boy he had barely attended school, with the result that he wasn't even functionally literate. At the time of their wedding he had been working as a laborer in the Dushanbe beer factory, which allowed him to drink as much as he liked. Often when drunk he would beat and/or rape his wife. However, in 1985 he had contracted emphysema and was put on disability. The doctor warned him that drinking could seriously exacerbate his health problems. In any case, once he was no longer working at the factory he couldn't afford alcohol, so he stopped drinking.

Now he no longer beats Kutfi but he is still strict with her. She is not allowed to leave the house without permission and must explain where she is going and with whom each time she goes out. Jumabek's bad health makes physical activity difficult, so he rarely leaves the house himself. Most of the time he sits in the courtyard, supervising the children's work. Kutfi has taken the only job she could find—cleaning her children's school, which is situated opposite their house. It pays badly but at least brings in some cash.

Jumabek seems wary of the way he is regarded by their neighbors, particularly his contemporaries, who mock him for his lack of education and rural ways. During Soviet times he was the only one who raised cows and sheep. However, since independence his neighbors have lost their jobs, and now they keep livestock too. Jumabek believes they envy him his large herd. This makes him feel better, but he comments on his neighbors in a belligerent manner and is obviously very touchy about them.

Jumabek's children are little keener on school than he was. His sons rarely attend, preferring to take the cattle to the mountains to graze or help their parents on the homestead. His daughters all attend school but don't do that well there. Most days after class the second daughter does her mother's school cleaning work while Kutfi sits and chats with her friends. The children are so busy helping their parents that they don't have time to do any homework, which further impedes their studies.

Most of the time, their parents pay little attention to the children, who play together with minimal oversight. I was once present when the nine-year-old picked up a large iron rod and hit his five-year-old sister over the head with it. While I tried to stop him, Kutfi and Jumabek looked on with indifference, ignoring my remonstrations and suggestions of the harm this could cause. When Jumabek finally decided to intervene, he did not appear to be doing so to protect his daughter, but merely to gain peace and quiet. He informed me that during

Soviet times, Russians had constantly tried to interfere with the way they were raising their children, but they had taken no notice, the inference being that he would take no notice of me either.

Most of the parents' interactions with their children seem to involve either putting them to work or disciplining them. Anytime they don't instantly obey, they shout at them, swearing and calling them names. If that doesn't have immediate effect, Kutfi will smack the child and threaten worse, such as a beating from their father. This usually works since, as Kutfi told me with apparent satisfaction, the children fear their father for his strictness and ability to hurt them. Although the children are permitted to be wild among themselves, when with adults they are expected to keep quiet and not intrude.

When I asked Jumabek about his principles of childrearing, he informed me that children had an obligation to obey their parents no matter what. Teaching them principles of conduct, however, is the school's responsibility. "In our day," he told me, "teachers were very strict and taught children manners and proper behavior. Now they neglect their duties. I don't think they have even tried to teach our children these things." When I asked who else should do it in that case, he merely shrugged and said he didn't know.

The boys are very rough. Except for having to help their father with farm work, they have few constraints on their behavior. The girls are much quieter. They are expected to spend most of their time outside classes helping their mother and in her presence are not permitted to be rambunctious.

When I was introduced to the family, the eldest daughter, Sadbarg, was sixteen and an apprentice in a knitting factory, where she worked three days a week.[1] On the other two she attended vocational high school in the center of Dushanbe.

Sadbarg felt uncomfortable at home. She disliked her brothers' violence and her parents' indifference to it. She also hated her parents' attitude to their children in general. She felt they did not treat them with affection, especially her father. She thought this might be why her siblings quarreled and fought all the time.

At school she had classes on childrearing. In addition, her favorite television programs gave her new perspectives on family life. Furthermore, visits to her more educated neighbors showed her that even traditional Tajik families could raise their children differently from the way she and her siblings were being brought up.

Her exposure to other ideas made Sadbarg determined that when she had children of her own she would not copy her parents. She would have a small family. Although she would ensure that her children obeyed her, she would do this through firm kindness and correct teaching, not through harshness like her parents. After marriage, she would not be like so many young women who leave

their children with their parents while they go out to work. She wanted her par-
ents and siblings to have as little as possible to do with her children. She would
hate them to grow up like her brothers and sisters, she informed me.

When we were alone, Sadbarg would show herself as strong and determined. I
was amazed at how different she looked when with her parents, quite meek and
humble. Despite her private criticisms she was careful to adopt an air of instant
compliance with all their orders. When she didn't see the point of them, she
would pretend to conform and secretly do what she thought best, at least insofar
as she could get away with it. For instance, she was supposed to go straight home
each day as soon as she got out of work or school. However, when the factory
closed early or didn't open at all, as often happened for lack of raw materials,
Sadbarg would accompany her girlfriends into town. If they had the money they
would enjoy themselves at the cinema. If not they might stroll around Lenin
Park or window shop.

Sadbarg was afraid her parents might choose her a husband who resembled
her brothers. The eldest one, for instance, informed me that when he married he
would beat his wife if she didn't instantly obey his mother. Sadbarg hoped so
much her husband would be different. However, she knew she wouldn't have any
say in picking him but would be forced to marry the man of her parents' choice,
and would have to obey him and probably her mother-in-law as well. Despite
this, she did not want the responsibility of choosing her own husband. If she did
so she would be on her own, she said. Her parents would very likely disown her.
It was far too risky. What if it didn't work out? Then where would she be?

Sadbarg believed her relationship with her mother-in-law would affect her
welfare more than that with her husband. As long as the latter did not beat her,
he probably would not be too bad. But her mother-in-law would have the power
to treat her however she liked, and Sadbarg would not be in a position to protest.
Moreover, she would be likely to spend far more time with her than with her
husband, since he would probably be away from home a lot. "We Tajiks have an
absolute law that we must at all costs obey our elders. We have no choice," she
told me. "If my husband is near my age he won't be able to boss me around so
much."

Sadbarg longed to travel and see the world. However, she knew she wouldn't
be allowed to go anywhere, although her two eldest brothers had both gone to
work in Russia. It was unfair that girls had so little freedom. Why wasn't she
born a boy? Unfortunately, all that awaited her was to remain at home until she
married and then to lead a domestic life looking after her husband and children.
This didn't attract her at all, but she saw no alternative. She didn't dare mention
her aspirations to her parents.

Sadbarg finished school at the end of that year and soon afterwards her par-
ents married her to a distant cousin. Her husband was kind to her and she was

happy with him. He was an orphan who was raising his younger siblings on his own, so that quite unexpectedly she found herself in the position of senior woman in the household, which she said was wonderful! Within a year she had a pretty daughter and a couple of years later gave birth to a son. She thinks she may now have completed her family but will make a decision on that together with her husband later on, she says. However, she won't have more than one or two more children.

Jumabek's and Kutfi's parenting style is probably a lot harsher than in a truly traditional family, where the roles of each person would be fully pre-scribed by custom (cf. Kenyatta 1965). Today, parental authority continues to be privileged, but the checks and balances that protected youngsters in tradi-tional societies, where every aspect of life was regulated and those who did not comply with the rules were punished, have vanished.

Thus, according to Tajik traditions, Sadbarg has no right to challenge her parents. The collectivist ethic prevalent in the culture reinforces this.

Harry Triandis defines collectivism as a cultural pattern common to those so strongly linked to their in-groups that they find group requirements more important than their own needs. Individualists, on the other hand, put their personal wants and goals first (Triandis 1995: 2, 12).

In Tajikistan, the most important collectivity, or in-group, is the family, and great stress is laid on putting the overall good of this group before the good of its constituent members (cf. Triandis 1995: xiii–xiv). Men are tied to their birth families for life and identify strongly with them. Women are in a somewhat dif-ferent position, since like Sadbarg they will move away at marriage and thus gain access to a second in-group. However, they are also raised to put the collec-tive good before their own. Hence, Sadbarg knows that irrespective of her own wishes she has at least to appear to obey her parents' demands.

Since she now gets on well with her marital family, she may be able to do without her parents' material support in the future. However, she is well aware that if she alienates her parents and something goes wrong with her marriage, she could be cast out from her marital family and refused readmit-tance to her natal one, thus finding herself in limbo. This means that it is still important for Sadbarg not to move too far from her parents' concept of the acceptable. She cannot afford to do anything that will lose her their support, as this might be crucial for her later survival. Moreover, despite her dislike of much of their behavior, she still loves her family, especially her mother, and does not want to lose them.

In Tajikistan, the in-group expands to encompass not only the extended family but also the clan or region. Multiple mechanisms are used to keep people under control, and these are applied through families, particularly male family heads. These are the people whose personal status is most highly bound up with family status, since conceptually they stand for their families in front of the community at large, in whose eyes they are responsible for the behavior of the other members. This is both a privilege, as it puts them in a superior power position, and a responsibility, since simultaneously it makes them dependent on the behavior of others, as I will explain later in this chapter.

The other important in-group for most people in Tajikistan is their local community. Sadbarg's neighbors, for instance, would spend a considerable amount of time in the street, spying on people and ensuring the social chastisement of anyone who transgressed. When in late 1994 a divorced woman living across from Sadbarg became a polygynous second wife to a man whose first wife lived a mere few houses away, the neighborhood women constantly found small ways to embarrass her, while the men would harass her small son by saying bad things about his new "father." In this case, it was not so much the fact that the man took a second wife that was the issue, as that he did so openly, right in front of his first wife and all her neighbors. The polygynous wife was considered at fault for acquiescing to such a situation much more the man involved[2] (Harris 2004: 69ff).

Through exerting pressures of the kind discussed above, communities help maintain the conformity so highly prized in this collective society (Singerman 1995: 50).

In such a setting, it is easier for people to maintain the norms by portraying themselves as stereotypes rather than complex human beings with unique characteristics. Sadbarg, for instance, would display herself in multiple different guises in order to appear to conform to the appropriate narrow set of local ideals considered appropriate for unmarried girls of her age. It was notable that there were considerable differences between the persona she displayed to me and that which she showed her parents.

Individualism works in the opposite way, with people expected to show their "true" selves to the world. As opposed to collectivist societies, where people display a multiplicity of images depending on occasion, members of individualist societies are supposed to have only one outward presentation, which should reflect their own authentic personalities (Giddens 1991: 74–78).[3]

GENDER IDENTITIES IN COLLECTIVIST TAJIKISTAN

It is not enough simply to internalize gender ideals; it is also necessary repeatedly to demonstrate adherence to them through one's behavior (Harris 2004: 14–15). In other words, people are expected to act appropriately within the norms considered acceptable for their sex and age in their particular social environment (Butler 1990: 24).[4] This is what Sadbarg was doing when she behaved submissively in front of her parents.

Like Sadbarg, young women in Tajikistan are expected to repress their ideas and wishes far more than are their brothers. It can therefore be hazardous for them to allow those in authority to see that they have thoughts that go beyond the norms.

Sadbarg feared her parents would watch her much more closely if they had any inkling that she did not simply acquiesce to their commands. She was extremely fearful that they might discover her outings with her girlfriends. She knew they would not believe in their essential harmlessness. According to popularly accepted notions, girls who transgressed the norms did so in order to meet boys, not simply to have the fun of an afternoon at the cinema or the park with their girlfriends.

Sadbarg's brothers did not have to be careful in the same way. Their mobility was not restricted. In fact, it was easier for them to get permission to go to Russia to work than for Sadbarg to be allowed to spend an hour in the park with her friends. Moreover, the boys were not monitored closely for daily conformity. As long as they obeyed all direct commands, especially in regard to major decision-making, Jumabek and Kutfi did not question what they did or thought.

This is because of the differences between gender identities. The most crucial issue for unmarried girls is the preservation of their virginity, something that has no male equivalent. This means that girls have to demonstrate over and over that they never do *or even think* anything that might put their virginity at risk in any way. One way to do this is for parental control to restrict their mobility so stringently it is impossible for them to transgress.

In fact, Sadbarg's parents were not significantly constraining her movements. Their control was more discursive than real. Sadbarg was permitted to go on her own into town every weekday to her factory and school. Her parents appeared to believe that as long as their daughter arrived at a time commensurate with the official times at which her school and work were supposed to finish each day, she had come straight home

It did not seem to occur to them that in those times of scarcity there were many days on which the factory did not have enough raw materials to keep the workers employed for a full working day. There were even times when it would remain closed for several days. Sadbarg would never tell her parents. She simply left home at the same time every day. On days when the factory was closed she would go out with her friends, who similarly did not inform their parents of the situation.

The ease with which they managed to get away with such transgressions demonstrates loopholes in the system. In fact, it only works properly in a truly traditional setting where girls are always under their mothers' eyes (cf. White 2002: 220). This gap between discourse and reality assumes special importance in the matter of boy-girl relationships, as I explain in Chapter 5.

In conformity with Tajik traditions, Sadbarg was expected publicly to acknowledge her parents' right to control her, most of all her father's right. As head of his household, Jumabek was supposed not only to exert control over his wife and children but also to make this control explicit and visible. Kutfi and the children had equally visibly to display their compliance.

Such traditions are part of Tajik gender norms. The most important masculine characteristic here is control over females and subordinate males by the dominant class of males—heads of families, invariably conceptualized as mature males.[5] Although today there are large numbers of female-headed households in Tajikistan, women can never be conceptualized as household heads. This is partly because they are supposed always to live under male control, but mostly because any loss of family honor becomes synonymous with the emasculation of the family head, since he is responsible for controlling subordinate family members.

This means that female household heads can never fully be held accountable for their subordinates' behavior, which opens the way for the existence of rogue households. In this respect, it is interesting to note that in the Khatlon villages where I worked with Ghamkhori, female heads of household were subjected to particular pressures from other senior women, presumably in an attempt to ensure the suppression of potential aberrations.

For a man, the most shaming of all is failure to control female sexuality. This accounts for the behavior of the men discussed in Chapter 2, who killed their unveiled womenfolk as the only way to regain their honor.[6] It also explains the importance of female seclusion.

Jumabek is trying to live up to this masculine ideal. His strictness is intended to show his neighbors that despite his lack of education and his disability, he is still able to exert appropriate control over his family. This may be why he is so harsh with his family and why Kutfi admires this. She does not want anyone to be able to suggest that her husband is not a "real" man, as this would reflect negatively on her.

Men unable to prevent the manifestation of deviant behavior on the part of a family member will be punished by their peers, among other things by mockery and jeering. This appears to be an extremely effective means of enforcing male social conformity, as Jumabek's sensitivity on the subject shows. It is not necessary for men to be at low social and educational levels for this to work. It can be applied at any social level, always provided the man in question accepts the Tajik definition of masculinity.[7]

Although at first glance it seems as if under this system all the power lies in the hands of men, in reality women are much more powerful than the discourse suggests. Masculinity is dependent on feminine agreement to display the visible maintenance of submissive virginity/chastity that is the most important feminine characteristic in this cultural system and the complement of male control. A female who refuses to conform can destroy her menfolk's masculinity, which is why girls must be closely guarded until they can be handed over to their husbands as virgins.[8]

This is so very crucial because the hymen is at the center of the rite of passage to manhood, which consists of its "public" penetration on the wedding night, confirmed through the display of a bloody cloth. The bleeding of the bride serves simultaneously as her passage to womanhood and the only wedding present she is required to bestow upon her husband. For this reason, it is essential she preserve her hymen for marriage, the time when sexual control over her symbolically passes from her father to her husband and his family. If she cannot demonstrate her virginity on her wedding night, she has shamed her father and shown him up as a failure. A real man would have kept his daughter under proper control.[9]

Girls not only must come to marriage chaste but also live in such a way that nobody can doubt this. Hence, like Sadbarg, they are usually subjected to restrictions in mobility in order to ensure a visible lack of opportunity to transgress. In addition, they are expected to show active acquiescence to such limitations and display modesty and submissiveness in front of dominant males and others in positions of authority.

Sadbarg clearly did not experience herself as submissive. In front of me she displayed strength, resolution, and individualistic longings for which she would have been penalized had her parents known of them. Her strength came through not just in her speech but also in the way she moved, held her head high, and looked me in the eyes. She behaved quite differently in front of her parents, hanging her head and avoiding eye contact. Her very face would look somehow softer. Thus, she projected different personalities in front of different "audiences."[10]

As women grow older they gain authority and thus have less often to resort to manifestations of submission. In fact, while in theory control over young people of both sexes remains with the male head of family, in practice it usually falls to the senior woman to exert daily control over them, since men spend much of their time away from home.

It is still common in Tajikistan for young couples to spend at least the first period of their married life, and sometimes the whole of it, in the home of the husband's parents, specially if he is the youngest son. In such a situation, brides find themselves subjected to their mothers-in-law as much as, and often more than, to their husbands.[11] This explains Sadbarg's apprehension before marriage and her enormous relief at finding herself without the constraint of a mother-in-law. Although in theory women also have to obey their husbands, when the two are of a similar age it is easier to negotiate with a husband, unless he is really violent. Mothers-in-law rarely permit negotiation. Like parents, they demand unquestioning obedience.

From the description of the chief gender characteristics given above, it is clear that in Tajikistan the ideal masculine and feminine identities coincide with those of the mature adult male and the young female. In other words, the power differential between the sexes is accentuated by the generational distinction. Young women find themselves in the lowest power positions, especially immediately after marriage when they are likely to find themselves incomers (virtually interlopers) in an alien family where they have no established relationships (cf. Baştuğ and Hortaşçu 2000).

However, young men do not have it easy either. As males they are supposed to be powerful but they are also supposed to honor and obey their elders. This means that while they can exert control only over females of their own age and younger people of both sexes, older women have authority over them. In other words, young men are confronted with the need to live up to the ideal of the mature male while being kept in thrall to both parents, in front of whom they have to demonstrate submission only marginally less humbly than do their sisters. As they grow older, they gain in power until eventually, in maturity, they can become heads of family in their own right. However, as long as their parents are alive, they will still have to obey them.

As was suggested above, even more thoroughly than men women are supposed to suppress their inner selves while young. Like their brothers, however, they also increase their power base as they age, until they reach the point when as mothers-in-law they have *kelins* of their own to rule over. In reality, as I just explained, they also rule over their sons. However, this concept does not enter public discourse, since it contradicts the gender norms of submissive females and domineering males.

In fact, although not publicly spoken of, mature women take on many characteristics usually attributed to males. At the same time, young men have to negotiate between living up to the masculine ideal of the mature male while simultaneously demonstrating subservience (usually associated with femininity) to their elders. The result is that in Tajikistan both young men and women have held out to them the promise of the patriarchal bargain that exacts submission to elders in youth, in exchange for power when they are older (Kandiyoti 1991: 32–33).

The problem is that this system breaks down when couples have no sons. If they have daughters it may be possible to negotiate with one of their daughters' husbands to live with them after marriage to allow them some measure of family continuity and support in old age. However, this means that the mother will never be able to attach herself to an adult son, nor have a *kelin* of her own, and it is through these means that mature women gain their real power base.

Men are also penalized if they are unable to produce sons, since they are not considered "real" men. This is why so many Tajik men insist on having child after child until a son is born. In fact, because sons are so important for the status of both parents, women may also be willing to try very hard to have one.

Worst of all, of course, is infertility, which becomes both a cultural and an economic disaster in the Tajik context, as in other similar settings[12] (cf. Inhorn 1996).

COLLECTIVISM AND CHILDREARING

In Tajikistan, where collectivism is expressed through hierarchical, gerontocratic power relationships, young people are expected not to have a voice of their own. Sadbarg, for instance, knows she is supposed to obey her parents unquestioningly and should not think for herself or make her own decisions.

According to Western psychological theory, authoritarian childrearing like that which Jumabek and Kutfi practice facilitates young people's submission to parental decision-making and makes it difficult for them to separate from their parents (Grotevant and Cooper 1998). In the middle-class Western terms in which most psychological theory is couched, such parenting is considered negative.

This is because mainstream psychological theory has typically ignored social context and assumed that everyone subscribes to the same ideals as the white Western middle classes. However, recently the growth of cultural and cross-cultural psychology has shown that child development occurs differentially across societies, depending on context-specific childrearing practices, and that different material conditions demand different types of childrearing in order to maximize survival.

In other words, each type of society prioritizes child-rearing methods suited to its particular material conditions. Jumabek and Kutfi needed their children's labor and valued their material contributions to family welfare. They put less stress on the emotional relationship. This is consistent with findings from traditionally inclined families elsewhere that prioritize utility values in family relations (see Chapter 6).

From her schooling and her television viewing, Sadbarg learned to think in a more urbanized and educated context, in which children are valued more for their emotional than their utility value (Kağıtçıbaşı 1996: 81–89). This put her at cross-purposes with her parents. After marriage Sadbarg was determined to follow a more modernistic lifestyle and especially to develop strong emotional ties with her children. She also intended to have a small family so she could concentrate her attention on each child.

For the last few decades Tajiks have tended to favor large families. This was a response both to the very high child mortality rates of the early part of the twentieth century and to Soviet policies that greatly rewarded mothers of large numbers of children. However, since the breakup of the Soviet Union, parents can no longer afford to have many children, and therefore there has been a general tendency towards smaller families (Harris 2002). So far there has not been a corresponding change in approaches to parenting.

It has been suggested that in agrarian societies with high infant and child mortality, authoritarian childrearing styles make sense because in such a context children's obedience gives more chance of survival than their independence (Levine 1974, 1988 in Kağıtçıbaşı 1996: 29–30). Historically, this is the type of society that existed in Tajikistan, which may in part explain the origin of local parenting styles.

The dictatorial Soviet regime, with its frequent waves of purges, may well have been another reason for parents to teach obedience. It was no doubt considered important to ensure young people's public conformity in order to avoid trouble. In these circumstances, it is almost inevitable that Tajik parenting would be authoritarian. Like Jumabek and Kutfi, the majority of parents I knew in Tajikistan insisted on automatic obedience from their children.

In white Western middle-class families, parenting styles tend to teach early independence and reinforce boundaries between individuals (Benjamin 1995: 49ff). Mothers learn that it is wrong to merge with their young children because it hinders their correct development. This is because in individualistic societies people maintain strong interpersonal boundaries. In Tajikistan, families prefer to keep the boundaries between members weak and fluid in order to foster interpersonal dependency and close family bonds (cf. Kağıtçıbaşı 1996: 69–70).

Childrearing practices are strongly sex specific. Girls are kept at home and learn about domestic chores and caring for children from watching their mothers and older sisters. From early puberty onwards, they are closely guarded as an important repository of family honor. Boys, on the other hand, spend much of their time outside in the street, playing with their peers. Carla Makhlouf observed the same phenomenon in Yemen (Makhlouf 1979: 24). This differential influences the development of gender identities, since such experiences are implicated in how children learn to behave in gender-appropriate ways (Butler 1999: 19).

Kutfi had so many children she had had little time to pay attention to the early development of any particular one. However, even when they were older she spent little time interacting with them. She and Jumabek tended mainly to pay attention when the children bothered them. It is considered negative in this setting for children to disturb their parents by attracting attention to themselves. Hence, when Jumabek scolded his children in front of me, this was not because of their violence but because they were disturbing us adults (cf. Kağıtçıbaşı 1996: 45).

In the more traditionalistic Tajik families, children are expected to learn not from parental explanation but by example and observation. This means they do not need large amounts of individual attention to become socially competent adults. Thus, Kutfi was able to raise Sadbarg and her other children to function perfectly well within their environment. Unfortunately, this system works well only as long as the traditional context is maintained. Adaptation to new circumstances is difficult since the system does not support the transfer of skills to new types of tasks (Kağıtçıbaşı 1996: 36–37).

In contrast to people from more traditionally inclined families, the more modernistic of my Tajik acquaintances tended to have fewer children and to use verbal communication to encourage their development, in a manner similar to middle-class Western practices.

COLLECTIVISM IN TRANSITIONAL TAJIKISTAN

Collectivism puts the responsibility for deciding what comprises the good of an in-group in the hands of its leader. As we have seen, in the case of the most important Tajik in-group—the family—the leader is the male family head. It is therefore *his* right to decide what the good of this family will be.

However, family heads are not permitted to choose this arbitrarily. They are under pressure to ensure that what is defined as the good of the family conforms to community norms, as we have seen. This will ensure that practices within each family strengthen the wider collective. Thus, conforming to the family head's concept of good should automatically encompass appropriate demonstration of adherence to community norms. This will keep a family's status high within the community, which is beneficial to all its members.

Community norms allow a certain measure of leeway on the part of each family, depending on status. The most socially secure will have the widest margins within which their members are permitted to act. Low-status families, such as that of Jumabek, are under greater pressure to conform (Ginat 1982: 180).

However, since parents do not control every minute of their children's lives, and since in the transitional world of Tajikistan today children are exposed to multiple influences outside the family, they may well seek spaces within which to maneuver outside the narrow confines of the family and develop their own personalities. Thus, Sadbarg was able to make use of her schooling and her observations of the different lifestyles of her neighbors, as well as her exposure to television to develop new ideas and opinions of her own that moved her some distance from her parents' conceptual world, even while she was still bound by their material sphere. In this way, she had psychologically moved beyond conformity to the collective in which she had been raised. The same thing was true when she expressed her longing to travel and see the world.

One of the continua I described in the Introduction had collectivism at one end and individualism at the other. This is closely related but not identical to the continuum running between traditionalism and modernism, which I discussed in Chapter 2.

The fact that she was able to express personal desires that clashed with community values shows that Sadbarg was moving away from the collectivist end of this continuum, as she was from the traditionalist end of the other one. Nevertheless, she did not wish to become an individualist in the Western sense. She was strongly committed to being part of her family and very aware of how vulnerable she could become without their support. Moreover, marriage had now positioned her within her husband's collective, where she had to show conformity also. Thus, collectivism was as vital for her survival in marriage as it had been in girlhood.

The fact that Sadbarg had ideas that went beyond the collective does not mean she sought to adopt an individualistic lifestyle. On the contrary, the very thought was frightening because this would force her to take on responsibilities she was completely unprepared for. Similarly, she did not intend to raise her children as individualists, which she viewed as egotistical. She would bring them up to respect their parents and to be good and productive family members.

Life without her family, whether marital or natal, was unthinkable for Sadbarg. Irrespective of any emotional attachment, she knew they would remain mutually dependent for life in the material sense. In this social setting, where pensions have become so eroded they barely buy a few loaves of bread and where medical care is no longer free, family support in old age or sickness is essential for all but the richest. Even a hospital stay is impossible without family contributions, since food is rarely provided, and all comforts for patients must be brought in from the outside. Often this will include medications and even bedding.

Moreover, family support is important for young people, not just for the elderly. As we shall see in the next chapter, without this it is difficult to enter higher education or gain employment. In other words, family support is crucial for material survival throughout one's lifespan.

Those people I knew in Tajikistan who had lost all their family members in the war, or who were stranded far from home and family, found themselves in a very difficult situation. Their fate constituted a potent warning for young people tempted to believe themselves capable of living independently, as did also the increasing numbers of children living in orphanages and the growing body of street children, often forced into prostitution to survive.

Despite support from aid organizations, their situation is dire. They have nowhere to live, no support to gain income-generating skills, no way of finding a job, and nobody to arrange a marriage for them. Conforming to collectivist ethics appeared to Sadbarg a small price to pay for remaining safe from such a fate.

Collectivism, then, is one answer to the lack of a social safety net to keep the poor and vulnerable from slipping into destitution. In times of reasonable prosperity and stability it works well, since most families will have sufficient resources to help their most vulnerable members. The problem is that resources can be overstretched when income-generating opportunities have become as limited and uncertain as they currently are in Tajikistan. As a result, many families are unable to comply with all their obligations. Nevertheless, the poorest Tajiks are considerably better off in this dire economic situation than poverty-stricken Russians, whose family relationships are based on individualism.

The elderly Russians who were mentioned in Chapter 2 as having been abandoned by their families were clearly in an exceedingly bad state. In the mid-1990s, during my first few visits to Tajikistan, their numbers were visibly diminishing, almost by the week. Some were no doubt sent for by their children in Russia, but many more died of starvation and neglect.

When pensions were not paid or became worth too little to live on, and they were unable to procure sufficient aid to compensate, they would have no recourse but to beg. Most adult beggars were elderly Russians, or Tajiks who had lost their families in the war. This was another warning of the dangers of individualism.

Sadbarg admired the independent, autonomous women portrayed in her favorite Latin American soap operas. At the same time, she realized that such a lifestyle was not for her. She did not want to live for herself alone, nor did she wish to make all her own decisions. She knew she could not have it both ways. Either she set out to travel the world, bearing the consequences of almost certain alienation from her family, or she accepted the constraints of collectivism in return for reaping the advantages.[13]

In the West young people would not normally be forced to abandon their families in order to seek their dreams. This is because the concept of pursuing individual goals is coherent with local parenting styles. It is an accepted part of childrearing in the individualist environment of the United States, for instance, to encourage young people to develop agency, make their own decisions, and, when old enough, earn their own living and lead an independent life.

In Sadbarg's circle, it would be social death for a young person to assert her right to autonomy, and she understands this very well.[14] This is not what she is looking for. She is simply one of a growing number of young people, particularly in Dushanbe, who have been exposed to ideas of individualism and modernity and who would like their families to make at least a small concession to this. These youngsters do not wish to be individualists—they do not wish to fend for themselves, make their own decisions, or be responsible for their own lives. However, they do want their parents at least to consider their wishes and needs; they long to be treated with greater equality and respect than they are at present. In other words, they want to move out of their family's current lifestyle to one that more nearly resembles Kağıtçıbaşı's emotionally interdependent family, commonly found among educated families in Turkey and other countries of the Asian south.[15]

In Tajikistan the discrepancy between parental insistence on authoritarianism and the desires of today's young people to share in decision-making has not led to actual rebellion, for the reasons described above. It is simply not feasible for young people to rebel without the material basis for it. This is especially true for girls, who have very little latitude in behavior if they want to be eligible for marriage with a decent family. Thus, they are virtually obliged to acquiesce to their parents' demands and obey their wishes.

Young men who really do not wish to submit now have one potential escape route unavailable to their unmarried sisters. They can migrate to the Russian Federation.[16] Moving to Russia allows these men to experiment with freedom without cutting themselves permanently off from their families. It is impossible to know how many actually have this in mind when they leave. However, large numbers seem to prefer life there despite their attachment to their families in Tajikistan, since they spend more and more time out of the country. Increasingly, one hears of men like Sadbarg's eldest brother, who left for Russia and no longer communicates with his family.

For an unmarried girl to work even short-term in Russia would be problematic. Since her parents would no longer be able to guarantee her virginity, they might not be willing to take her back. To do so would shame them and thus lose them status in the community. Moreover, Tajik girls are not allowed to marry Russian men because their religion forbids them to marry non-Muslims. Such a marriage would separate them forever from their families and make them pariahs in their home communities, although their brothers can return to Tajikistan at any time, even with a Russian wife and children.

CONCLUSION

The tensions that Sadbarg experienced were due to her wish for the chance to have at least a small say in her own future, coupled with a dislike of her family's lifestyle. Nevertheless, her collective upbringing had not prepared her for an independent life, nor was this what she was really seeking. Her dreams of traveling and leading a different lifestyle from what her parents had planned for her were more wishful thinking than something she could actually imagine doing. It would have been far too risky. She realized only too well how important family support and a collective ethic were for material as well as emotional survival.

Individualism is just not attractive to most people in Tajikistan. Thus, what Sadbarg and her friends seem to be looking for, as we shall see in the following chapters, is not so much autonomy as a way of sharing power with the older generation, so that the collective good represents more fairly the good of all members of the in-group. They would also like their parents, husbands, and marital family to value them more for their emotional than their utility value.

CHAPTER FOUR

EDUCATION AND EMPLOYMENT

Contemporary forms of secular education and competitive job markets are strongly linked to the modern individualist worldview that developed in conjunction with capitalism. While these two institutions have now spread over most of the world, local values greatly influence their functioning.

In Central Asia, the Bolsheviks set up educational establishments and provided formal employment opportunities. These differed from their capitalist equivalents in that they depended less on individual competitiveness than on bureaucratic decisions (Bronfenbrenner 1970). Nevertheless, they were also supposed to depend on personal ability.

In Tajikistan, the population had their own way of dealing with this. One way was to buy their children's education. According to friends in Moscow, the republic was notorious in Soviet times for selling university degrees, at both undergraduate and graduate levels. This moved education from an individualistic to a collectivist enterprise, one where parents provided their children with the necessary qualifications rather than encouraging them to study and learn independently.

Today the situation is especially difficult because the government cannot afford to provide decent schooling. Particularly in rural areas, schools lack even the most basic amenities such as toilets, and textbooks have barely changed since Soviet times. Teachers work under difficult conditions for low pay and as a result most of the best ones have left the profession (ICG 2003).

The situation is therefore very discouraging for young people. On the one hand they are bored by the poor teaching; on the other they know that studying hard will not necessarily help them get good grades. These are more likely to depend on how much students can pay their instructors. Moreover, for all but the very best of them, entrance to tertiary education and the attainment of degrees are also dependent on money, not ability. Finally, with unemployment running at over 30 percent (ICG 2003), young people with few connections or resources fear they will have little access to work in the formal sector.

Since Soviet times, patron-client relations[1] have been important for access to good jobs in Central Asia, and today they are even more vital. There are few employment opportunities in Tajikistan for which appropriately qualified persons can compete on equal terms. People gain jobs not through having the appropriate skills but because of whom they know, or how much they are able to pay to obtain the position.

The following story relates the fortunes of a group of siblings from a family with few economic resources or useful connections, and tells of the difficulties they face in negotiating the barriers to gaining an education and subsequently earning a living.

When we became neighbors in early 1995, Nahdiya was a widow and mother of five children, Farhod, Tahmina, Jahongul, Farukh, and Bahorgul, whose ages at that time ranged from twenty-two to twelve years old, respectively.

Nahdiya's husband had been murdered nearly thirteen years before in connection with his work as a factory inspector. Their marriage had been arranged, but they had loved each other dearly, and all these years later she still missed him dreadfully. He had been an educated man with a master's degree, determined to see that his children were well educated too.

As a teenager, Nahdiya had wanted to go to university herself, but her mother hadn't seen any point in educating girls, who, after all, would just get married and become housewives. Wage earning was men's responsibility.

After Nahdiya had her first two children, her husband suggested she apply for university and told her he would support her studies, but she was no longer interested. After his death she regretted this, as her low level of education made it difficult to cope with Soviet bureaucracy or find decently paid work. For this reason, as well as because of her husband's wishes, Nahdiya was determined to send all her children to university, including the girls.

After her husband's death, Nahdiya took a job in a jewelry workshop. The family managed to survive reasonably well on her wages and the allowances she received from the government as a widow and mother of five. Their serious problems started after independence, when the workshop closed down and the allowances became almost worthless.

Nahdiya started working as a trader. She would buy cloth at the cheapest place in Dushanbe, travel down to her sister's place in Qurghonteppa, and sell it in the market there. However, this soon became too much for her health, especially during the cold winter months, so she was forced to stop. Later she worked as a cleaner, but for very low wages.

By this time, it had become impossible for any but the very best students to pass the higher-education entrance exams without paying a "fee," which Nahdiya simply could not afford. As a result, both Farhod and Tahmina failed to get into university. After several attempts, Farhod gave up trying. It was time for him to get married, and he needed to start earning money. Tahmina, however, was desperate to get a degree, so the family asked all their neighbors and friends with connections at the university if they could help. One of them said she thought she could get Tahmina accepted through her mother, a professor in the department where Tahmina wanted to study.

It was shortly after the main fighting in the civil war had ended and the news was full of stories of girls being abducted and raped. This scared Nahdiya so much that she decided the safest thing to do was to marry her daughter to remove her from danger. She could study later, when things quieted down. Tahmina was horrified, but she didn't dare tell her mother how upset she was. Nahdiya realized her daughter wasn't happy with her decision but was sure it was for the best. She arranged a marriage for her with a family living in a village in Hissor, whose son was studying economics at the university in Dushanbe.

Before completing the arrangements, Nahdiya extracted a promise from Tahmina's prospective parents-in-law that they would allow the young couple to live in Dushanbe and would help her daughter enter university. However, after the wedding they reneged on their promise and forced Tahmina to live in the village with them. They needed her for the housework, they said, and had no intention of sending her to study. Without a powerful man to support her, Nahdiya was unable to force them to keep their promise. She was very distressed and deeply regretted the marriage, but it was too late.

I became acquainted with Tahmina some two years after her wedding. She had come to her mother's place for a visit and was considering whether to ask for a divorce. She told me how much she hated living with her in-laws. She said they treated her like a slave, forcing her to work day and night. If she asked to listen to music or watch television in the evenings, she would be scolded and told that she was not there for entertainment. She felt that she was being treated like a servant.

Tahmina's younger sister Jahongul was sixteen and in her last year of high school. She very much wanted to achieve what her older siblings had not; that is, to study for a profession. However, first she had to complete her school exams and figure out how to be accepted into university. She wasn't at all sure whether she could achieve this, in view of her older siblings' failures.

Like her sister, Jahongul was studying at a Tajik[2] high school. The majority of girls in her class were preparing to marry, she told me. Their parents had informed them that this would happen immediately after graduation, irrespective of whether they wanted to continue their education. Most of them were upset about this. They knew they might well have similar problems to those Tahmina had faced in getting their marital families to permit them to study. Without such agreement they would have no option but to become housewives (sidit' doma). However, there were a few girls who thought there would be no point in studying if their husband earned enough to support his family well.

Jahongul had computer lessons at school, but she said they only did a little DOS and simple BASIC programming. She didn't really understand anything about computers because the teacher never explained properly. In any case, no one learned much at school anymore. The teachers gave whatever marks they felt like, the students attended class whenever they wanted, and nobody seemed to bother much about anything.

Jahongul was constantly being called out of class to help the teachers with tasks such as typing. This caused her to miss many lessons, including most of her English classes. She didn't think this mattered, since, in return for her help, she would be given a good grade. If a teacher suggested she might fail the subject, Jahongul would offer her services in return for being promised a four.[3] This was the lowest grade she could afford to get if she were going to be accepted into college. The previous year she had received a four in algebra and a five in Tajik literature, despite not studying at all. Even though Jahongul and her friends didn't have much money to spare, before each exam they brought their teachers food, as added insurance.

I asked Jahongul what the point of good grades was if she didn't learn anything. She insisted the classes weren't worth attending anyway. The teachers didn't exert themselves now that their pay was almost worthless, and there was no control over standards. Jahongul had little motivation to learn, since the highest grades went to those who gave the most expensive presents or provided the most valuable services for their teachers, not to those who gave the best answers.

Moreover, good grades were no guarantee of acceptance into university. Most of those who went on to tertiary education did so through family connections or by paying bribes. Only five out of the previous year's graduating class had managed to get into university. A large group who had failed the entrance exams came back and asked their teachers why they had even bothered attending school.

Meanwhile, Jahongul's own preparation was so poor that she was unable to answer more than half the questions on the previous year's Russian and Tajik language entrance papers.

In Jahongul's home the only reading materials were the children's school-books. Sometimes when she came over to my place she would look at my small library. She clearly found it strange that I had such a thing, especially considering I was just there for a few months. Although I offered to loan her books in Russian or Tajik, she never accepted. She explained that in her scant spare time, she preferred to sleep or watch television.

Indeed, Jahongul really was very busy. Nahdiya didn't do any housework now that she had daughters old enough to do it, and since Tahmina was rarely there, it mostly fell on Jahongul's shoulders. Bahorgul was too young.

Thus, Jahongul had little time to spare for studying. If her mother needed something, or if guests arrived, Jahongul was obliged to put her books aside. Her brothers also expected her to put their needs before her own, demanding that she mend their clothes or prepare a meal for them, regardless of whether she had schoolwork to do. Jahongul said she really didn't care that much because she didn't believe it was important anyway.

In the end, like her elder siblings, she also failed the exams, and her mother arranged for her to marry immediately on graduation. However, afterwards Nahdiya managed to enroll her in technical school, where she studied bookkeep-ing and accounting.

By the time she finished, her first child had been born. He had a health prob-lem, and it took all Jahongul's time and energy to take him for treatment and do therapy with him at home. Thus, she didn't even look for a job. After her second child was born, she abandoned all thought of employment for the moment in fa-vor of fulltime motherhood.

Tahmina's husband was a student in the economics department at the Tajik State University. His courses mainly addressed the organization of a planned economy, he said, but the department intended to start teaching market econ-omy sometime in the near future. The young man didn't seem particularly con-cerned about his courses' lack of relevance to the contemporary world. His parents were paying for his exams, so he was scarcely bothering to attend classes anyway. It was only the degree that counted, he told me; there was nothing to be gained by studying.

He thought it would be good if Tahmina could get a degree in the same way. However, his parents refused to pay for their kelin's education.

Some five years after Tahmina's marriage, Nahdiya managed to pull strings to get her registered as an external student in the department of Tajik philology. External students don't follow the normal semester system, but instead have two short, intensive sessions of classes a year, each lasting some forty days. Tahmina was just able to manage this, but the rest of the year her time was occupied with *domestic tasks. Except during the period of classes, she never opened a book, she said. External students were not expected to study outside the sessions.*

To get her younger son, Farukh, into university, Nahdiya borrowed $500—a fortune, representing her wages for over four years. By this time very few instructors were giving students passing grades without payment. The family was struggling financially and could not afford to pay to get him through all the exams, so after a couple of years Farukh was forced to abandon his studies and seek work in Russia. By 2003 he had found a job as a builder and was sending money home to pay off their many debts.

From the time she was very young, Bahorgul's best friend had been Russian. To ensure that her daughter received a good education, her friend's mother decided to send her to the best possible secondary school. She persuaded Nahdiya that it would be to Bahorgul's advantage to accompany her friend. Unlike her siblings' secondary school, this one was Russian.

When I first met her as a twelve-year-old, Bahorgul had been no more interested in studying than her sisters. However, the influence of teachers and fellow students at her new school caused her to change her attitude. She started to find learning interesting and even to read for pleasure.

One reason her school was better than that attended by her sisters was that the director categorically refused to allow teachers to demand bribes. To compensate, she arranged for parents to pay a monthly fee, which she used to supplement wages. In this way she was able to maintain standards. This made a tremendous difference to the attitudes of both teachers and students, and it kept the academic level high. In addition, when she reached the top two grades, Bahorgul was offered extra classes at the Turkish High School,[4] probably the best school in the country, and this helped her even more. Here she learned Turkish and a little English.

Bahorgul's school friends were mostly from highly educated and even elite families, where girls were relatively free in their movements. As a result, by the time she was in the upper classes of high school, Bahorgul found the limitations her family wanted to impose on her mobility very frustrating. The most annoying was the way Farukh was constantly censuring her clothes and behavior. She finally had to ask her mother to make him stop.

By this time Dushanbe had become much less dangerous. The war was over, and it was no longer common to see men with Kalashnikovs in the streets. Bahorgul thought she should be trusted to go out by herself after school. She said she would never do anything to dishonor her family, but she wanted to be able to spend time with her friends just as her classmates did. Nahdiya said she trusted her daughter and insisted that Farukh leave her alone.

Another problem for Bahorgul was the fact that as the only daughter living at home, she had to do all the housework and attend to guests. This often made it difficult to finish her schoolwork. Nahdiya couldn't understand why it was necessary for her to do so much of it. Her other children never had, and she considered it a waste of time. To avoid arguments, Bahorgul took to doing her schoolwork at night after the family was in bed.

She had seen her sisters married at age seventeen to men they didn't care for and witnessed their subsequent misery. She didn't want to suffer the same fate. She was determined to study and make herself financially independent; she would marry only when she was ready and would pick her own husband.

Despite Bahorgul's much higher academic standards, she was still unable to get into university. This time, rather than marrying her daughter off, with great difficulty Nahdiya found her a job with a colleague of her late husband, who managed a private business. Despite minimal typing and computer skills, Bahorgul was hired as a secretary. At first, she told me, she was very slow and clumsy, but she learned fast and soon became the quickest and most accurate word processor in the firm. As a result she received a promotion. By 2003 she was earning one hundred somoni a month, over three times what her mother was making as a cleaner with the same firm.[5]

A year after graduating from high school, Bahorgul had saved enough to be able to pay for acceptance into the Tajik State University's department of economics as an external student. She studied very hard for her classes, helped by being able to use the computer and Internet at work. Her boss gave her time off with pay during the two yearly sessions, so she considered herself lucky. Still, it was a huge struggle to complete all the work at a high standard. She was determined to do well enough in her exams so that she would not have to pay to pass them, but this was something only the top few students could manage.

There were many obstacles in the way. For a start, there were hardly any textbooks available, and the teachers often didn't come to class. The physical conditions in the university were very poor—some of the windows had no glass, which was especially bad in the wintertime. There was no heating, and at times they almost froze. Teaching standards were low. The instructors knew practically nothing of market economics. Most of their textbooks dated from Soviet times, so a great deal of what they were studying was irrelevant to current conditions. Nevertheless, Bahorgul was determined to continue and get her degree. Her ambition was somehow to get a scholarship so she could study for her master's degree abroad.

Although a number of families approached her mother with offers of marriage, Bahorgul always refused. She insisted she would marry only when she found a man she really liked. Naydiya willingly agreed because she wanted so much to see one of her daughters happy. She told me she hoped Bahorgul would marry a foreigner. Tajik men were bad, she said. They used to be fine, but since independence they had all been corrupted.

When I last visited in 2003, Tahmina was living at her mother's place with her two children, while her husband was in Russia. Her daughter had just turned six, and it was time for her to start school. Her parents-in-law wanted them to move back to the village and send the child to school there, but Tahmina refused. She knew that the village school was useless and that her daughter would learn much more in Dushanbe. Her in-laws could not see why this was important and tried to insist on her returning to the village. But Tahmina told them the child was her daughter, and she would decide for her. Besides, it was her family that was paying all the costs.[6]

While all the members of this family believed in the importance of education, their reasons varied. Tahmina and Jahongul's poor level of schooling meant they put more stress on gaining a diploma than on learning, although their attitude changed regarding their children's education. Thus, Tahmina insisted that her daughter go to the best school available, even though she was only just starting first grade.

Bahorgul's viewpoint was the result of her superior schooling, which had made her interested in learning for its own sake. This was being undermined by her degree course, which was less well taught than her high school classes had been, but she was convinced she would enjoy studying at a good university—hence her ambition to study abroad.

Nahdiya believed it was her children's duty to support her in any way she demanded, but she also thought she had duties towards them, including providing them with access to higher education and jobs. However, her lack of education made it difficult for her to grasp the point of studying and to understand why her youngest daughter put so much stress on it. Following the traditions and providing appropriate levels of hospitality for friends and family were vital for building social capital, and thus they seemed more valuable than schoolwork.

The family members' differing outlooks arose from their different cultural exposure. Nahdiya grew up in the provinces, where she had little contact with Russians. She was raised in a traditionalist family, and her years of living in Dushanbe have done little to change her way of thinking, although her husband's influence at least made her appreciate the importance of good qualifications, even if she did not understand the point of learning.

Bahorgul, on the other hand, grew up around her Russian friend's family; her schooling helped to Russify her further. As a result, she thinks in a very different way from her mother and even from her older sisters, and her outlook is much more modernistic and individualistic.

Education Systems

Contemporary education systems tend to be based on those developed in the West, which are organized around rationality, scientific knowledge, and a secular worldview (Acar and Ayata 2002). Their main function is to prepare young people for participation in modern society, and particularly for successful competition in a capitalist job market. They were developed according to modernistic, individualistic ideology and are organized accordingly.

Students are judged mainly through supposedly impartial examinations intended to give all participants a level playing field. Using such tactics as reading exam questions beforehand to gain a personal advantage is considered cheating and is thus condemned.

Examinations are used to assess students' abilities, including whether they are fit to continue to higher education. They also determine students' final qualifications and levels of entry into the job market.

Such a system is contrary to the way traditional societies function—through personal interaction rather than impersonal bureaucracies. Moreover, in a truly traditional society, a secular education system has little point. Young people learn all necessary skills at home, since they usually follow the same trades as their parents. Such schooling as exists is likely to be aimed at providing religious competence, as was the case in Central Asia before the Russian conquest.

In the late nineteenth century, secular schools were established by Russians and Tatars. However, these reached very small numbers. After the Revolution the Bolsheviks established an education system along similar lines to the Western one described above, intended to reach the entire population. Their goal was both to prepare young people for employment in the new state and to indoctrinate them in Soviet ideology. Later instruction in communist morality was added. Children were taught how to deal with each aspect of their daily lives in the "correct" manner, both in and out of school. They were also supposed to join the appropriate youth groups, such as the Young Pioneers or the Komsomol'.

Uniform curricula were developed for all schools in the union, irrespective of whether they were in Moscow or the most isolated Central Asian village. Textbooks were produced in Moscow and therefore used symbols familiar to Russian children, which were often unintelligible to those in the very different geocultural climate of Central Asia (Pearson 1990). Moreover, rural teachers in Tajikistan did not always fully understand the syllabi themselves, let alone know how to teach them effectively.

Special additional classes were introduced in Central Asian schools for the purpose of combating the pernicious effect of local cultures. The inculcation of atheism was an important component, as was instruction in Soviet behavioral ideals to counteract those taught at home.

Most important here were gender identities. The Soviet system generally taught that girls and boys were different, and aimed to encourage the appropriate feminine and masculine behavior in young children (Attwood 1985, 1990; Kon 1995). However, it also taught that men and women should participate equally in the workforce (Bronfenbrenner 1970; Pearson 1990). In Central Asia, schools further taught that girls should have the same rights as boys, especially in the matter of mobility and education. They should participate equally in sports and other after-school activities.

Since the majority of teachers were locals, it is hardly surprising that these topics were often not covered in the way the regime expected, even in most Russian-language schools. Nevertheless, many Tajik parents viewed the education system with unease and felt it to be a threat to the preservation of their culture, in particular where the teaching of girls was concerned. Thus, in the early days they strongly resisted sending their children to school (Rakowska-Harmstone 1970: 43–44). It took some decades before parents started doing this as a matter of course. However, by the time of independence almost all children were in school, usually remaining at least through eighth grade (ICG 2003).

Like Karomat's, other parents also counteracted the pernicious effects of the education system by reinforcing local norms and values. For instance, one of Kutfi's neighbors told me that as a child she had found it very confusing to be taught at school that there was no such entity as God, while at home she was informed it was her duty to revere Allah and obey His precepts. Since as an adult she considered herself a good Muslim, it seems her parents' influence was the stronger.

The contradictions between the school teachings and the Tajik traditions were one reason for parents preferring to remove their daughters from school as early as possible[7] (Tolmacheva 1993: 537–38). In addition, it seemed pointless for them to learn things that would be of little use in the future, since the vast majority would not enter formal employment. Parents felt the time would be better spent preparing them for their future roles as *kelins* and mothers.

Certainly the women we taught in Ghamkhori's rural development project appeared to have received little benefit from their eight to ten years of education, other than basic literacy and numeracy skills. For many, even these had been little used in their adult lives. In some of the classes participants were asked to write, and it was common for women to tell us this was the first time since their school years they had done so (Harris 1999).

The indifference Tajik families show towards schooling may also be due to differences between learning styles. As was pointed out in Chapter 3, in traditional societies children are expected to absorb skills by observing the same-sex parent at work, the aim being to develop social competence, rather than cognitive or verbal skills. However, since the latter are vital for secular education, children from families that do not encourage their development may be seriously handicapped at school (Kağıtçıbaşı 1996: 35ff). It was only by dint of great efforts that Bahorgul was able to benefit from the teaching of her Russian school and overcome the disadvantages of her background, including the lack of books at home.

COLLECTIVISM, INDIVIDUALISM, AND EDUCATION

Another reason for the clash between Tajik values and those represented by the Soviet school system is the difference between a collectivist and an individualist ethic. Sovietized Russian culture did not privilege individualism in the American sense of sharp separation from the group. Rather, it encouraged a collective type of individualism. People were expected to serve group interests as the regime demanded. However, Russians also kept clearly differentiated selves and were encouraged to develop their personal abilities (Triandis 1995: 44–47, 143).

Salient differences between Russian/Soviet and Tajik cultures included ways in which boundaries were drawn among collectives and between members of collectives. The Soviet regime constructed community boundaries in such a way as to further its ideological mission of the moment. Citizens might be asked one day to collaborate with their neighbors in cleaning up their apartment block, and the next to demonstrate loyalty to their workplace. Neither of these in-groups has strong boundaries. Even the Russian family has permeable boundaries that permit the relatively easy entry of new members, such as a child's spouse. However, Russians draw fairly strong boundaries around individuals.

For Tajiks, on the other hand, membership in their collectives, of which the most important are family and region of origin, is crucial for their personal identity. They draw tight boundaries between these in-groups and the rest of the world, which greatly hinders the acceptance of outsiders. However, the boundaries between members of these collectives are permeable, particularly between family members[8] (cf. Geertz 1975; Kağıtçıbaşı 1996: 53).

Soviet schools stressed the concept of students working as a collective (Bronfenbrenner 1970; Pearson 1990), but they also put emphasis on individual achievements and high marks. Parents were expected to help their children with homework and to encourage them to achieve scholastic excellence.

In Tajikistan, however, even if they wanted to, uneducated parents like Nahdiya, Jumabek, or Kutfi would be unable to help their children with schoolwork. In any case, it is rare for Tajik parents to encourage their children to excel at school. This is hardly surprising, since their collectivist outlook means they do not value those who stand out from the crowd (Triandis 1995: 44) and therefore rarely prize personal achievements in their children. In fact, they play them down, endeavoring to keep young people from seeking independence.

Moreover, people in Tajikistan do not necessarily believe academic achievements are meaningful, especially for females, since learning culturally appropriate social competence and housework skills is a better preparation for the domestic future that is supposed to be their lot (cf. Kağıtçıbaşı 1996: 36). After all, Tajik women are not conceptualized as participants in the workforce, as I discuss later on.

Kağıtçıbaşı (1996: 62) makes the point that competitive schooling is incompatible with a collectivist ethic. This is echoed in other settings. For instance, in Yemen in the 1970s, as Carla Makhlouf discovered, teachers were viewed as part of children's families. As such, it seemed logical they should want to help their students. They were therefore expected to do such things as reveal examination questions in advance. Teachers who did not feel comfortable doing this would find themselves in a difficult situation, since *their* students would miss out, while students from other classes would be well prepared. The result was that most teachers found themselves compelled to go along with what was essentially the subversion of the individualistic and competitive nature of the system (Makhlouf 1979: 71).

Since the idea of school as a place where each child is individually responsible for his or her own work is alien to collectivist thinking, it seems natural for parents to intervene, for instance, by giving gifts to teachers to encourage them to reciprocate in the matter of their children's grades. This practice has long existed in Tajikistan, as indeed in other parts of Central Asia (Lubin 1984; Nazpary 2002).

Russians see this as corruption and look upon it with great disdain. Viewed from a collectivist standpoint, however, it makes sense. Children are not supposed to have to confront the world alone, without support from their in-group. Giving a gift to boost their marks is a logical way of dealing with the individualistic education system.

Of course, if parents help their children in this way, it not only makes praise for good marks meaningless but also makes it difficult for children to learn to rely on their own abilities, as these are never tested. But why should they be? In a collectivist setting people are not supposed to have to rely on themselves alone.

During Soviet times providing teachers with gifts supplemented incomes, which although low were at least sufficient to pay for the necessities of life. This is no longer the case. Since independence, the government of Tajikistan has been hard pressed to pay teachers' salaries at all. During the 1990s, levels

of remuneration rapidly fell from a reasonable living wage to one barely sufficient to purchase a couple of loaves of bread a month. Many teachers left the
profession and became traders or migrant laborers (ICG 2003). As was the
case in Jahongul's school, those who remained started charging students to
take examinations, offering the best grades to those who paid the most. When
it became clear that this was going to be a long-term situation, a few of the
best schools, such as that which Bahorgul attended, started to charge monthly
fees in order to preserve academic standards, paying their teachers for their
work rather than for exam results.

In Central Asia, payment for university entry has long been considered a
logical response to a system that expects students to enter tertiary education
by passing examinations. Subsequently, payments to course instructors to ensure good exam results reflected further parental contributions towards their
children's degrees. Such practices enabled university teachers in some disciplines to earn as much as ten to twenty times their salaries (Lubin 1984: 192;
Nazpary 2002).

In Tajikistan today, the cost of entering higher education ranges from several thousand dollars for law and medicine down to almost free for the least
desirable disciplines. Like Tahmina's husband, many students whose parents
can afford to pay their way through school scarcely bother to attend classes at
all, and very often the teachers do not either.

The Slovyansky University in Dushanbe is one of the few institutions that
has tried to maintain standards.[9] It has two tracks: The first is for the best students and is free as long as they keep a high grade point average. The second
is for lesser-achieving students who can afford to pay for their studies. All the
entrance exams are difficult, and competition for the first track is fierce.

The vast majority who are unable to achieve such high standards are left to
use collectivist approaches and arrange their studies through *blat* or bribes.
This effectively bars students like Jahongul, who were unable to pass the exams under their own steam and have neither wealth nor useful contacts, from
entering a good institution.

The education situation is similar in the other Central Asian republics.
Few courses have up-to-date textbooks in local languages. New books are
mainly imported from Russia, or even occasionally from the West, in English,
and are correspondingly expensive. In any case, instructors are not trained to
teach new concepts or methodologies and are too poorly paid to bother improving their skills. Despite the recent introduction of paid tertiary education
in some republics, the system of paying bribes for entering universities and
passing exams appears to be continuing (ICG 2003).

A very few foreign institutions exist, such as the Turkish High Schools in
Tajikistan and Uzbekistan and the American University in Bishkek, to which
entrance can be gained only through truly competitive examinations, and

where teaching levels are high. Their students tend to come from relatively individualistic families that prize the development of academic excellence in their children and encourage them to succeed through their own efforts. Most of the best students in Tajikistan come from such backgrounds, including my acquaintances in the first track at the Slovyansky. Even in other universities, the very best students are usually allowed to pass exams without payment, so that the tiny minority who manage to achieve the requisite standards can in fact earn their degrees without paying bribes.

While Jahongul had little belief in her ability to cope independently with tertiary education, Bahorgul was much more self-assured. Good schooling and modernistic friends had given her somewhat of an individualistic outlook. She had been obliged to pass her high school examinations on her own merit. This gave her the assurance that she could do the same at the university too. She was determined to continue this throughout her degree course, if at all possible.

Summing up the situation in regard to education in Tajikistan, it can be said that the large number of students dependent on their collective rather than on their personal ability to pass exams is a result of both the lack of emphasis families place on individual attainments and poor levels of education that neither prepare students adequately nor interest them in studying. As a result, people are mainly concerned with gaining qualifications, which are a prerequisite for many jobs.

Many of the poorest and least educated families, who know they will be unable to help their children gain skilled employment, have simply stopped sending them to school at all (ICG 2003).

Skills and Employment

One downside to all this is that it effectively negates the use of education for the attainment of knowledge and skills for employment purposes. Central Asia has long had a problem in regard to the disjunction between skills and employment. Soviet officials complained that in Central Asia people's qualifications often did not match their actual jobs. In other words, the disciplines in which students gained their diplomas were not necessarily related to the jobs they sought after graduation. The officials were concerned, since it implied either that the field of study was irrelevant, that people were not properly trained for the work they were doing, or both (Lubin 1984).

In the post-Soviet period in Tajikistan, this issue has been further complicated by the fact that the education system is in many respects so out of date that what is studied bears almost no relevance to contemporary conditions. The Tajik government has not had sufficient resources to retrain its teachers or publish new textbooks. UNICEF has helped with some basic books, and a

Figure 4.1 Rural primary school in Khatlon

few other organizations have followed suit, but most subjects are still taught just as they were in Soviet times. In some disciplines this may not much matter, but others are now so outdated they make very little sense.

Among the subjects that most need updating is economics. More than a decade after the end of the socialist system, Bahorgul's course still taught Soviet principles, despite the promise to Tahmina's husband's class some seven years earlier that the next cohort would study market economics. When I looked through Bahorgul's textbooks in 2003, I saw no mention of the market.

In such a situation, it is very understandable that students do not take studying seriously. Bahorgul says she has learned more about economics through her job than from anything she has studied at university, and no doubt she is not alone in this.

Since independence, the labor market in Tajikistan has undergone tremendous transformations. State institutions are much less dominant, although a relatively large number of people continue to work for the state. As might be expected, private firms comprise an increasingly significant proportion of enterprises. However, there is an enormous shortfall in employment opportunities compared with the numbers seeking work.

In the last decades of the Soviet era, there was already significant unemployment and underemployment (Akiner 2001; Fierman 1991b). This has now greatly increased, mainly because of lack of jobs but also because the mismatch in skills between those seeking work and those seeking employees has continued and even grown (Fierman 1991a: 20; ICG 2003).

EMPLOYMENT IN A COLLECTIVE ENVIRONMENT

Bribes and *blat* have the same importance for entering employment in Tajikistan as they do for education. Even those who have honestly earned their degrees will probably still have to use connections or else purchase a position. I was told, for instance, that each clinic in Dushanbe had its own scale of payments for physicians seeking a post there. The size of the fee was dependent on how much each position was estimated to bring the practitioner in sub-rosa fees.[10]

In private firms, hiring occurs only through connections. Moreover, when the persons who provided the job leave, all those who received employment through them may be laid off to make room for the new bosses' associates. Bahorgul feared suffering the same fate. Her mother had found her the job through a former colleague of her father's, who manages the firm where she now works. Bahorgul knows that if the owner brings in another manager, it is very unlikely she will be invited to remain.

As for state jobs, the top positions everywhere are now routinely given to Kulobis—that is, to people from the region President Rakhmonov comes from—if not to people from his native village. This occurs even when it means removing more competent and experienced people from other regions from their posts. This expanded form of nepotism is in fact a kind of collectivism. Even when the president himself does not intervene, Kulobis appear to consider it their right to make use of their membership in the president's collective to gain benefits.

In such circumstances, it is not surprising that increasing numbers of the less privileged are emigrating to places such as the Russian Federation, where it is easier to find work. It has been estimated that around a third of the Tajik labor force is currently employed in the Russian Federation (ICG 2003: 32). Certainly, Tahmina's husband, her two brothers, the eldest brother's wife and her family all now live there more or less permanently. Sadbarg's two oldest brothers and many of her neighbors are there, too. More and more of the men and even some of the women from the Khatlon villages served by Ghamkhori now work in Russia for at least part of each year. Even there, since most Tajik citizens are working illegally, they usually only manage to gain employment through connections. Thus, people from one Tajik village are likely to work in the same Russian town, having all been recruited by the same person.

TENSIONS AROUND WOMEN'S EMPLOYMENT

As I have mentioned before, levels of female employment have always been low in Tajikistan, and there is still considerable prejudice against it. In some circles it is even considered a sin for women to go out to work (Harris 2004: 82–84). Thus, the discourse around feminine gender ideals suggests that they should not be employed outside the home. In actual fact, since the numbers of both female-headed households and single women are rapidly increasing (ICG 2003), more and more women are forced to earn their living. Unfortunately, the gap between discourse and reality means that females are rarely given the chance to acquire useful qualifications. Women therefore tend to be ill prepared for employment, so that they end up in low-paying jobs that keep them and their families below the poverty line.

Today girls usually marry right after leaving high school, so it is their marital families who decide whether they may study and/or enter the workforce. Besides producing children, the main function of a *kelin* in traditionalist families is to provide domestic services. This is especially important for those living in *havlis* like Kutfi's and Jumabek's, which resemble tiny farms requiring considerable labor to keep them going.

Mothers-in-law in such surroundings usually refuse to allow their *kelins* to enter the workforce, as they need their labor at home. This is one reason they prefer uneducated girls, who supposedly will have little interest in getting a job. Moreover, it is feared that a woman with a high level of education, or one who is financially independent, might decide to challenge the system whereby young women are subordinated to their families[11] (cf. Badran 1995: 165; Kağıtçıbaşı 1996: 37). This explains why many Tajik parents prefer not to educate their daughters, and why Tajikistan had the lowest female employment levels of any former Soviet republic (UNDP 1995: 44).

Young Tajik women who do hold a job are often still expected to perform the domestic tasks commonly demanded of a *kelin,* irrespective of the fact that they are contributing to the family income and that they have much less time at home than *kelins* without outside employment. In-laws are not sympathetic to this issue. Their thinking tends to be that they are doing their *kelins* a favor by allowing them to work outside the house, and that they should work extra hard inside it to show their gratitude. After all, their proper function is not to earn a living but to contribute their labor.

In other words, there is considerable suspicion of female employment, and women who work outside the home are carefully watched in order to ensure they do not take advantage of the situation to increase their power position.

The problem is that today many women have no choice but to become breadwinners. This happened to Nahdiya after her husband was killed, and to Kutfi after her husband became disabled. Their high levels of social competence as *kelins* were of little use to them in the Soviet employment arena. For lack of qualifications, neither was able to find a decently paid job. Such situations are increasing today with the growth in male labor migration. Their low education levels put Tajik women at a distinct disadvantage. During Soviet times, they were typically employed on collective and state farms as laborers, while their husbands worked as mechanics, drove tractors and harvesters, or took jobs in the nearest urban centers. Since independence, work on the farms is even less well paid and considerably physically harder because there is little machinery left in working order. Women working in the cotton fields would tell me in disgust that they were doing work formerly assigned to tractors. However, they cannot avoid this, because both the houses they live in and the private plots they feed their families from are on land belonging to the kolkhoz or sovkhoz. In compensation at least one family member has to contribute their labor to the farm. This is usually left to the women, since men look for better-paid work elsewhere, whereas women have few other options (cf. Tokhtakhodjaeva 1995: 114–15). Besides farm laboring, trading and dressmaking have become common ways for women to earn money. However, the returns are often negligible (Harris 1998).

It is in order to save her daughters from such a situation that Nahdiya has tried so hard to help them gain formal qualifications. Nevertheless, in choosing a wife for her elder son, Farhod, Nahdiya stuck to the convention that a bride should be submissive and obedient, rather than a financial support for her family, so she chose an almost illiterate girl. Her social competence was of little use when it came to helping her family financially. However, Nahdiya picked her before the extent of the economic distress in Tajikistan became apparent.

When I asked high school and university students whether they would prefer to have a paid job after graduation or to be housewives, almost all of them said they wanted to get a degree and then seek employment. However, they added the rider that this would depend on their husbands. It is the marital family that decides whether or not *kelins* will study and/or work. As I suggested above, all too often mothers-in-law see no benefit to having their *kelins* employed outside the home. They would rather have them at hand to do the housework.

Husbands also prefer their wives to stay at home. This is first because they believe that *real* men should be able to support their wives, and second because they want to prevent their wives from having any opportunity to meet men, since they fear this might tempt them to stray. Thus, a woman going out to work is seen as an indication of her husband's failure to live up to the standards of Muslim masculinity, according to which economic support is supposed to be men's responsibility (WHO 2000: 23) and female seclusion is the only effective way of preventing women from indulging in extramarital relations.

For both these reasons, Tahmina's husband wanted her to live in his family village, despite the fact that he was almost never there himself. When she insisted on remaining in her mother's household, he still tried to stop her from taking employment, despite the fact that during the ten years of their marriage he has never supported her or their two children.

Tahmina's husband had been living in Russia for more than three years, during which time he had scarcely been home. Two years previously, when he had paid a visit to his parents he asked Tahmina to join him and they slept together. She had not been prepared and became pregnant. She decided to get an abortion because she believed they couldn't afford another child, but her husband insisted that if she had a son he would take her and her children to Russia to live with him.

However, when Tahmina went through with the pregnancy and bore a son, nothing changed. Not only did her husband not send for her, neither he nor his family gave her any financial support. Since the boy's birth the only money he has sent his wife is a couple of hundred dollars for the child's medical expenses once when he was very sick.

Tahmina and her children were barely surviving on her family's charity. In 2003 one of their contacts offered her a job as a Tajik–Russian translator. Not only was this well paid, but attached to the facility was a kindergarten where her children could be cared for during the day. Tahmina's husband told her that if she took the job he would divorce her. It was his business to provide for the family, not hers. A good Muslim wife would not go out to work. So she turned the offer down. Later she realized her husband would never help her and decided to take the job after all, but it was too late, and after that she was unable to find another.

Bahorgul was disgusted and said that her sister had no guts. She believed that Tahmina's husband would have respected her more and treated her better had she defied him and taken the job. She thought it was incredible that Tahmina was so spineless that she allowed her husband to get away with neither providing for his family nor allowing her to work.

Although Tahmina's husband called on religion to justify his refusal to allow his wife to take the job, in fact, Islam does not give him the right to prevent her working. Actually, he is the one contravening religious law, since it is his duty to support his wife and children. In other Muslim settings, such as Egypt, if a man does not fulfill these duties, his wife is considered released from her obligations to him, including that of obedience (Hoodfar 1997; Watson 1994).

In Tajikistan this is not the case. Regardless of their husbands' behavior, women are expected to comply with their marital duties (Khegai 2002: 62–63). This puts pressure on Tahmina to obey her husband no matter what he does.

However, in today's difficult economic situation, Bahorgul is very likely right. Had Tahmina ignored his opinion and taken the job offer, few people would have condemned her for it, and her husband might not have divorced her either. After all, someone has to provide for her and her children. If he will not do it, then she is going to have to earn her own money. In such a case it may be possible to contravene the norms, provided this is not done in a publicly confrontational manner, especially since Tahmina can prove her husband has never fulfilled his obligations to her.

In this environment, where marriage is a family affair and masculinity very strongly dependent on the correct performance of femininity, the tensions around women's employment are directly connected to their gender identities. Girls are deprived of the chance to gain qualifications by parents who worry that education will reduce their daughters' chances of marriage. Wives are later prevented from working so as not to put their husbands' masculinity at risk.

CONCLUSION

Today the Tajik education system is in a particularly difficult situation. It is still a great deal better than the systems in many developing countries; however, this situation may not last long, since only about 2 percent of the gross domestic product (GDP) of Tajikistan goes towards education. This is insufficient to maintain any sort of decent level.

Numbers of those attending school have also decreased. In some parts of the country, notably in some of the rural areas, secondary school attendance dropped from close to 100 percent before the civil war to 50 percent in 2003. Girls are the most affected (ICG 2003: ii), since, as we have seen, many parents do not see educating them as beneficial. Despite overwhelming evidence (including skyrocketing divorce rates) that women can no longer depend on the financial support of husbands, the discourse that suggests that women's place is in the home continues to affect practices. Early marriages further reduce girls' opportunity to gain an education, since in-laws have nothing to gain by allowing their *kelins* to study.

Moreover, the system of bribes not only makes it difficult for most families to provide their children with tertiary education or find them good employment, it also serves to keep young people dependent on their parents. In other words, while the collectivist system protects children from facing the world alone, it also prevents them from independent action and thus forces them to remain within the collective. Even those from families with more individualistic leanings find themselves in this situation, which puts them at a great disadvantage compared with their peers in other Muslim capital cities, as we shall see in the next chapter.

In any case, the Tajik education system is very far from meeting requirements to provide requisite skills for those seeking employment. At the same time, the fact that jobs are largely gained through bribes reduces the incentive to acquire skills.

In regard to both education and employment, the transitional setting of Tajikistan is thus proving very negative. Pressures to adhere to traditionalist gender identities are making an already difficult situation even worse.

The tensions between individualist and collectivist outlooks in regard to education are not clear-cut. It frequently happens that people in Tajikistan from strongly collectivist backgrounds who have been exposed to high-quality education become interested in learning, and if given the opportunity they may continue to tertiary education and study seriously, like Bahorgul. Or people who were not well educated themselves may learn to prize this for their children, as Tahmina did.

Many of my educated acquaintances in Tajikistan originally came from strongly collective families, but exposure to education produced changes in their attitudes. They have not moved all the way towards the individualistic end of the continuum, but they are much further along it than their parents. One sure sign is that they tend to expect their children to get on in life through their own abilities rather than through paying bribes for them. As a result, educated parents are more likely to expect their children to take studying seriously than uneducated ones like Nahdiya.

As for employment, the government of Tajikistan sets a clear precedent for elevating patronage over skills when they remove from their positions those who know their work and replace them with Kulobis unskilled in that area. The result of this system has been that even the most individualistically inclined are forced to use patronage networks, since there is no other way to obtain employment.

Foreign enterprises in Central Asia looking for skilled employees at managerial levels, especially those who require them to work independently, often face problems. Parental authoritarianism and the Soviet-style education system have trained people never openly to question their bosses' demands. This does not prepare them well for the demands of working as managers in globalized industry. Another frequently voiced complaint is that Central Asian workers do not know how to assess risks so as to be capable of making informed decisions (ICG 2003: 12).

In the absence of both efforts to transform the education system so it can provide a pool of skilled labor and an economic policy able to create sufficient jobs to employ even half of those seeking work, it is difficult to conceive of significant improvements occurring in the near future.

CHAPTER FIVE

ROMANTIC FRIENDSHIPS

*U*med is a second-year student at the Slovyansky University. His family is
quite modern, and Umed knows he will be allowed to choose his own wife.
His parents may want some input but will not try to choose for him. He thinks
he is very lucky in this respect, because few of his fellow students will have the
same luxury.

*As yet Umed has not met a girl he really likes, but he is in no hurry. He is still
young and has plenty of time. Knowing how complicated it would be to have a
girlfriend without intending marriage, he does not even try. However, a large
number of his classmates do have such friendships. Umed says he knows that
some of the boys, especially the wealthiest, have explicitly informed their girlfriends that they haven't the slightest intention of marrying them, but this does
not appear to deter the girls. Umed thinks this may be because they secretly believe that if their friends come to love them enough, they will eventually change
their minds and marry them after all.*

*According to Umed this is very unlikely. He believes that if this is why the girls
have such friendships, they are deceiving themselves. Most boys he knows prefer
to marry modest girls, ones who have never dated. However, even if they wanted
to marry their girlfriends, they would have both their own parents and those of
the girls to contend with. In Umed's opinion, few of his classmates have sufficient
power or are skilled enough at manipulation to manage this. Nevertheless, his
female classmates continue to have boyfriends.*

Umed says that nowadays a girl who breaks up with her friend is not necessarily stigmatized if later she goes with a different boy, but he knows this is due to the comparatively modern outlook of the students in their university, and that this attitude is not common elsewhere. A girl who is known to have had many boyfriends would certainly be considered bad, even at the Slovyansky.

His female classmates confide in Umed that they are chiefly interested in boyfriends from wealthy families, hoping in this way to gain well-to-do husbands. This makes him sad, because everyone knows that such families often treat their women badly. They greatly constrain their mobility and refuse to allow them to take jobs. They may even be violent towards them. Irrespective of the girls' own plans, Umed is sure that at least half of the students in his class will marry by arrangement, and at least half of the women will be forced to stay home after marriage, although all of them claim they won't allow this to happen.

In his opinion, the more modern boys will probably choose their own wives and allow them to work outside the house. However, by his reckoning, at the very, very outside, 50 percent of the Tajik students at the Slovyansky are this modern—in reality probably a good deal fewer.

Unlike the girls he knows, Umed's male friends don't look for rich wives, and he thinks most boys don't. His male classmates are in general more interested in marrying a modest wife who will agree to stay home and do what she is told than one from a wealthy family.

Umed says his classmates have a lot of parties. The better brought-up girls leave early, which takes a lot of the fun out of it for the boys. Even so, many girls do not dare tell their parents where they are going, instead pretending they will be studying at a girlfriend's place.

Since the parties are restricted to their classmates, students can only attend as couples if they are dating someone in the same class. This does not often happen, since the tendency is for girls to date boys older than them. They rarely get their boyfriends' permission to go to parties without them. Umed thinks this is partly because boys fear their girlfriends may meet someone they like better and partly to show their power over them. Sometimes the girls tell their boyfriends the same thing they tell their parents and go to the parties anyway.

Because courses are taught in Russian, the majority of Slovyansky students are from urban areas, and therefore the student body is the most progressive in Tajikistan.[1] Perhaps this is why so many girls have boyfriends. Nevertheless, Umed doesn't think the boys are all that modern. Many of his classmates seem to think they have a right to tell their girlfriends where they can go and what they can do, just like traditionally minded males.

Umed is sure that those boys who don't allow their girlfriends freedom of movement won't allow their wives any either. These are mostly the richer boys, because the girls wouldn't pay attention to any others.

ROMANTIC FRIENDSHIP IN A MUSLIM COLLECTIVE

As we have seen, prior to the Soviet era, social relations in the area of Tajikistan were very different from what Umed describes. All contact between people of the opposite sex was prohibited, except among close relatives. Even after most women stopped wearing the veil, they still did not socialize with men.

As long as females remained in seclusion, it was not hard to keep boys and girls apart, although there were always loopholes. Karomat remembered her mother telling her that when she was a child in the early years of the twentieth century, occasionally girls in their village would manage to escape their parents' vigilance and start a friendship with a boy. Sometimes one of them would even get pregnant. In that case her punishment would be stoning to death for dishonoring her family.[2]

One of the main reasons compulsory education was so strongly challenged by Tajik parents was the opportunity it provided for contact between the sexes.[3] For a long time after universal secondary education was established, the strictest parents removed their daughters from school at puberty to keep them away from contact with boys. Unmarried girls were kept under close supervision at all times.

It was not necessary for them actually to have sex to be shamed. Merely appearing to have the slightest contact with a male was sufficient (Tadjbakhsh 1998). This is why the more conservative families from outside Dushanbe were often reluctant to allow daughters to study there, especially if this would involve living in a coed dormitory. It was feared that without proper control, they might start a romantic friendship and could even lose their virginity.

Parents were justified in their fears. Once young people started studying and working together, boys and girls managed to figure out ways of getting acquainted, friendships blossomed, and some girls did end up pregnant. This happened despite attempts to keep girls segregated at all times when not in class.

There was little if any relaxation of the authoritarian manner of contracting marriages. It was assumed that parents had the right to be the sole arbiters of their children's fate and most of them took that literally. Arranged marriages remained the norm and young couples often did not meet before marriage. This still happens; Tahmina, for instance, saw her husband for the first time at their wedding.

Thus, Soviet teaching that young people had a right to decide their own futures was negated by the strictness of the collective norms. Similarly, the material changes that allowed relatively easy contact between the sexes were not matched by changes in behavioral ideals. Today, when it is not always possible for families to control their daughters' activities outside class, this has become particularly problematic.

Ethnographic and historical accounts from other Muslim countries suggest that in similar cultural settings elsewhere, the introduction of coeducation and exposure to new ideas brought about a measure of relaxation in regard to family decision-making and allowed a very restrained form of courtship to become socially acceptable. This was a significant change from earlier times, when sexual segregation was the norm and marriages were arranged between couples who had never even seen each other.

In Istanbul significant social change started to occur as early as the late nineteenth century. At that point, young men and women from the most progressive families were able to meet, perhaps not entirely openly but at least without condemnation if this were discovered. On occasion, they were also able to carry on secret romances, similar in scope to, but somewhat more sophisticated than, the kinds of contact that Karomat and Khudoydod managed in Tajikistan in the 1940s.

By the turn of the twentieth century, progressive Istanbul families had started to permit significant social contact between engaged couples, and the concept of love as a basis for marriage entered public discourse among the middle and upper classes, based to a large extent on the influence of French literature. How much this discourse reflected reality, it is hard to say. However, it seems that by the late 1920s women from more liberated Istanbul families were permitted considerable input into the choice of a husband (Duben and Behar 1991: 96–103).

Despite this, the concept that girls married a family rather than an individual remained prevalent in most social circles in Istanbul, as it did in Tajikistan. This underlines the gap between the strongly collectivist ideals of the majority and the somewhat more individualist practices of the progressive few. In Turkey the numbers of the latter grew throughout the early twentieth century, encouraged by the modernizing political environment but almost entirely restricted to urban areas (Duben and Behar 1991; Kandiyoti 1997). Today Istanbul continues to be far more modern than most of the rest of Turkey, and romantic friendships between young people are acceptable in many circles there (Acar and Ayata 2002).

By the 1970s, in the Moroccan town studied by Davis and Davis (1988), girls' attendance at secondary school was making courtship possible, inspired to a large extent by the introduction of foreign media. The most popular print media were Arabic translations of European comic strips portraying love relationships and showing the exchange of kisses and caresses. Television had also just been introduced and was airing programs portraying romantic love.[4]

At first courtships had to be carried out clandestinely, but eventually they were accepted as a legitimate path to marriage. The youngsters who experimented in this way were the first generation to attend secondary school, and their mainly illiterate parents felt obliged to allow them more freedoms than they had been permitted in their youth (Davis and Davis 1988: 102ff).

In North Yemen in the 1970s, once girls started attending secondary school and going on to professional employment, allowing them some say in their choice of marriage partner logically followed. This was a time when the generation gap was very large. Mothers spent most of their time in the private and segregated world of women, while their daughters moved into the public world. Just as with Nahdiya and the Moroccan parents studied by the Davises, in these circumstances mothers doubted their competence to decide their daughters' futures and therefore permitted them to make their own decisions (Makhlouf 1979). Here also, there was considerable Western influence from mass media, travel, or both.

In Tajikistan, secondary education and professional employment for women have been common for some generations. However, children's entry into education and formal employment was not accompanied by parental concessions in regard to decision-making.

This is no doubt because of the very different history of Central Asia. Tajikistan was part of the conservative world of the Soviet Union, where the education system, the media, and employment were all under strict state control (Mickiewicz 1980). Openness to the outside world, which formed the trigger for the relaxation of the formerly strict rules of segregation in the countries discussed above, was nonexistent (Tokhtakhodjaeva 1995: 71). Moreover, in Tajikistan education was imposed by the colonial rulers. It was not seen as conferring benefits but rather as corrupting youth and threatening traditions. As a result, it had much less effect on the general population than in the countries described above and to this day courting in Tajikistan is still strongly frowned upon in all but a tiny minority of progressive families. It has, therefore, to be much more carefully concealed from public view than in the Davises' Moroccan town, even by Umed's fellow Slovyansky students.

The Soviet Union is no longer in control, and Tajikistan is governed by its own people. However, as Nandy (1983) suggests, it is a much more complex and lengthy process to end psychological than political colonialism. In Tajikistan this has meant that the population has not yet relaxed the protective stance toward their culture that they assumed in the early Soviet period. In fact, it is unlikely they will soon do so, since the current exposure to globalization is already proving far more destructive to this culture than the heaviest of Soviet pressures.

In this respect the situation of Tajikistan in many ways resembles that of Muslim families in Western Europe. Most come from rural or poor working-class backgrounds, where the norms of sexual segregation continue to be strict. In Europe parents are forced to send their children to coed schools. Here they mix with the Western majority, who come from individualist backgrounds where dating is perfectly acceptable and sex before marriage may even be encouraged. Muslim parents have typically reacted by coming up with their own invented traditions, especially in regard to gender identities, which greatly resemble those of Tajikistan. The resulting intergenerational tensions have been at least as strong, as many studies have shown (see De Vries 1988; Jacobson 1998; Sunier 1998; Vertovec and Rogers 1998).

Muslim parents in Europe try their best to control their daughters' movements outside class. They do not always succeed. The same is true in Dushanbe, where the irregularities of the school system make it almost impossible for parents to keep tabs on their daughters' movements. Although, like Jumabek and Kutfi, parents take care to find out the official time classes finish each day, the frequent absences of teachers mean that classes usually finish much earlier than planned. This gives youngsters like Sadbarg considerably more freedom than their parents realize.

University students have even greater latitude, as Umed's story suggests. The Slovyansky students are the most progressive in Tajikistan. Therefore, it is to be expected that they will have the highest rates of male-female friendships. However, romantic friendships are starting to occur even among high school students, especially those studying in central Dushanbe.

ROMANTIC FRIENDSHIPS AND GENDER DIFFERENCES

Over the last few years, the most stringent controls on girls have eased a little, at least among my Dushanbe acquaintances. However, any public contact between the sexes still causes gossip. If this gets back to a girl's family, she may find herself in serious trouble unless she can come up with a good explanation. This was one reason why Tahmina and Jahongul rejected all their high school suitors. Despite her greater freedom, Bahorgul has never had a boyfriend either.

Girls from the more traditionalist families have a great deal to lose if it is discovered that they have boyfriends. However, some of them take the risk anyway. The chief reason the girls I spoke to gave for doing so is that this was the only way they could participate in choosing their husbands.

This is because they hope their boyfriends will ask their parents to offer for them. Essentially, they are looking to achieve what Karomat did—to maneuver their parents into accepting an offer, without their realizing the young couple is already acquainted. One girl told me that after her parents accepted her friend's offer, her mother said to her, "I hope you have not been meeting him. It is not respectable for you to meet with a boy before your wedding." Of course, the girl reassured her she had not. What else could she do?

Thus, girls see romantic friendships as a way of playing an active role in choosing their husbands while appearing to acquiesce passively to their families' choice. This allows parents the chance to vet their daughters' boyfriends and thus to put their seal of approval on the relationship.

Such actions imply that these girls do not consent to the collectivist ethic that any male their parents choose will be an acceptable husband. Rather, they are concerned with their own and their future husband's particular personalities and seek a companionate relationship with a compatible mate.

But what of the boys? Umed does not think most cooperate. According to him, girls who tried to use their friendships in this way were likely at best to be disappointed, at worst to be disgraced by pregnancy. Of course, girls realize there are dangers, and this very much preoccupies those considering whether or not to agree to start a romantic friendship.

In 1997, when I helped provide sex education for upper-level classes in a Dushanbe high school, one of the students posed the following question: What do boys really want when they ask someone to be their girlfriend? The ensuing discussion showed considerable differences between the sexes.

The girls said that many of their female classmates saw romantic friendships as a way to choose their husbands, while the boys indicated that for them the point of having a relationship was to have a good time. The girls were very annoyed at this indication of the boys' lack of seriousness. They said they had heard from older friends that rather than trying to get their parents to offer for their girlfriends, boys frequently end their relationships upon graduation, using the excuse that their parents refuse to agree to their marriage plans. The girls found this extremely worrying and accused the boys of cowardice. They felt that as males they should be powerful enough to get their own way. If they really love their friends, they should fight to marry them. If they don't, they should never have started the relationship in the first place.

Part of the problem is that unless they will be immediately continuing to tertiary education, girls are usually married on graduating from high school, while boys are rarely married before their twenties (WHO 2000). Thus, to attain their goals, the girls would need boyfriends some five years older than them, but this rarely seems to occur. In this school, at any rate, almost all the girls who dated had friends in the same class, or at the most two classes above. This meant that the age difference was so small that the two were unlikely to be ready for marriage at the same time.

Thus, if girls' purpose is to choose their own husbands, it would seem that they are risking a great deal for a potentially small return. They are putting their reputations on the line and possibly exposing themselves to very serious censure. Another issue is that even those who succeed are not necessarily happier than women in arranged marriages.

Ruzikhol and Bahreddin met at university. They took many of the same classes, so they would often see each other. Ruzikhol was an excellent student and always at the top of the class, while Bahreddin did much less well. Despite these differences, they became sufficiently good friends so that when graduation time approached, Bahreddin persuaded his parents to ask Ruzikhol's family for her hand in marriage.

Bahreddin had been so kind and sweet to her that Ruzikhol had come to care for him a great deal. She thought they would be able to develop the kind of companionate marriage her Russian friends enjoyed. So she encouraged her mother to accept on condition that she be allowed to go on to graduate school and subsequently seek a job.

Shortly after their wedding Ruzikhol enrolled for her master's degree, while Bahreddin found himself employment as a gardener. Within a few weeks, he started to change. He became very autocratic and would demand Ruzikhol wait on him all the time she was at home. He kept her so busy she had no time to study and her grades started to slip. The only way she managed to get any work done was to go to the library after class, but this made Bahreddin furious. He constantly accused her of meeting a lover there.

Bahreddin's suspicions continued to grow, until he could stand it no more. To ensure she would not run off with a lover, he insisted on getting his wife pregnant rather than waiting for her to complete her studies as they had previously decided. In order to keep the peace Ruzikhol agreed. However, when she was near the end of her first trimester, Bahreddin started to beat her. He battered her so badly that she landed in the hospital and almost lost her daughter.

Despite her husband's behavior, Ruzikhol managed to study hard enough to graduate cum laude.[5] Afterwards she was invited to join the university department where she had studied, with a salary much higher than that of her gardener husband.

Soon afterwards, Ruzikhol bore a son. Meanwhile, Bahreddin had started drinking heavily and would beat his wife whenever he got drunk. When she could stand it no longer, Ruzikhol would run to her mother and ask to move back in with her. Her mother never took any notice of her pleas. "Bahreddin is a good man," she would tell her, "You must have done something bad or he wouldn't have beaten you." After a few days Bahreddin would turn up with flowers in his hands to fetch her home, crying and saying he hadn't meant it and would never

do it again. So Ruzikhol would go back, only for the cycle to start over. The vio-
lence only stopped once her son became old enough to protect her.

As her daughter entered puberty, Ruzikhol watched her closely and made ab-
solutely sure she had no chance to meet with a boy. She had analyzed her own sit-
uation and decided that she had ruined her chance of happiness by making two
big mistakes—she should neither have gone to university nor married for love.

Ruzikhol was determined her daughter would not make the same errors.
Therefore, after she completed tenth grade Ruzikhol arranged her marriage to a
cousin. She told me this had turned out well and her daughter was happy.
Ruzikhol attributed this to her foresight in ensuring that her son-in-law was bet-
ter educated than his wife and that he feared his mother-in-law too much to
dare maltreat her daughter. This would not have happened in a love match, she
believed.

Ruzikhol's personal experiences convinced her that marriage in the Tajik
culture was only likely to work well if organized in the traditional manner,
and if the wife stuck to her traditional roles. She was sure any attempt to step
outside these would end up hurting the woman. It was just not worth trying
to increase women's power position, as this could only make their lives more
difficult.

Whatever one may think of this as a general proposition, evidence suggests
Ruzikhol was correct in her conclusions that women in love matches were often less happy than those in arranged ones. This may be because of the tensions between this way of contracting marriages and Tajik culture. When
parents do not choose their sons' wives, they tend to be particularly cold towards their *kelins* because they feel that they have undermined their parental
authority. As a result, they may even encourage their sons to be violent towards them. The young women's own parents may provide little support,
since they also may feel their authority to have been flouted by the love
match. Even if they do not think this way, like Ruzikhol's mother they rarely
take the marital violence seriously, even when their daughters end up in the
hospital, as happened to Ruzikhol on a number of occasions.

Moreover, all but the most modern of husbands tend to subscribe to the
popular concept that women who have once sought love may easily do so
again, thus cuckolding their husbands. Rather than making them anxious to
ensure their wives' happiness so they will have no wish to stray, this seems to
encourage husbands like Bahreddin to be highly suspicious and to use various forms of violence, including forced pregnancies, to try to forestall potential unfaithfulness.

Women in arranged marriages are supposedly less demanding and therefore
more easily content with a less satisfactory relationship. Tahmina, for instance,

does not appear to have had any great expectations of marriage. According to Tajik thinking, this makes her likely to be faithful, because she will not look for more out of the marriage than her husband can give her and thus will be little interested in seeing if another man would offer more.

Today it may no longer be true that young women in arranged marriages have no expectations. Girls the age of Tahmina's youngest sister, even those who do not date, appear to have thought about what they want from marriage. This is especially the case for students in higher education, who strongly favor the position that the choice of partner should lie in the hands of the young people themselves, since they are the ones who will have to live together.

What the girls say they are seeking from marriage not only subverts the traditions, but also differs in many ways from the notions of their male peers. In December 2003, I held a discussion with a group of students at the Dushanbe Pedagogical Institute. As with the majority of youngsters I talked to during that trip, the word *modern* clearly bore positive connotations that were somehow connected with international youth culture. However, at least as far as the boys were concerned, this appeared only marginally to influence attitudes towards gender identities and lifestyles.

At the start of our discussion, most of the group claimed to be in favor of moder- nity. One boy told me he was "totally modern, hip, and with-it," although he could not explain what he meant by this.

When I raised issues concerning the nature of marital relationships, all the girls and those of the boys who self-identified as modern said they wanted a love relationship. In fact, there was general agreement that it was preferable to choose one's own spouse, but they knew few of them would be allowed to do this, probably only those whose parents were educated, long-time Dushanbe residents.

One girl who claimed to be from a reasonably modern family said she was very concerned about her future husband. She would do all she could to become acquainted with prospective suitors before giving her consent. She also said that almost more important than her future husband's character would be the chance to live separately from his parents.

All the girls were in agreement that it made a big difference whether or not they would be expected to live with their in-laws. It would be much easier to have a good marriage if the young couple lived by themselves. The boys con- curred; no woman ever wanted to live with her in-laws, they said. It was differ- ent for men. Patrilocal marriage meant that they did not have to leave their homes to live in an alien setting. Most of the boys had nothing against living with their parents; some even preferred it.

Next the students started to argue over who should be boss in their marital relationships. The girls said they wanted equality. They didn't see why one partner should have power over the other. The boys categorically disagreed. Even the one who had defined himself as hip was adamant he would be in charge. He would make all decisions and saw no need even to consult his wife. One or two of the boys did say that if they lived on their own and their wives were employed, they might well agree to help with the housework, but not if they lived with their parents.

One boy, who identified himself as a traditionalist, said his wife would have to obey him in everything. Unless she had a university degree, he would not allow her to work for a living and would only permit her to leave the house when absolutely necessary. He said he would greatly prefer an uneducated wife, because she would be easier to control. He would watch her closely and check her friends to see if they were suitable. The more modern-minded of the boys mocked him for this, but he maintained his stance that such behavior would make for a stable and lasting marriage, in which both partners would know their place.

The girls were upset at hearing this, and especially at the idea that one of their classmates wanted an uneducated wife. They all said they could not imagine being able to have a good relationship with an uneducated man. They would have too many problems understanding each other.

At first, the boys did not grasp what the girls were getting at. After some explanation, they still appeared bewildered. Mr. Hip-and-Cool said he believed in love at first sight. He didn't think it was possible to fall in love any other way. However, he didn't understand why he should care about the educational level of the object of his affections. It was her looks and character that would count, not her brain.

When the girls informed him that they expected to be able to hold interesting conversations with their husbands, the boy simply stared. "Why on earth would anyone want to do that?" he asked. "I have [male] friends for conversation. My relationship with my wife will be about completely different things." The other boys agreed. They couldn't see that this should figure into the criteria for selecting a spouse. Much to the girls' dismay, the idea appeared irrelevant, even strange, to their male classmates.

Further discussion elicited the fact that the boys were aware that their ability to earn an income sufficient to support their families would probably be limited, which would leave them dependent on their parents for years to come. This would reduce their power to negotiate over the subject of marriage. Only the economically independent or those from very modern families would be able to hold out for a love match. Of course, another option would be to seek work in Russia.

Even those boys who claimed to be modern seemed to be strongly influenced by the importance of maintaining traditionalist forms of masculinity. This accounts for the large gulf between the sexes, the boys favoring a climate of male authority, while the girls were arguing for a qualitatively different relationship, one based on mutual understanding, romantic love, and intimacy. The relationships of autonomy and democracy that these girls imagined (cf. Giddens 1992: 188–191) and the ways they reflected on their own identities and those of a potential spouse were considerably more modern than the visions of their male classmates (cf. Giddens 1991: 91–92).

Returning to the comments of the high school students with which this book opened, it should be noted that almost all the female students from the Pedagogical Institute were dressed in modern style. The boys' clothes, however, closely resembled those of Soviet times. That is to say, they were dressed like the young men in Figure 5.1—in loose-fitting pants, tennis shoes, shirts, and jackets. This is typical of menswear in Tajikistan, where to outline the shape of the legs is considered immodest and therefore against the tenets of Islam.

Umed and his friends from the Slovyansky cultivate a more Western look, but the most modern-looking of all are the boys who had studied in the United States. According to Kamirjon, who had spent his last year of high school there and still dressed very much like an American, he and his friends who had also studied in the United States were seen as freaks even in the Slovyansky. Other students would come up to them and make pejorative remarks about their being different.

In other words, there actually are ways to distinguish modernistic boys by their clothes, and it is perhaps an indication of the differences between the sexes that the girl students who called themselves modern dressed accordingly, while the boys had made no significant changes to their style of clothing. Of course, they do not wear the truly traditional clothes worn by many rural men (see Figure 5.2), but neither do they dress as the young men they see on television from Moscow and other more Western environments.

I believe it is an indicator of how very small are the numbers of modernistic boys that such a tiny number dress in a modern style. It is also interesting that those who do tend to have lived in relatively modern environments. Boys like Umed and especially Kamirjon have a mindset qualitatively different from the majority. They invariably want to marry for love, expect to live separately from their parents, and are in favor of greater freedoms for girls and women than their traditionally minded peers. It is perhaps the fear of the implications of this for masculine identity that brings other boys to mock them, possibly in the hope of forcing them to recant their subversive attitudes along with their stylish clothes.

Figure 5.1 Young men wearing Soviet-style clothing

The boys from the Pedagogical Institute appeared caught between modernistic longings and a fear of abandoning traditional forms of masculinity. Above all they seemed to fear relinquishing male control.

Their female peers, on the other hand, had little to lose from abandoning traditional concepts of submissive femininity. They had eagerly embraced the notion of marriage as primarily an emotional relationship, unlike many of the older women I knew, who thought of marriage as a pragmatic and practical affair.

For the reasons discussed above, marriage for love is generally thought to encourage female infidelity. Thus, the very concept tends to make boys feel insecure. As a result, many tend to be only too glad to accept their parents' choice of bride, believing that a girl who has come to them in what Karomat called "the clean Tajik way" would be less likely to betray them. In any case, since the boys had little chance of becoming economically independent for some time to come, they knew they would have little choice but to acquiesce to their parents' decisions.

In the other Central Asian republics, young people are expected to be financially independent before marriage. This gives them a certain measure of freedom (Storey et al. 1997: 4, 13, 29, 45, 64). Tajikistan was the least Sovietized of all the republics, which probably accounts for the high percentage of traditionally inclined families. It is also the poorest. This makes it difficult for young people to become independent. Because sons' wives are likely to live with their in-laws for at least part of their married lives, even educated mothers will have a particular stake in choosing their *kelins*.

This attitude is illustrated by the vehement declaration of a respected member of the Academy of Sciences: "I want my daughter-in-law to fit in with my way of doing things, so she must be well acquainted with our local customs and able to prepare our local dishes.[6] Therefore, I am not going to permit my son to choose his own wife. He might pick someone from outside our village or even from another region!" This suggests that the students were correct in thinking that they might not have more freedom than their sisters to choose their spouse.

Of course, the arranged marriage is not peculiar to Tajikistan, Central Asia, or even Muslims. This has been the commonest way to contract marriage worldwide. It is not so long since it was also found in Europe, at least among the upper classes, where very often alliances were arranged for the strategic or financial benefits of the families concerned.

I have not been able to figure out exactly on what basis parents in Tajikistan choose their children's spouses, other than that, as in many other Central Asian and Middle Eastern cultures, there is a strong preference for first cousins. As far as I have been able to tell, unlike more capitalist-oriented settings, incomes play a small part here. This is no doubt due to the relatively small economic differentiation under the Soviet system. The most desirable quality for a Tajik bride seems to be submissiveness. There are no special qualities demanded of a bridegroom, not even the ability to earn a living, since his parents are expected to provide for the young couple.

Due first to the war and later to labor migration, for the last decade or so there has been a significant imbalance in numbers between young men and

Figure 5.2 Rural men wearing national dress

women. As a result, parents of girls are usually so thankful to get them off their hands that they gladly accept the first offer that comes along, often without too much inquiry into the family's character. The slightest hint of doubt regarding a daughter's virginity, however, will disgrace her parents and make it impossible to make a good match for her. It may even force parents to agree to allow their daughter to become a polygynous second, or even third, wife.

Given this situation one cannot help but ask why so many girls risk disgrace by having boyfriends. Do they really believe that the chance of finding happiness in this way is worth it?

Two elements seem to play an important role here. First, I found that girls did not seem to understand that boys were only marginally less constrained than they were. They had internalized the concept of male power without realizing how much it was age dependent. Since boys were more powerful than their girlfriends, the latter thought of them as on equal footing with their elders, not understanding how far this was from reality. Thus, girls may consider boys' capacity to persuade their parents to offer for them much greater than it actually is. They may equally overestimate their eagerness to do so.

Second, girls today are developing a new idea of self, qualitatively different from that of earlier generations. This perhaps makes them feel that they are not taking such a huge risk after all. The students I met in 2003 talked about the desirability of modernity in a way unavailable even to their older sisters. This is due to two interrelated phenomena, both relatively new to Tajikistan: youth-oriented mass media and access to a wide range of consumer goods.

MASS MEDIA AND THE CONSUMER SOCIETY

Mass media, especially film media, can have a powerful influence on concepts of selfhood and behavior (Abu Lughod 2002). This was illustrated in a series of retrospective documentaries on the twentieth century broadcast by the BBC in 1999.[7] Among them was one dealing with the influence of the cinema on comportment. In one scene, an elderly Italian woman reminisced about life in her village before World War II. She and her friends, she mused, had learned how to behave on a date, including how to kiss, from watching movies.

The Bolsheviks were very aware of the media's potential for transforming behavior, and they made frequent use of this in those regions they considered backward. Thus, from the 1920s on, the Soviet regime used media to teach new lifestyles to the peoples of Central Asia. They educated women about hygiene, nutrition, and other health-related issues through books and newspapers, but most of all through the cinema, magic lantern shows, and dramatizations (Lubin 1984: 220–223; Nukhrat 1930: 22–25; Raskreposhchenie 1971: 65).[8]

The films that Karomat and her friends watched and the Soviet novels they read as teenagers depicted chaste romances between kolkhoz workers. Karomat said it was watching these movies that suggested to her and her girlfriends the possibility of the kind of circumspect and innocent dating they indulged in.

The concept of marriage for love was not introduced into Central Asia by the Bolsheviks. It had figured in the discourse of Tatar immigrants in the late nineteenth century (Kamp 1998: 76). However, it does not seem to have made significant inroads into the imagination of the population until much later. It took modern media, especially cinema and later television, to popularize the idea of romantic love. I found out how important this had become for Tajik girls when so many of them asked me whether I had married for love and then looked markedly wistful when I informed them that most people in the West did so.

In the twenty-first century, the days of the chaste Soviet romance are long gone. Today, Moscow television broadcasts programs from a multitude of different sources, both domestic and foreign, ranging from torrid romances to outright pornography.

Much has been written about the influence of foreign media on youth in the former Soviet Union.[9] Soap operas in particular have made an impact on the way young people understand human relationships. As one of Kathleen Kuehnast's Kyrgyz acquaintances expressed it, "We are especially interested in the relationships between men and women in the West [that we see on television]. . . . Although I think women are more influenced by western television programs than are men, the [conservative] Turkish television station is beginning to affect men's attitudes [towards their wives] as well"[10] (Kuehnast 1997: 273). Similarly, in Tajikistan women are typically influenced by different viewing from men, but both have learned new types of behavior from the media.

In 1994 and 1995, during my first visit to the republic, the Mexican *telenovela Simply Maria*[11] and its sequel, *Wild Rosa*, formed the most popular viewing of adolescent girls and young women. Later, *telenovelas* from other Latin American countries, such as Brazil, achieved similar levels of popularity.[12]

These shows portrayed worlds of wealth and romance completely outside the personal experience of their Tajik viewers. They depicted love as the principal mover in relationships between the sexes and as the basis for contracting marriage. Women's emotions were strongly on display. Novel notions of masculinity were also represented. For instance, men were shown taking care of women, protecting them, and displaying overt affection towards them, even occasionally waiting on them. This was so unlike male behavior in Tajikistan that Karomat decided the stories could not possibly be true, simply on the grounds that men did not do such things.[13]

It was the emotional aspects of women's lives that so much attracted the girls I knew. On the one hand, they were charmed by Maria's and Rosa's friendships with men. This made them long for romance in their own lives, despite knowing this was likely to be impossibly far from the reality of their own futures, which they feared would be more likely to hold indifferent or violent husbands and dominating mothers-in-law.

On the other hand, they yearned for stronger emotional ties with their natal families. When at the end of the series Maria's mother discovered her long-lost daughter, their tender reconciliation moved everyone to tears. My young friends talked about this for months afterwards, making clear their longing for such an expression of love from their own mothers. Sadbarg was strongly affected, since her family relationships were unusually harsh. Perhaps as a result, she adored these programs and never missed an episode.

There was a general tendency for the girls to see these dramas as portraying real life, but in a setting so far removed from their own that they could not imagine themselves participating in it. However, they found the notion that such lives existed somewhere in the world highly comforting.

Such shows allowed them to imagine a way of life where girls counted as persons, their views were heard, they were wooed for who they were, and they could have a marriage that had nothing to do with either being good *kelin* material or conforming to the restrictive gender norms expected of Tajik girls. In other words, their television viewing was revealing an emotional dimension to family relationships the girls had not experienced in their own lives, one significantly different from the utilitarian one of the collective setting of traditionalist Tajikistan.

In fact, this was probably the chief factor that brought Sadbarg to question her family relationships. What she was learning at school and had seen in the homes of her neighbors served merely to reinforce her television viewing.

The generation younger than that of Sadbarg is even more affected by television. Bahorgul—twenty-one at the end of 2003—has been watching foreign television shows since she was small. In addition to soap operas and *telenovelas*, she enjoys rock concerts and other programs from Moscow that present international youth culture.

The Tajik media have been changing also. Sexually explicit programs had been broadcast from Moscow for some time. In many Tajik households these had been for adult male viewing only. In 2003, along with Bahorgul, Tahmina, and the latter's children, I watched on one of the Tajik channels, in simple language intelligible to all, a series of video clips portraying what were evidently local young couples. They were holding hands and quite suggestively behaving in a romantic, almost but not quite explicitly sexual manner, nearly, but not quite, kissing.

My coviewers appeared simultaneously fascinated and repelled by these scenes, which were accompanied by repetitive and hypnotic music. This was sung by young and handsome men, shown in the intervals between scenes standing with their hands held invitingly out to the audience.[14] My friends were critical of the couples' behavior, saying that nobody in Tajikistan would ever do such things in public. When I said I had seen young couples walking arm in arm, if not hand in hand, in Dushanbe, they told me it was dreadful and immoral. Those must be married couples; no unmarried girl would dare do such a thing. It was out of the question. It would ruin her reputation, they insisted.

I agreed with them that this was new. Hitherto, the slightest physical contact, even between married couples, had been limited to that most private of settings, the bedroom. I wondered how much the relaxed standards of behavior I had seen were the result of the influence of shows and love songs like those described above that were becoming popular with the youth. How was this influencing girls' ideas of what was permissible? Was it giving them implicit permission to indulge in romantic friendships? Did they think, "If those young Tajiks can behave in such a way, if they can do this in Lenin Park, right in the center of Dushanbe, then surely it can't be so bad if I have a boyfriend"?[15]

These broadcasts are linking locals to the international youth scene depicted on Russian television. It is the first time young people in Tajikistan have been exposed to global culture in this way. Many girls have reacted by trying to emulate the dress and behavior of their peers elsewhere.

Those I spoke to were avid consumers not just of new ways of forming relationships but also of new ways of displaying the female body. They were no longer prevented either by traditions or by a lack of available merchandise from dressing as they pleased. Even though the choice is more limited and more conservative than in Moscow or other major capitals, Tajik girls can now buy clothes only a little more modest than those they see on television.

For the young women Kuehnast met in Kyrgyzstan, the most prized freedom of the post-Soviet period was neither political nor ideological, but rather the right to express their individuality through the purchase of consumer goods, particularly clothes (Kuehnast 1998: 641). It took somewhat longer for these to arrive in Tajikistan, mainly due to the civil war. However, now that they have done so, Tajik girls are latching on to them in much the same way and for much the same reasons as Kuehnast's Kyrgyz girls.

It is now possible to individualize one's appearance through varying clothing styles and makeup, in ways unavailable only a few years ago in Soviet times (cf. Giddens 1991: 172). The most modernistic girls now have a way of dressing that is completely different from that of their elders. The first signs of the future are visible in Dushanbe as the girls shop for pretty sweaters and skirts, for jewelry and makeup—deciding which suit them personally and how to combine them with what they already have.

In Kyrgyzstan and Kazakhstan young people shop for individualistic clothing, too, but they are also by and large earning their own living. This is not the case in Tajikistan, nor is it likely to be as long as unemployment remains so high. This makes it more difficult for girls there to buy any but the cheapest goods, and it acts as a brake on the development of modernity compared with other parts of Central Asia, especially Kyrgyzstan and Kazakhstan (Kuehnast 1997, 1998; Nazpary 2002).

Nevertheless, while 99 percent of Tajik parents still expect to choose their offspring's spouses unilaterally (WHO 2000: 13), almost all my young female acquaintances, urban and rural alike, and even some of my male ones, were busy imagining a new kind of marital relationship—one in which they would have a hand in choosing their own spouse. This type of imagination is in itself individualistic, and its continued development seems likely to transform the collective ideal. Indeed, the way the young girls in the markets preened, regarded themselves in the mirrors, tried out new types of makeup, and eagerly posed for photos suggests that new and more individualistic concepts have to some extent already arrived.

This does not prevent the older generation from continuing to pressure young people into keeping the traditions, and thus it does not remove the element of risk from having a boyfriend. While television viewing may portray romantic friendships as idealized—a walking off into the sunset in a soft and rosy haze—in real-life Tajikistan, girls are much more likely to find themselves in a violent marital relationship, or in disgrace for having dated, than happily married to the man of their dreams.

LOVE BEFORE MARRIAGE

In contradistinction to the young people, those parents I talked to opposed the concept of love matches for their children. They would firmly declare that for Muslims love was not supposed to form the basis for contracting marriage. It would grow afterwards. However, I sensed they added this last as a concession to the modernistic ideal of marital love that had been imposed on Central Asians since Bolshevik times, rather than because they saw love as an important ingredient of marital life. Admitting the possibility of its development was intended to make their determination to arrange their children's marriages appear more acceptable.

Despite this attitude, it was obvious that many older women in the villages where Ghamkhori worked hungered for love. They would frequently choose it as a subject for discussion sessions. This was never in relation to their children's marriages but rather to their own love for boys they had known long ago. Considering that in these villages women had been virtually in seclusion right up to the civil war, it was fascinating to hear one after the other talk about how she had secretly fallen in love, only to have her parents marry her to someone else.

As girls, they had not even contemplated asking if they could marry the boy they were interested in. Rather, they had agreed without protest to their parents' choice and in most cases had never seen their beloved again. However, they continued to dream of him. They carried his image in their hearts and considered him an ideal to which their husband had singularly failed to measure up.

There appeared to be a disconnect in the minds of these women between their feelings of love and the concept of the arranged marriage. Many of them had daughters approaching marriageable age who, like their mothers, believed themselves to be in love. These girls could not even imagine discussing this with their mothers. They were far too frightened of being accused of shaming the family. Almost certainly they, too, will accept their mothers' choice of husband without overt protest.

In an attempt to help the girls, Ghamkhori's staff would encourage their mothers to consider alternative scenarios. They would ask how they would feel if their daughter told them she fancied a certain boy. Would they consider allowing her to marry him, or would they force her to marry someone else? The women would typically say they would not take any notice of their daughters' wishes. They were too young to judge who would make them a good husband. The women did not appear to see any contradiction between this and their insistence that they themselves would have been happier married to the men they had loved than to those chosen by their parents.

If anyone questioned their right to impose their wishes on their children, their reply would be that for Muslims, it was a sin for children to disobey their parents (cf. Altorki 1986). However, although it is true that the Qur'an speaks of the obligation to honor parents, it also states that women have a right to make their own decisions regarding spouse selection, and that if a girl forced into marriage as a minor is not happy, on reaching the age of majority she may ask for her marriage to be annulled and then choose for herself (Omran 1992: 49ff).

In the more modernistic of social groups in Turkey, Yemen, and Egypt, young people have been permitted to meet and decide on their own marriage partners for some decades, even though they still need their parents' consent (Duben and Behar 1991; Hoodfar 1997; Makhlouf 1979; Wikan 1980). In the capitals of the other Central Asian republics this is also possible, although arranged marriages are still common there (Hortaşcu and Baştuğ 2000; Kuehnast 1998; Nazpary 2002). Except for the elite, in Tajikistan this is only possible in a few of the most modernistic families. For the rest, even highly educated parents often look askance at such behavior. In many ways, the comportment expected of young people in Dushanbe is more in line with that expected of the rural population in Turkey (Sunier 1998) than of the inhabitants of other capital cities.

This is very likely due to the history that has prevented Dushanbe from developing into an influential cultural center. In the 1920s Stalin gave the region's most important historical cities to the powerful and influential Uzbeks, thus depriving Tajikistan of a true metropolis.[16] Dushanbe essentially became a Slavic town, its Tajik population very much in the minority. This only changed after independence, when the majority of Slavs emigrated and their place was taken by rural migrants.

The result is that there is no numerically significant group of sophisticated Tajiks to provide cultural leadership and counterbalance the rigidity of traditionalist mores. In many families decades of intermarrying between rural and urban branches have minimized lifestyle differences between them, so that many Dushanbe families live almost identically to their rural cousins (cf. Lubin 1991: 51). The result is that, compared with parents in the Muslim societies discussed above, most Tajik parents have remained relatively rigid.

Their children do not dare openly challenge parental authority and so are careful to keep any romantic friendships secret. They have only been able to establish these in the first place owing to the comparative freedom girls in Dushanbe now have to go around unsupervised, as we have seen. The result is that there is an increasing gulf between the discourse that insists that girls must be kept under parental control until marriage and the reality that they spend large amounts of time outside the home unsupervised.

Girls have few precedents to tell them how to behave in such circumstances; rather than learning how to act around members of the opposite sex, they have been physically kept away from them since puberty. They may therefore be easy prey for boys who want to convince them to start a friendship or even to persuade them to have sex.

This is in many ways reminiscent of the situation confronting their great-grandmothers in the early days after unveiling. Joshua Kunitz, a traveler in the region in the early 1930s, met a Central Asian woman who had recently unveiled and joined the Communist Party. She told him just how difficult she had found her situation. After having been secluded all her life, she had had no idea how to behave around men. Her male comrades had treated her with great friendliness but also with equivocal remarks and persistent advances. At first she did not understand what was going on. However, eventually she realized that whenever men and women were together, the atmosphere became charged with "passion, jealousy, and fear." This woman did not know how to deal with this and eventually found herself in a disastrous situation, which she believed greater experience would have helped her avoid. When she finally realized the implications of the way the men had been treating her— that because she was unveiled they thought of her as more or less a prostitute—she felt debased and affronted (Kunitz 1936: 298–299).

This is not much different from the situation girls in Dushanbe may find themselves in today when they start seeing a boy. The secrecy that of necessity surrounds such relationships is highly problematic. It leads couples to be frightened of being seen together and makes the relationship extremely stressful (cf. Al-Khayyat 1990: 69ff). It also isolates the girls, leaving them unprotected. Just as in the case of Kunitz's acquaintance, girls who date are often considered little better than prostitutes, as they are supposedly agreeing to some form of sexual relationship.

Indeed, boys often seek a girlfriend precisely for this purpose. This gives them great cachet with their peer group, as it makes them into "real" men. Therefore, they frequently try to pressure their friends into sex and the girls do not always resist. The situation is made more complicated by their lack of knowledge about sex. If boys start fooling around, their girlfriends may not realize what is going on nor have any idea how to protect themselves.

From time to time girls have come to Ghamkhori's Women's Center very upset because, they said, a boy had done something bad to them. They were not really sure what exactly had happened but it usually turned out to have been vaginal penetration. Judging by my conversations with girls in Dushanbe, many of them are no better informed than Ghamkhori's clients.[17]

Interestingly, it is usually the more traditional boys who seek sex in this manner. Modern-minded boys like Umed and Kamirjon, who put great store on choosing their own wives, take great care to avoid possible sexual complications for fear of ending up forced into a shotgun wedding.

In any case, many boys know only marginally more about sex than their girlfriends. They are unlikely to understand much about the reproductive system, to know how to prevent pregnancy, or to be informed about how diseases are spread. Although condoms are available, it is unclear that boys understand their function, much less how to use them. Even adult male participants in Ghamkhori's projects rarely knew this. In other words, young people in Dushanbe now live in a situation that facilitates relations between the sexes, while being denied access to information that could protect them from the consequences.

Ozoda and Abduvali got to know each other when they were living in student dormitories in Dushanbe. By their senior year they were dating and eventually started going to bed together. Since they knew little about the mechanism of sex and nothing about contraceptives, they took no precautions, and Ozoda soon became pregnant. When the young couple realized what had happened, they had no idea what to do.

When she could conceal her pregnancy no longer, Ozoda was forced to drop out of university. Ozoda's parents lived in an isolated village and had sent their daughter when quite young to live with a widowed aunt in Norak, hoping she would receive a better education there. Ozoda couldn't return to them in this condition. Instead, she went to her aunt, telling her that she and Abduvali had celebrated their marriage by nikâh, *and that as soon as Abduvali could break the news to his parents, they would also be married at the ZAGS office. Ozoda's aunt agreed to allow her to stay with her and not to inform her parents until Ozoda was acknowledged by Abduvali's family as his wife. A few months later Ozoda gave birth to a daughter.*

Meanwhile, after graduation Abduvali went home to his parents and broached the subject of his marriage. They told him they had already betrothed him to one of his cousins. Dismayed, Abduvali tried to explain that he loved another woman. His parents refused to listen, insisting that if he married against their will, they would disown him. Unable to decide how to handle the situation but too scared to tell them about Ozoda and his daughter, Abduvali put off his wedding, saying he was going to Russia to work.

On the way, he went to Norak to tell Ozoda what had happened. She was desperately upset and tried to persuade him to go to the ZAGS office with her to register their marriage, saying his parents would have to accept the fait accompli. However, Abduvali was unable to bring himself to defy his parents in this way and told her to wait. Somehow or other he would persuade them to agree to their marriage.

He then went off to Russia, from where he sent Ozoda money to keep her and their child. Whenever he was in Tajikistan he would secretly visit them, while continuing to resist parental pressures to marry. Nevertheless, he still did not confess his situation. Meanwhile, when Ozoda visited her own parents, she always left her child with her aunt, pretending still to be a virgin. They were concerned that she was still unmarried at her age and it took all her aunt's assurances that she had the matter in hand to keep them from arranging a marriage for her.

After some years of this, neither Ozoda nor her aunt believed Abduvali would ever marry her. However, Ozoda was stuck in a situation from which she could only escape by giving up her child. She could not bring herself even to consider this, although she was sure her parents would never forgive her if they found out what had happened. She was aware that many girls ended up on the streets after having been cast out by their families. She knew she had been incredibly lucky to find refuge with her aunt, but she realized she could not continue in this way indefinitely.[18]

This story amply illustrates the pitfalls of the transition period in Tajikistan. On the surface it is business as usual. However, the former material controls whereby girls were physically kept away from members of the opposite sex no longer exist. In their absence, young people need information and support to be able to handle the new circumstances. As this story suggests, the lack of communication between children and parents and the insistence of the latter on unconditional obedience, together with young people's ignorance on sexual matters, can result in tragedy.

The extra level of freedom this particular couple had, owing to the complaisant aunt and Abduvali's migratory stratagems, allowed them to postpone dealing with their problems in a way unavailable to most of their peers. Although this saved them from immediate ruin, in the long run it made the situation worse.

There were numerous points at which resolute action might have saved the situation. For instance, Ozoda could have had an abortion. Her aunt could have gone to Abduvali's parents and threatened to take them to court if he did not marry his pregnant girlfriend. Or Abduvali could have risked his parents' ire and told them what had happened. But they did none of these. In the end, their indecisiveness ended up losing them all possible chances of remedying the situation. Ozoda and her daughter are suspended in a limbo from which they will only be able to escape with great difficulty, and Abduvali is scarcely better off.

Unfortunately, there is little in the way of counseling services to help those in problematic situations. They did not exist under the Soviet regime and have not been developed by Rakhmonov's government. Ghamkhori's Women's Center is one of the few places people can go to for confidential advice.

Such services are desperately needed. Turning to older siblings or friends may be of little help to young Tajiks. In the first place, confidantes are notorious for giving away the secrets entrusted to them. In the second place, the problems are often so complex it is hard to find anyone experienced enough to help. This leaves youngsters trying to cope with very difficult issues on their own. It is not surprising, then, that there have been many women who, like Ozoda, have found themselves in untenable situations.[19]

SEX EDUCATION

It is not easy for young Tajiks to get information on sex, as they cannot ask direct questions. Since premarital sex is prohibited, they should not need to know anything about it.

Almost without exception, the youngsters with whom I discussed the subject told me that no adult had ever given them information about it. A few years ago I asked one highly educated woman what she had told her twenty-year-old student daughter about dating and sex. "Nothing," she said. "Why not?" I asked. "What would I say to her? She probably knows more about these things than I do and would just laugh at me." "I think you really ought to have a word with her," I insisted. "What will you do if she gets pregnant?" My friend did not know. All she could say was she hoped it would not happen.

This woman was sure that giving girls information about sex was more likely to encourage them to experiment than to help them avoid dangerous situations. In Tajikistan it was considered inappropriate to provide information on sex until just before marriage. I pointed out that her daughter had many more opportunities to transgress than previous generations. She was out studying all day and often spent part of the evening with her classmates. Her mother had no idea what she was up to then. My friend interjected that she hoped it was nothing bad.

I explained that in the West, the countries where girls are best informed about sexual matters—for instance, the Netherlands—have very low teenage pregnancy rates. The United States, on the other hand, where sex education in schools is minimal or nonexistent, has the world's highest percentage of pregnancies among unmarried teenagers, with the UK coming a close second for the same reasons (Feijoo 2001; Henshaw 2004).

My explanation did nothing to persuade my friend to change her mind. During the course of our conversation, it became clear that despite marriage and childbirth she had learned little either about sex or reproductive processes. She felt she would not know what to tell her daughter and would be unable to answer her questions. This accounted for much of her reluctance to discuss these matters with her.

Girls in Egypt, Morocco, and Yemen were allowed to be present during the older generation's discussions of sexual matters. In this way they were able to learn something about them (Davis and Davis 1988: 109; Hoodfar 1997; Makhlouf 1979). This was not the case in Tajikistan, where the subject was almost never voluntarily discussed in public.[20]

There seems to have been a general ignorance of sex throughout the former Soviet Union. This was the result of Soviet puritanism, which prohibited all talk of sex (Kon 1995). A study of Muscovites in the late 1980s showed that even the more educated knew very little. For instance, a twenty-four-year-old female editor claimed, "[O]n the first night of marriage I did not suspect that I could get pregnant as a result of sex"[21] (Geiges and Suvorova 1989: 33).

A national survey carried out in the Soviet Union in early 1991 showed that only 10 percent of boys and 15 percent of girls had received any information at all about sex from their parents, while there were no sex education courses in the schools and little, if any, access to literature on the subject (Kon 1995: 92, 117).[22] My own experiences in Tajikistan, with a variety of groups, showed that few adults in Tajikistan knew much more about sex than the friend mentioned above.

Under the circumstances, it is hardly surprising if Ozoda had little idea how pregnancy occurred and understood still less how to prevent it. She was a student in the early post-independence years when contraceptives were not readily available, but in any case it is doubtful if either she or Abduvali would have known of their existence. Few of those who came to Ghamkhori for family planning services, even the married couples, knew much about birth control. Many physicians knew little more.

Such lack of access to information on sex is having very negative consequences in the transitional setting of Tajikistan, exacerbated by the complete lack of communication between parents and children on this subject. While such silence is typical of traditional societies, in the more advanced transitional ones parent-child communication on such subjects tends to be somewhat greater (Altorki 1986; Kağıtçıbaşı 1996).

Hampered as it is by its history, Tajikistan has not yet reached this point. It is unlikely to do so in the near future unless parents are also appropriately informed. Some schools now have sex education programs, but these are rare and tend to reflect their presenters' difficulties in discussing such matters openly. The same is true of the books for teenagers I saw for sale in Dushanbe. Among the few exceptions are the sex education courses given by people trained by me, since I insist on their providing explicit information to help youngsters protect themselves from unwanted sex, undesired pregnancies, and sexually transmitted diseases.

A girl only has to make a very tiny slip to end up pregnant and thereby bring deep shame on her family. In such a setting, when new freedoms are coupled with a complete lack of information, the results are likely to be tragic, especially for girls from the most traditionally minded families. Among the consequences of maintaining silence are a significant increase in teenage abortions, a rapid rise in HIV infection, and heightened suicide rates (Harris 2005, 2005a).[23]

CONCLUSION

Romantic friendships represent perhaps the single greatest challenge to both traditionalism and collectivism, as well as to the gender norms of this Muslim society. They are at odds with the custom of male/female spatial separation, which in prerevolutionary times was reinforced by female seclusion and veiling. As a way of deciding on a marriage partner romantic friendships are highly individualistic, contravening the idea of marriage for the benefit of the family as a whole.

Love matches challenge parental control in the families of young people of both sexes, although this is most negative for parents of girls. Dating is an obvious sign that a girl has transgressed the unwritten contract stating she must not only *be* a virgin at marriage but must also look as if she never had the slightest opportunity of being otherwise. Having romantic friendships is the antithesis of this and thus a very serious threat to the honor of the male family head.

Adolescent boys establish their masculinity in the eyes of their peers by visibly giving themselves opportunities to have sex. One reason that having a girlfriend is important to them is that this is tantamount to a proof of their virility. The corollary is that a girl who has a boyfriend has as good as declared her refusal to comply with the traditions that demand she show herself to have had no contact with a member of the opposite sex before her wedding night.

Irrespective of whether or not girls actually have sexual relations, the very fact of having a boyfriend strongly implies their willingness to have some form of physical contact. This alone can be sufficient to condemn them; it also explains why their boyfriends are unlikely to want to marry them. Even before the wedding, they feel as if their masculinity has been compromised because their future wife is not entering marriage *pure* as a good Tajik girl should.

There is a considerable difference between this kind of relationship, in which the couple consider themselves embroiled in a romantic friendship and meet surreptitiously in unsupervised settings that permit physical contact and possibly even sex, and the types of friendships in which there is no such formal acknowledgment and encounters are limited to public places. This last kind was the type Ruzikhol and Bahreddin, and Zebi and Qodil (Chapter 6) were involved with. Boys in relationships that never progress beyond friendship will be less likely to lose respect for their friend and as a result are more likely to ask their parents to offer for her.

In theory, romantic friendships should break down the most conservative elements of the traditionalist/collectivist lifestyle and open up new opportunities for young people to shape their own lives. Unfortunately, as we have seen, this rarely happens. Even when young men want to marry their friends, as Abduvali did, they may not have the power to defy their parents in order to do so. More often, they do not hold the same opinion about this as their girl-friends and therefore do not seek to marry them.

While for girls marriage for love is an ideal, boys may feel it puts their honor at risk. Even those whose premarital relationship, like Bahreddin's, remained at the formal level may feel vulnerable after making a love match. Only the most modernleaning and individualistic-thinking males will have a different concept of masculinity—one that will not be threatened by marriage to the woman they love.[24] This shows how much the tensions between traditionalist and modernistic, collectivist and individualistic outlooks occur between the sexes as well as the generations.

CHAPTER SIX

MARRIAGE AND THE FAMILY

MARRIAGE FOR LOVE

Love matches disturb the hierarchical order and threaten the traditions that permit parents to exact obedience from their children for life. Worse, they may create a situation in which the marital tie becomes stronger than that between a man and his natal family.

Such an outcome is not inevitable, of course. As we saw in the previous chapter, Ruzikhol and Bahreddin's marriage did not result in a strong bond. However, there is a definite expectation, especially on the part of prospective brides, that a love match will be a rewarding, warm, and positive emotional experience that will bring them and their husbands close together.

In Tajikistan today, both collectivist ethics and the current economic problems make it difficult, if not impossible, for newly married couples to live on their own. This gives parents considerable power. A mother determined to force her *kelin* to submit to her authority at all costs can easily destroy her son's marriage.

When the couple come from significantly different backgrounds, living with the groom's parents can be even more problematic than usual, particularly when a bride from a modernistic setting is asked to conform to the expectations of traditionalistic in-laws.

Zebi is a young woman in her early twenties from a southern Dushanbe suburb. Her mother, Khayma, is a high school mathematics teacher; her father, Fazil, teaches Russian language and literature in another high school.

Zebi has three sisters and a brother. Her eldest sister is a Russian teacher like her father. Her next younger sister and her brother are studying information technology, and her youngest two sisters are still in high school.

Fazil's siblings think he is crazy to send his daughters to university today when it is so expensive. It was not a problem during Soviet times, when education was free, but it is a waste to spend good money on girls. They will only marry and then belong to another family. Fazil does not agree. He believes it is important to give his daughters the best possible preparation for life. They may live with another family, but they will always be his children, come what may. He loves them and wants the best possible life for them. For this reason, although he believes discipline is important, he also treats his children as friends.

Fazil says he is different from his siblings. He attributes this to the influence of his studies. Years of working with Russians and of reading Russian literature have caused him to value many of their ideas over what he was taught as a child. Khayma was a traditionalist when she married, but her husband's influence has changed her outlook and she has embraced many of his notions.

Like her mother, Zebi has a degree in mathematics from the Tajik State University. During her time there she became friendly with a fellow student, Qodil. They didn't date, but would see each other in class and talk from time to time in the corridors. Qodil liked Zebi so much he decided he wanted to marry her.

Qodil lives in a large compound on the outskirts of Qurghonteppa with his parents, his eldest sister, his five brothers and the latter's wives and children. Three more sisters are married and live elsewhere.

After Qodil's graduation, his parents told him it was time to marry. Qodil said he didn't want to marry anybody but Zebi and begged his parents to arrange this. They were not really in favor, but in the end they gave in and went to Zebi's parents to ask for her hand in marriage.

Khayma and Fazil were not at all sure they wanted their daughter marrying outside Dushanbe and cautioned her that Qodil's background might not be compatible with theirs. However, Zebi wouldn't listen. She really liked Qodil and very much wanted to marry him.

Khayma and Fazil were invited to Qodil's house to meet his family. They were well received. The compound looked in excellent shape and the family seemed to be doing well economically. Fazil told his daughter's prospective in-laws that Zebi had a university degree and intended to look for a job after marriage. They replied that their other kelins were educated also—one was a kindergarten teacher, for instance—and they had no objection to Zebi's working. Still not too happy about it, but persuaded by their daughter's pleas, Fazil and Khayma agreed to the marriage.

Zebi's parents wanted to register their daughter's marriage with ZAGS. Qodil's, however, insisted on first doing nikâh. They could go to the registry office

Figure 6.1 The apartment block in which Zebi's family lives in southern Dushanbe

later, they said. So as not to cause their daughter problems, Khayma and Fazil reluctantly agreed. In fact, the marriage never was registered.

After the wedding, Zebi was told that she should wait to look for a job. She agreed, thinking it would be better first to settle into her new home. She was very happy with Qodil. However, she soon started having problems with his family. Her mother-in-law was extremely authoritarian and ruled the household with an iron fist.

She ran it like a Soviet meeting, Zebi said. Every morning the six kelins *had to line up; their previous day's work would be criticized and they would be told how to improve it. Then they would be given that day's duties. None of the* kelins *was allowed outside the compound on her own. They were told they were slaves, there to serve the family. They had no rights, so they shouldn't think it would get them anywhere to complain.*

Zebi learned to milk cows, process cow pats[1] and carry out other rural tasks that as an urban apartment dweller she had previously been completely unfamiliar with. Her hands became rough and chapped. She lost weight, her face was burned black by the sun, and much of the time she felt depressed.

Zebi's parents frequently came to visit her, and they found their daughter's appearance very upsetting. This was not at all what they had expected her to look like after marriage to the man she claimed to love, especially during the honeymoon period. On her early visits, Khayma always inquired why Zebi and Qodil were not going into Qurghonteppa, or even coming to Dushanbe, to enjoy themselves by going to parks, cinemas, and other places of entertainment. This would embarrass Zebi, who would say, "Hush, mum. Don't talk like that." Each time Khayma left, Zebi's in-laws would tell her it was shameful for her mother to be thinking of pleasure so much. They were also shocked by the fact that she sat in the front of the car next to Fazil, not in the back as a good wife should.

Sometimes during her parents' visits Zebi would cry and cry. She never explained what the matter was, and Khayma was at a loss to understand what was going on. After all, her daughter was an educated adult. Surely, she should be able to tell her mother if something were seriously wrong? But Zebi said nothing. She knew her mother-in-law was hovering nearby, listening to her every word. If she complained she would be punished.

Zebi was hardly ever allowed to visit her parents. When she did she was always accompanied by her mother-in-law, who wouldn't leave her alone with her family even for a minute, so she couldn't talk to them there either.

One day Qodil fell ill and had to go to the hospital. When he heard about this, Fazil decided it was a good opportunity for Zebi to come home for a long visit, so he went to fetch her. They had only just set off when her mother-in-law came out of the havli, *accompanied by four of her sons, and demanded that Fazil bring their* kelin *back, saying he had no right to take her away, so he was forced to leave her there. Shortly afterwards, Zebi got hepatitis, and the doctors said she should spend a month in the hospital. However, her in-laws wouldn't allow this. They insisted on taking her straight back home.*

Despite her good relationship with her husband, Zebi was miserable. So were the other kelins. Although several had postsecondary education, they also hadn't been allowed to take jobs after marriage, so they had no financial resources. By the time Zebi joined the family, the others all had children. Moreover, their in-laws' aggressive behavior had almost completely severed all contact with their natal families. This made them completely dependent on their in-laws.

Figure 6.2 Qodil's family's *havli*

Zebi's in-laws hated the fact that her parents were not behaving like those of the other kelins and that they continued to visit her frequently, taking no notice of hints to leave their daughter alone. One day Qodil told his wife she should forget about her family; she had now joined his. Zebi said she would agree to forget about her family if he would forget about his, and leave the havli *so they could live on their own. Qodil was horrified. Except when he lived in the university dorm as a student, he had always been with his parents. Even then, he had gone home every weekend. He could not imagine leaving his family permanently.*

Several months went by. Rather than settling down, Zebi became increasingly restless and unhappy. Day by day she found the treatment harder to bear. Finally, she couldn't stand it any longer. Early one morning she quietly slipped out of the compound, leaving all her possessions behind, and took a bus to Dushanbe. This time her in-laws didn't come to fetch her. In fact, she hasn't seen or heard from any of them since, not even from Qodil. Zebi still loves him and is unhappy at the way things turned out, but she cannot stand the thought of living there again. It was like being in hell.

When she first came home, Zebi was very depressed and would sleep all day. After a few weeks Khayma found her daughter a teaching job, and working has helped her feel somewhat better. However, she thinks about Qodil all the time and longs to see him. She hasn't tried to contact him because she knows it's pointless. She won't go back to live with his family, no matter how nice he is to her, and she is sure he will never leave them. Luckily she didn't get pregnant, so she doesn't have a child to deal with.

Zebi's eldest sister says she is not interested in marrying because there are no decent men today. Her parents agree. Fazil says there are few families like theirs, who allow their children the freedom to make their own decisions and are happy for their daughters to live with them for life like their sons. He believes almost none of their neighbors and acquaintances care as much for their daughters as he and Khayma do. They are more concerned for their honor than for their children's happiness.

Zebi's experience has made Khayma and Fazil worried about the future of all their daughters, and they are adamant that they will never again allow any of them to marry outside Dushanbe. They feel it is less likely an urban family would abuse a kelin *in that way.*

TRADITIONALISTIC VERSUS
MODERNISTIC MARRIAGE

The two families in this story might be said to represent the extreme ends of the traditionalist–modernist continuum in Tajikistan. To clarify what I mean by this, I have used their characteristics to derive a model containing two family types. The traditionalist family, based on Qodil's, is by far the most common in Tajikistan, even if few families are as extreme as this. The modernist family, based on Zebi's, is a type that as yet has few adherents.

I have drawn here on work of Çiğdem Kağıtçıbaşı. Kağıtçıbaşı's dynamic model of the family synthesizes context, both cultural and socioeconomic, together with different family systems. She uses it to present three different family types. Her independent family is typical of the West and thus not relevant to Tajikistan. Her other two types—interdependence and emotional interdependence—correspond to types of families found in many Southern societies (Kağıtçıbaşı 1996: 72–90). They bear a strong resemblance to my traditionalist and modernist family types respectively.

I have made my model somewhat simpler than Kağıtçıbaşı's. It is static and includes only those characteristics salient to the arguments in this book. Following Kağıtçıbaşı, I have outlined these characteristics in two tables. The first gives the context, which consists of both material conditions and family structures. The second shows family systems, including the values placed on different kinds of socialization, as well as the typical socialization practices of such families.

A comparison between my model and Kağıtçıbaşı's shows great similarities, but also some important differences, most especially in regard to economic status.

Model of family styles (after Kağıtçıbaşı 1996: 72–90).

TABLE 1

Context	Traditionalist	Modernist
Culture	Strongly collectivist	Weakly collectivist, with some degree of individualism
Living conditions	Rural peri-urban *havli* dwellers/apartment dwellers	Urban apartment dwellers
Educational levels	Low-medium	Medium-high
Family structure		
Family type	Extended patrilocal	Mainly neolocal
Wealth flows	Towards parents	More towards children
Family ties	Stronger patrilineal and weaker matrilineal (mothers choose sons' wives from among their own cousins)	Nuclear with strong kin ties
Fertility levels	Medium – High	Low – Medium
Gender identities	Traditionalist – strong male control over females	Modernist – weak male control over females

TABLE 2

Family systems	Traditionalist	Modernist
Socialization values		
Loyalties	Strong in-group loyalties	In-group plus individual loyalties
Dependence-independence values	Strong interdependence values	Weak interdependence values
Basis for valuing family members	Utility values	Emotional values
Degree of son preference	Sons confer status and security	Both sons and daughters confer status and security
Way marriage is contracted	Arranged marriages	Children have considerable say in the choice of spouse and love matches are acceptable.
Value put on sons' wives	*Kelins* belong to the whole family. They are the mother-in-law's to command.	*Kelins* are important in the family as a whole but their marital relationships are primary.
Basis for choice of sons' wives	Chosen for utilitarian values, such as submission and willingness to work.	Chosen for emotional values, such as compatibility and companionship.
Family interactions		
Parenting styles	Strongly authoritarian	Mildly authoritarian
Childrearing orientations	Obedience-dependence	Dependence plus a degree of autonomy
Chief direction of power relations	Strongly gerontocratic power relations coupled with strong gendered ones	Mild gerontocratic and gendered power relations
Practices around divorce	Abused wives strongly discouraged from abandoning marriage. Divorced daughters forced into remarriage.	Divorce not encouraged but abused daughters allowed to return home and remain there.
Interpersonal dependence/independence	Strong interpersonal interdependence	Weak interpersonal interdependence
Orientation of self	Orientation towards relational self	Relational self coexists with some degree of autonomy

Economic Issues

While for Kağıtçıbaşı economic status is crucial for distinguishing these two family types, my model omits economic indicators altogether. This is because I have not been able to find any direct correlation between economic resources and family types in Tajikistan. This is no doubt because Kağıtçıbaşı's model is based on Turkey and other Southern societies that have long been embedded in the capitalist world system. Her family types are strongly related to social class. Her emotionally interdependent family type is essentially middle class, and her interdependent type is typically found among peasant and working-class families.

This distinction does not exist in Tajikistan, as I explained in the Introduction. Capitalism has not made sufficient inroads into the republic's socioeconomic structures for a class system to have formed. Until it does, it is likely that families like Zebi's will remain rare, since at present neither the sociocultural nor the material conditions for their formation exist.

As Kağıtçıbaşı suggests, in capitalist-influenced settings, affluence is a prerequisite for the development of the modernist family. This almost always goes hand in hand with a middle-class environment. It is therefore quite striking to see how different the situation is in Tajikistan, as is demonstrated by the fact that Qodil's traditionalistic family is considerably better off financially than Zebi's. This reverses the relationship between educational levels and income found elsewhere[2] (Kağıtçıbaşı 1996).

During Soviet times, there was often no direct correlation between education and income levels. In Central Asia, many families living in *havlis* had access to extra income, for instance through the sale of produce from their plots,[3] making them considerably wealthier than those dependent on their wages, even those in highly skilled jobs. This meant that the more modern-leaning families were often considerably less affluent than traditionally inclined ones (Lubin 1984). In Tajikistan today, the same holds true.

In this setting, income does not hold the same significance for determining social levels as in capitalist-oriented societies. A better indicator can be found in attitudes towards education. Families in which parents put a high value on their children's academic achievements, and seek to help them gain knowledge and skills, have modernistic tendencies, irrespective of income. Those who put no value on education, or who are happy to purchase their children's diplomas, are on the traditionalistic side.

The fact that Qodil and his brothers graduated from university does not mean that they and their family valued education for its own sake, as we saw in Chapter 4. In Zebi's family, however, not only did all the adult members study at institutions of higher education, they were also expected to gain their degrees as far as possible through their own endeavors. Fazil and Khayma help their children with their schoolwork and encourage them to study independently. The apartment is full of books, and reading is considered a normal part of everyday life.

Wealth in Qodil's family flows from the children to their parents. That is to say, the parents manage the family resources, and spend relatively little on their children, who from childhood have been expected to contribute their labor for the family's benefit. Fazil and Khayma, on the other hand, have made considerable effort to educate their children so that in general wealth flows from them towards their children, as in my modernist family type. However, those young people who have completed their studies and remain at home are expected to contribute towards family upkeep so that wealth circulates relatively equally among the adults.

The amount of labor each of the females is expected to contribute in the modernist home is relatively small, since they all share the workload, and much less effort is involved in keeping up an apartment than a *havli*. Moreover, as it is not a productive unit, all food will have to be purchased. Therefore, it is important that family members bring in money, and every adult is expected to work for a living, including the women. Without this, the family would find it difficult to survive. In such a setting, there is insufficient housework to warrant even one woman remaining at home all day, unless she is needed to look after small children.

Although neolocal residence is usually preferred by modernist families such as Zebi's, the material conditions of Tajikistan do not always permit this. There is simply not enough housing to go round. Therefore, young men are not infrequently forced to live with their parents for a considerable period after marriage. In Soviet times, it would usually take some time to get to the top of the housing list. Now that apartments can be purchased on the open market, they have become more inaccessible than ever for all but the wealthiest. Thus, Zebi's brother will probably also start married life in his parents' home.

Basis for Valuing Family Members

No doubt the original reason for prioritizing utilitarian family values was the need for labor. Before the Revolution, multiple generations of Tajiks would live in one large *havli*, which required considerable labor to keep it going, especially in rural areas where farms were large. Although the contemporary peri-urban *havli* is smaller, it still requires a great deal of labor to be fully productive, as we saw in Chapter 3, since most work is done manually, both on the farm and in the house, and there are no appliances or convenience foods to lighten domestic tasks.

In Qodil's home, almost all the work was carried out by the *kelins*. Their labor was vital, so the family could not afford to allow them to take outside

Figure 6.3 Traditional open-air kitchen

jobs. Since his mother was responsible for keeping the *havli* going, it is hardly surprising that she was more concerned with his wife's contribution to family welfare than with the quality of her son's marriage.

From the perspective of someone for whom utility values were more important than emotional ones, Qodil's attachment to Zebi might have been difficult to comprehend. In fact, from that viewpoint he is an aberration, although quite likely his anachronistic tendencies are now in the process of being knocked out of him. Presumably his mother has replaced their nonconformist *kelin* with one who will be malleable and work hard. Here the individual is not important; what is needed is someone willing to play the appropriate role.

Their labor needs make it almost inevitable that Qodil's family would prioritize the utility values of their members. Even though apartment dwellers do not have the same requirements for labor, many women living in them feel the same way. Once their eldest son is married, they think they should no longer have to carry out domestic chores. For this reason, they also tend to choose their *kelins* based chiefly on utility values. In such a setting it is usual for the eldest son to remain in the family apartment after marriage until he can afford a place of his own, after which the next son will be married and the process repeated. The youngest son will remain in the family home and inherit it after his parents' death.

In modernistic families such as Zebi's, domestic chores may be shared by all family members, even the males, so that there is no need for sons to marry to provide their mothers with a source of labor. Such families therefore have the luxury of being able to afford to emphasize emotional values.

Gender, Love, and the Development of the Self

There are significant differences between the gender norms of these two families. The importance that Qodil's mother gives to women conforming to appropriate feminine behavior patterns, exemplified by the concept that they should sit meekly in the back of the car, typifies a traditionalistic mindset. As has been noted before, in these circles it is important for women to display public submission to their husbands in such a way as to acknowledge their right of control.

This does not mean that women are *actually* submissive, a fact amply demonstrated by the strong persona Qodil's mother displays in private.[4] Her action in forcing Fazil to bring his daughter back to the *havli* demonstrates her real power and shows her ability to co-opt her sons to follow her commands. However, since this kind of power is not validated by discourse, it has to remain hidden. Thus, Qodil's mother conceals her private authoritarian self behind public displays of meekness.

Since Fazil does not feel the need to make a public display of control over his womenfolk, Khayma and her daughters do not have to demonstrate corresponding public submission. Thus, they may sit in the front of the car and, unlike the women in Qodil's household, are granted the same level of mobility as the men. Since these women do not have to assume a particular mien in public as opposed to private, they can present their personas relatively authentically, almost like people from individualistic societies (see Chapter 3). Nevertheless, all family members, including Khayma, wait on

Fazil. Moreover, Khayma also expects her children to acknowledge her authority over them, albeit with considerably less force than Qodil's mother.

Because they believe in their children's right to make their own decisions, Fazil and Khayma have made no attempt to marry Zebi's older sister, although she is now in her late twenties and therefore in Tajik terms already on the shelf (WHO 2000: 23). However, they still expect to be consulted and to have their opinions taken seriously. Had they forbidden Zebi to marry Qodil, they would have expected her to resign herself to their edict, but they would not have done this without very good reasons, which they would have discussed with her. They have nothing against their children marrying for love, and accept the idea that their primary loyalty will subsequently be to their spouse.

This is quite different from the attitude of Qodil's family. Given their need for labor power, it is surprising that he was permitted to choose his own wife, especially one from such a different background. Perhaps his mother allowed him more leeway than usual because he was the youngest son. In any case, she probably thought Zebi would quickly knuckle under and fit into the pattern of the other *kelins*, and that Qodil was so strongly bound to his family that his loyalties would remain with them.

This last assumption seems to have been correct. The fact that Qodil never contacted his wife after she walked out suggests he was unwilling or unable to defy his parents. Very probably he has already allowed them to choose him another wife, one more suitable for their purposes.

The differences in parenting styles and childrearing practices between these two families feed into the differences in self orientation. The authoritarian approach of Qodil's family is intended to guarantee the maintenance of interdependence, while the more relaxed but still reasonably authoritarian attitude of Zebi's parents serves to maintain a high degree of group interconnectedness, while encouraging a certain degree of autonomy.

These differences have many implications. For instance, in regard to education, the more autonomous youngsters are likely to be able and willing to take responsibility for their own achievements. For children reared in strongly authoritarian families such as Qodil's, this will be more difficult. They will probably have to struggle hard to be permitted to express their own ideas openly or move beyond their parents' worldview.

It was the combination of emotional family values, modernistic gender identities, and permission to exhibit personal autonomy that made it possible for Zebi to abandon her marriage. If one of Qodil's sisters were to walk out on her marital family, her own family would almost certainly force her to return, irrespective of the level of abuse. They would consider it highly shaming for a daughter to take the initiative to leave her husband (cf. WHO 2000: 23). Were the problem merely an authoritarian mother-in-law, the young woman would be expected to endure. However, if her husband were physically violent towards her, the family would most probably take steps to protect her, for instance by sending Qodil and his brothers to threaten her husband with negative consequences were the abuse to continue.

Fazil does not have this kind of muscle power at his disposal. All he can do to help his daughter is allow her to remain at home. At the same time, his definition of abuse is different from that of Qodil's family and includes the kinds of treatment meted out by Zebi's in-laws. He would not allow his daughter to return to the *havli* even if she expressed a wish to do so.

Thus, Fazil's definition of what is acceptable in a family relationship differs significantly from that of Qodil's parents. When two families are so far apart in outlook, it is not surprising if their members have serious problems dealing with each other's lifestyles.

OTHER MAPPINGS TO THE MODEL

As I indicated above, the two families whose story starts this chapter are extreme family types. Clearly, not all families fit these patterns so exactly. For most there is much more overlap between traditionalist and modernist characteristics. Moreover, I had no personal contact with Qodil's family and only knew Zebi's for a few weeks. Therefore, my model is a snapshot in time and less nuanced than it would have been had I analyzed families with whom I had had longer contact, such as that of Nahdiya.

Using the model to examine the characteristics of this family, based on their story as told in Chapter 4, we can see not only that they are not as clear-cut as those of my two prototypical families, but also that they vary over time. Having started on the traditionalist side, they are slowly moving towards greater modernity.

When I first met the family in 1995, Nahdiya still firmly believed in her right to determine her children's lives. She had raised them to obey her and not to dare oppose her decisions. She had recently forced Tahmina into a very much unwanted marriage and was determined to marry Jahongul as soon as she left high school. However, Tahmina's unhappiness was already beginning to affect her mother. By the time Jahongul finished high school some six months later, Nahdiya had softened her stance in so far as to allow her some input into the choice of a husband.

The criteria Jahongul used for judging her suitors were related to her sister's situation. Thus, she was determined to live apart from her in-laws and not to marry into a rural family. As a result, she agreed to accept the first offer they received, solely on the grounds that the prospective groom and his family lived in Dushanbe and that he already had his own apartment. Unfortunately, this marriage turned out unhappier than Tahmina's, because the young man beat her. In fact, Jahongul got on better with her mother-in-law than with her husband, so that this way of judging a marriage prospect had not served her well.

The result was that Nahdiya began to doubt the traditional setup whereby decisions had to made based on purely material grounds, since young people were not allowed to get to know each other before marriage. She decided to stop interfering and permit her youngest two children to make their own marital choices. Nevertheless, they were supposed to do this without dating, which was still considered shameful.

Nahdiya did not stop believing in the rightness of the Tajik traditions that insisted that children had to obey their parents, who would make all decisions for them. She simply decided that the current circumstances were exceptional. Tajikistan was in turmoil. The economic situation was so poor that the most enterprising young men had left the republic. Those available to families like theirs, with neither money nor good connections, were, as she put it, the dregs. She did not want to be responsible for her youngest daughter having a miserable marriage also. She even thought it would be preferable for her to marry a foreigner, seeing that the Tajik men her sisters had married had turned out so badly. One of their friends had married a European Muslim with whom she was very happy, and Nahdiya seemed to be hoping Bahorgul would be lucky enough to do likewise.

Looking at the model in light of this and the rest of this family's story as narrated in Chapter 4, one can see that they fall generally to the traditionalist side of the model, but with distinct exceptions. The family also started out strongly collectivist, but this has now somewhat weakened, albeit not to the extent of Fazil's family.

In 1995 Nahdiya lived alone in her apartment with her unmarried children; at that time her elder son was living in his wife's village, and Tahmina in her husband's. The family was thus nuclear but with very strong kin ties.

Nahdiya's own educational level is low, but that of her children is medium to high. Farhod had no postsecondary education, but Farukh had several years of full-time university education. Jahongul had attended technical college full-time, while her two sisters were completing external university degrees.

Wealth in this family flows in both directions. Nahdiya tried her best to find money to educate her children, and in that sense money flowed towards them. However, as she earns so little, her unmarried children have had to help pay off the debts incurred by their mother, and they are now also supporting her and Tahmina. In this sense the family tends towards collective modernity.

There have also been changes over the years regarding gender identities. When I first knew the family, the sons would help their mother keep the daughters strongly under control. Jahongul used to complain bitterly about this. In Bahorgul's case, Nahdiya forced her sons to stop this behavior, and

she allows her far more freedom of movement than most parents allow unmarried girls. She told me she would even be happy for her to study abroad
should the opportunity arise.

For Nahdiya, her children's happiness is as important as their material circumstances. Thus, her elder daughters' poor marital relationships troubled
her very much. She would lie awake at night trying to think how to help
them. Unlike most parents I knew, Nahdiya has never forced Tahmina to return to her husband's village. Instead she has allowed her to make her own
decisions.

From the economic perspective, the presence of Tahmina and her children
makes things harder, as the family is very poor. However, the strength of their
emotional bonds is such that this has not produced the same level of strain as
would have been the case in a traditionally inclined family.

For Nahdiya, both daughters and sons are important. She loves their *kelin*,
Farhod's wife, and sees her not as depriving her of a son but as providing her
with grandchildren. She expects any of the young women around to do the
housework, but she does not force them to do it.

Nahdiya's relative flexibility may be due to the absence of a husband. As a
woman she cannot be shamed in the same way as a man can, and she is not
expected to exert the same level of control over her children. Moreover, had
her husband lived, the family might well have developed along similar lines to
Fazil's.

His early death meant that his widow ended up raising the children in the
traditional pattern she was familiar with. However, as they grew up and times
changed, she has modified her stance towards the traditions. As a result, Bahorgul has much more freedom than did either of her sisters, and her mother
has been willing to relinquish some of her authority in order to allow her
youngest two children more power. No doubt the fact that they supply most
of the family's income plays a significant role here also.

The early loss of her modernistic husband may have retarded Nahdiya's
development of such tendencies, but at least her widowhood meant that there
was no authoritarian and inflexible male family head, such as Jumabek, to
force the family to maintain traditional patterns. Moreover, since living in an
apartment meant that Nahdiya did not need as much labor as Qodil's
mother, to a certain extent she could afford to put her emotional relationship
with her children above their utility value. Nevertheless, she could not allow
her family to become too individualistic; given their unequal earning capacity, this would have made the survival of the most vulnerable much more difficult. Thus, the orientation of this family is still mainly towards the relational
self but with an increasing degree of autonomy.

To sum up, Nahdiya's family does not fit neatly into one side or other of my
model but rather crosses the dividing line between the types. It simultaneously

displays characteristics both modernistic and traditionalistic, collectivist and individualistic, which change over time.

With this example I have tried to show that my two family types are not intended to be rigid molds into which all Tajik families automatically fit. A large number of families will, like Nahdiya's, straddle the line, displaying characteristics found in both family types. The model can also serve as a yardstick to help assess the positions of different families in relation to the continua.

MOTHER-IN-LAW–*KELIN* RELATIONSHIPS

As I have suggested, the very concept of the *kelin* is traditionalist. In a modernistic household the spousal relationship is primary and the wife is regarded as an integral member of the husband's family, so the word *kelin* hardly applies.

In families like Qodil's, however, the relationship between mother-in-law and *kelin* is of primary importance. The women are likely to spend much more time together than with their husbands, since men often spend most of their waking hours outside the home. In this situation, the use of the word *kelin* underlines the younger woman's incomer status. The question is whether such a relationship is always and invariably utilitarian and negative, or whether some measure of positive emotional relationship can coexist even within a basically traditionalist setting.

In many places where the patrilocal extended family is common, there are myths around the figure of the harsh mother-in-law. In India, for instance, folksongs have long described violent murders of *kelins* by mothers-in-law, and their part in dowry deaths is well documented (Mukta 2000: 164).[5] Mothers-in-law are thus conceptualized not merely as authoritarian but as downright cruel.

Similar myths abound in Tajikistan. In these circumstances, it is hardly surprising that the figure of the mother-in-law has come to resemble a bogey in the minds of unmarried girls, especially if the myths portray mothers-in-law like Zebi's.

This kind of dominating behavior in older women has been excused as a reaction to the very low power position they occupied as brides. If they are submissive, become acceptable *kelins*, and do their duty by producing sons, they are promised a position of power when their sons marry and they get *kelins* of their own to boss around (see Chapter 3). However, this does not fully account for the brutality of mothers-in-law, nor indeed of sisters-in-law, both in India (Mukta 2000) and in Tajikistan.

In the work Ghamkhori carried out in the villages of Khatlon, the mother-in-law–*kelin* relationship was the subject of much discussion. *Kelins* would often complain bitterly of the treatment meted out to them. In their turn, mothers-in-law would grumble at the laziness of their daughters-in-law, their lack of appropriate skills, their refusal to be properly submissive, and so on. The fact that they had chosen these *kelins* themselves did not make the older women any more inclined to like them or behave well towards them. They also resented any sign of their sons' developing love for their wives and would do all they could to prevent this. To this end, they often complained to their sons of their *kelins'* behavior in order to drive a wedge between them.

During debates on the ethics of such conduct, some older women were adamant that they had a right to do whatever they liked and were not obliged to be any nicer to their *kelins* than their own mothers-in-law had been to them. The youngsters should not whine about it so much. They should accept the treatment, shut up, and bide their time, just as the older women had done. If they have sons, they will later gain in power and have *kelins* of their own to take out their frustrations on.

Several decades ago in Algeria, the same stereotype of the harsh mother-in-law existed. This was very similar to what we have seen in Tajikistan. Mothers would choose a bride for their sons, but after the marriage would turn on her and abuse her, supposedly in the name of their sons' interests. According to Minai, the real reason was probably their wish to ensure that their sons continued to put their mothers first. Like the Tajik mothers-in-law described here, Algerian ones also often decided to rid themselves of their *kelins*, even if this meant forcing their sons to divorce. Minai believed, however, that this kind of behavior was far from universal in Algeria, and that many older women there, as in other parts of the Middle East, sought harmony in their homes (Minai 1981: 196).

In Tajikistan both types of mothers-in-law exist. Although the majority of those in Ghamkhori's project villages insisted on their right to behave as harshly as they liked, a large minority said they felt sorry for their *kelins*. They remembered what it had been like for them when they were young, how unhappy they had been to be separated from their natal families and childhood friends, and how unpleasant it had been to be ill treated by the women of their marital families. They said they really made an effort to be nice to their *kelins* because they did not think it was right for them to suffer as they had.

A third group of women explained that they divided their *kelins* into two groups: Those who were close relatives they treated as family; the others were aliens, and they felt no obligation to treat them well. This goes to prove my earlier statements in regard to the permeability of traditionalist family boundaries. It speaks to the preference in Tajik culture for cousin marriages and explains why this is supposed to protect *kelins*.[6] A family may take years fully to accept a new *kelin* who is not related to them. In fact, it is really only when women have acquired *kelins* themselves that they become insiders. At that point they are no longer mere appendages to their in-laws. They are founding their own lineages.

Occasionally, when several married brothers live with their parents, their wives are able to band together to resist the worst of the tyranny. One young woman told me that the six *kelins* in her household had elaborated joint strategies for dealing with their mother-in-law. However, this is comparatively rare; it is more usual for mothers-in-law to succeed in ruling over their *kelins*, as Zebi's did.

Nevertheless, today young women are less willing to put up with bad treatment than in the past. This is no doubt because the new influences discussed in Chapter 5 have suggested to them that there are other ways to live.

At the same time, the patriarchal bargain (Chapter 3) is breaking down. Owing to socioeconomic pressures, marriage has become extremely unstable. For one thing, the imbalance between the sexes as a result of large-scale male labor migration means there is a sizable pool of unmarried girls, so that if families do not like one *kelin* they can easily get another.

Consequently, there are many young divorcées who have been returned to their parents, very often together with several children. Frequently, it seemed to be their mothers-in-law rather than their husbands who forced them out.

DIVORCE

Knowing their rights is not necessarily helping young women improve their lives. Refusal to kowtow to their mothers-in-law may well result not in better treatment, but in divorce.

In traditionally inclined families, divorced daughters are often considered shameful, since it appears they have not adhered to their correct gender identities. Moreover, they have failed in a woman's most important profession— that of marriage. Respondents in the WHO survey mentioned previously said that in popular discourse, being a divorcée is considered on a par with being a prostitute (2000: 23). However, the numbers of divorced women are currently so high that sooner or later this stigma is bound to decrease.

The problem is as much financial as cultural, since a divorced woman frequently becomes an unwanted charge on her natal family. Her brothers, or more often their wives, are likely to resent resources being diverted from them. While an unmarried daughter is more powerful in her natal family than a *kelin*, a divorced or widowed one is in a lower position, especially if she has no income of her own and depends on her parents and/or brothers for food and clothing for herself and her children.

Theoretically, in traditionalistic families parents and children bond for life (Kağıtçıbaşı 1996: 31); in practice this is getting increasingly difficult. The tough economic situation, combined with social instability, is causing the interdependency of the collective to break down.

It would seem that the high divorce rates would make parents realize the necessity of giving their daughters as good employment-related skills as sons, so that if they are left to fend for themselves they will be able to support their families. However, cultural values have not as yet caught up with the material circumstances. Instead of empowering women by encouraging them to develop skills to help them earn a living, the arbiters of community values prefer to preserve the status quo, even when this means forcing women to remain in violent marital situations or leaving them to face serious poverty.[7]

In the current situation, a divorced or widowed woman is likely to be remarried as soon as possible both to minimize the financial burden to her family and to get rid of the object of shame. This may place her in the hands of yet another mother-in-law whom she will have to try hard to please, in the hope that this marriage will last and she will not soon find herself back home again.

I have known a few young women who went through this four, five, or even more times before either they managed to make a marriage stick or their parents gave up. In this respect, Zebi and Tahmina have been exceptionally lucky to have families who care more about their happiness than about either the potential shame or the financial hardship involved.

The Transition: Traditionalistic or Modernistic?

Given the history of Tajikistan and the way globalization appears to encourage the development of modernity and individualism, it would seem logical for people to move from the traditionalistic towards the modernistic. It is possible that there is a very slow-moving overall trend in this direction. However, it also frequently happens that people move in the opposite direction.

We saw in Chapter 2 that Karomat's exposure to Sovietization did not result in her deciding to reject the traditions and wholeheartedly adopt modernity. On the contrary, after vacillating between the two most of her life, in her last years she came down decisively on the side of the traditions. Moreover, she did her best to compel the rest of her family to do the same, irrespective of the fact that most of them were far more educated than she was.

I have also seen people move away from an even more solidly modernistic outlook after years of living in a traditionalistic family setting. The same applies to collectivism and individualism. In other words, people can and do move along the continua in both directions and may even on occasion reverse direction. How much changes in the outlook of one family member will affect others depends on their relative power positions and the weight of the pressures for or against change. In addition, since material context plays a significant role here, the factors that predominate at any one time are likely to vary.

Nevertheless, as Nahdiya's story suggests, changes are definitely taking place. This raises questions such as under what conditions families make a transition from one style to another, and whether this tends to occur among the members as a group or singly. How much of a role is played by such factors as gender and age? And what is the relationship between material conditions and family styles?

As I pointed out above, material settings encourage particular styles but do not determine them. Thus, it is perfectly possible for a modernistic family to live in a *havli,* although this is much more suited to a traditionalistic lifestyle, while apartments lend themselves to either.

In practice, modernistic adults tend to live in urban areas. Moreover, during Soviet times their workplaces often provided them with apartments. The result has been that it is rare to find such families living in a *havli.*

Since apartments are usually considerably smaller than *havlis,* there is no room for a family of the size of Qodil's. It would also be financially disadvantageous to have to provide for so many people in the nonproductive setting of an apartment. Thus, these tend to be inhabited by relatively small families, and most of the children move out as soon after marriage as they can find a place to live.

This facilitates the development of modernistic and individualistic characteristics, since it lessens parental influence, increases the importance of the husband-wife relationship, and allows the married couple to organize their daily lives according to their own ideas, even if major decisions are still taken in family council. Obviously, this does not mean that everyone living in an apartment will be modernistic or that parents will not be able to control children who live separately if they are determined to do so. It simply explains why living in an apartment gives people a greater chance of producing a modernistic/individualistic outlook than does living in a *havli.*

No single factor can explain what motivates people to move along the continua of transition. However, if I had to single one out, I would say that the most important is likely to be education, as I suggested above. Gender tied to age is also a significant indicator of position on the continua.

As we saw with the students in the previous chapter, young women are inclined towards individualism and modernity, since these appear beneficial to them. However, as they age they may come to prefer greater collectivism and a more traditional style, because this gives them more power. In other words, young women in traditionalistic families start at a lower status level than in modernistic ones, but as they age they gain in status to the point that older women in traditionalistic, collectively minded families hold more power than their modernistic peers.

This potential to gain in power is a good reason for young women to embrace traditionalism and accept collectivism even when these may appear at first glance to be against their interests. As I pointed out earlier, however, given current levels of social instability, far fewer of today's young women are likely to find themselves in a power position such as that of Qodil's mother than in previous generations. This means that it may make sense for young women today to take a more positive attitude towards modernization and individualism than it did for their mothers.

In regard to men, those with high educational levels have also been influenced to some degree by Russo-Soviet concepts of the more bounded self and personal attainments. They are likely to be in respected professions that provide them with status; therefore, maintaining strict control over family members may be less important to them than to their less-educated peers.

I am not suggesting that all highly educated men are inclined towards modernity, but rather that almost all those so inclined are highly educated. In fact, the number of modernists in the male population is much smaller than the number of highly educated men, and I know men with graduate degrees who are just as traditionally inclined as Jumabek.

Although their mix of characteristics means that, like Nahdiya's, many families do not clearly fit within one or the other of the types in my model, certain indicators are suggestive of the overall trend. One such indicator is parental willingness to allow children to participate in the selection of their spouses.

I believe that this single point speaks to a number of the different elements I have discussed in this chapter, including levels of authoritarianism, parenting styles, utility versus emotional value of family members, and degree of interdependence/autonomy. It can therefore serve as a useful indicator for estimating the percentage of Tajik families that tend towards the traditional.

Here I once again turn to the WHO survey. Its findings suggest that less than 1 percent of the nine hundred women interviewed countrywide were in favor of permitting their children any participation at all in decision-making around their marriages. Since only 17 percent of the WHO respondents were from Dushanbe, it is probable that the percentage of modernistic families from the capital is higher than the national figure, but it is unlikely to be much more than 5 to 10 percent. The great majority of parents from Dushanbe with whom I am acquainted are determined to make all decisions for their children, even for those with higher education, as my discussions with the students from the Pedagogical Institute demonstrated.

From multiple discussions and personal observation in both Dushanbe and Khatlon, it seems to me that, excluding the elite, no more than 1 percent of families in the conservative rural regions of Khatlon and at the most 10 percent of those living in central Dushanbe have some level of perceptible modernistic tendencies. In other words, the number of modernistic families in the republic is extremely small.

It should be noted also that the factors identified in my model are not intended to be deterministic, just as the points at which individuals can be found on the two continua are neither fixed nor static. Both are intended to show tendencies, not absolutes. Like Nahdiya's family, some will have characteristics that fall between the two styles, while others will have different ones not included in the model at all.

Moreover, the fact that a family privileges utilitarian values does not mean its members do not love one another. Similarly, a family that considers its relationships to be primarily emotional will still put some measure of utilitarian value on its members, for instance by stressing their domestic labor or earning capacities. Obviously, both the traditionalistic style epitomized by Qodil's family and the modernist one exemplified by Zebi's are in reality far more complex, dynamic, flexible, and shifting than my relatively static model suggests.

CONCLUSION

The traditionalistic and modernistic family types discussed in this chapter correspond very roughly to a traditionalistic/collectivist and a modernistic/individualist positioning on the continua of transition. A traditionalistic family style tends to support a collective ethic. A modernistic style favors interrelated individualism, in which family members become partially autonomous while maintaining an overall interest in preserving the collective good.

My analysis of how Nahdiya fits the model shows that families very often do not fall strictly to one side or other and that their positions change over time. Examining other families described in this book in light of the model would show further shadings and different kinds and speeds of shifting.

In previous chapters I discussed the positioning on the continua as if this were simply a matter of personal choice. While this certainly plays a role, family background and community pressures, as well as economic circumstances and education levels, are crucially important. Nevertheless, although people tend to stick to what they are familiar with, some do move away from their background, stand up to community pressures, and adopt new values, and the factors that bring them to do so cannot always be predicted.

Throughout this book we have seen happy and unhappy marriages both for couples in love matches and for those in arranged ones. In fact, whether marriages are contracted by parental arrangement or personal choice may be less important than whether the two are at similar points on the continua. It is this that will determine whether the young couple have compatible self-identities and aspirations. When one of the partners has strong modernistic tendencies while the other has more traditionalistic ones, the gulf between them can seem immense. This is especially problematic when, as in the case of so many women, their husbands try to force them to conform to traditionalistic gender norms. It can also be highly problematic, as Zebi's case shows, when a modernistic woman is forced to cohabit with a traditionally minded mother-in-law.

In Tajikistan today, the disjunction between the ideals of modernistic young women and those of their parents, in-laws, and even husbands, all of whom very often support a traditionalistic family style, is bound to make for tensions around marital expectations, and as a corollary is likely to lead to unhappiness for the person with the highest expectations from marriage, usually the young wife.

TENSIONS AND TRANSITIONS

In preconquest times, tensions among family members were almost certainly at a considerably lower level than they are today. The reason is that since traditional societies revere continuity, the pace of change tends to be slow. As a result, the conditions children are exposed to may vary little from those their parents experienced when young, which means there is no significant generation gap. Moreover, customs closely prescribe patterns of behavior, and conformity with the rules is enforced by the elders. Thus, abuse of the less powerful is minimized (cf. Kenyatta 1965).

It is my contention, as I suggested in Chapter 3, that upon significant contact with modernity, traditional societies quickly lose their detailed prescriptions for the everyday conduct of family and community relations. What remain are the overarching principles, including the preservation of power positions. Thus, the traditions Central Asians used to protect their culture from Russification maintained hierarchical power structures, while the mechanisms for protecting those at the bottom rapidly vanished. So did the flexibility that had formerly allowed people to adapt their customs in response to material changes.

After the Russian conquest, capitalist development speeded up the pace of change in Central Asia. Later, the institutionalization of socialism brought with it even more sweeping changes. This did not happen at an even pace. At some periods the speed of change was faster than at others. The faster the rate of change, the greater the differences between the environments in which parents and their children grew up and the sharper the intergenerational tensions that are the subject of this book were likely to be.

Karomat was born in the mid-1920s, at a time when the Bolsheviks were forcing very significant social and material changes on their Central Asian subjects. As a result, her childhood was immensely different from that of her mother's.

Karomat spent much of her youth in Dushanbe, where she attended a Soviet kindergarten, wore Russian clothing, had her hair cut short, and learned to sit on chairs. She subsequently completed five grades of primary schooling, most of them in a Russian coeducational school, and went on to work in a series of skilled jobs. From kindergarten on she was exposed to members of the opposite sex, first in school and later in the workplace. She had sufficient contact with males to be able to choose her own husband.

Her mother grew up in a village, sitting and sleeping on *kurpachas* and dressing according to local traditions, including full facial veiling. As a girl, she had no contact with men outside her family, and her marriage was arranged. She was in her late twenties and had already born several children by the time she removed her veil, started to attend school, learned to read and write, and first mixed with men. The only type of employment she ever held was as a primary school and literacy teacher, mainly in the villages of what is now Khatlon.

In other words, these two women were exposed to very different external influences. Karomat was raised to revere Tajik traditions. However, her Russian schooling and media viewing encouraged her to bend them by dating Khudoydod and organizing her own marriage, even if she took great care to do this in such a way as to preserve her good relationship with her mother, whom she adored.

The mothers of Sadbarg and Tahmina grew up in the 1970s in a period of comparative stability. They both attended secondary school, but neither was permitted to remain there until graduation. Instead, they were both married at age seventeen. Other than their desire to continue their schooling, they both told me, they had not thought much about their future but had passively accepted their parents' dictates. They would not admit to having had ideas outside the boundaries of the socially acceptable.[1] Their children were raised during perestroika and the early post-Soviet years, a time of tremendous upheavals. Consequently, the influences they were exposed to and the outlooks they developed were extremely different from those of their parents a generation before. Moreover, the pace of change was so rapid that it affected the youngest generation in another way from their siblings a few years older.

Unlike her mother, Tahmina had definite opinions about her future, and she did not see it as including early marriage. However, to have voiced a refusal to marry would have contradicted the norms—both the tradition of parental authority and the ethic of the collectivist good. Thus, she was forced to hide her psychological noncompliance behind a mask of reluctant conformity. This allowed Nahdiya to go ahead and arrange her daughter's marriage, taking her submissive exterior to imply consent. Between her desperation at being forced into an unwanted marriage and her obligation to comply with the norms, Tahmina found herself in a very painful situation, one that would never have happened had she been more traditionally minded.

Bahorgul had much firmer aspirations than her eldest sister. She was also much more determined to achieve them. Although she loved her mother and did not want to hurt her, she was also unwilling to assume the same compliant mien as Tahmina.

Her elder daughters' misery changed Nahdiya's outlook to the point where she began to question her own judgment. She realized she would have to make concessions to the changing times if she did not want Bahorgul to face similar problems. Sticking strictly to the traditions was clearly no longer useful. However, Nahdiya knew she had no other basis for decision-making. For this reason, she partially abdicated her authority in favor of permitting her youngest two children to make their own decisions.

Not all parents have reacted this way, of course. Qodil's mother is firmly determined to resist the slightest diminution of her authority. Jumabek also has not seen the changes as a sign for him to relax his behavior. On the contrary, they have strengthened his resolve to keep his children as far as possible under his control and to stick to the role of autocratic father that he feels will earn him respect in the community. Although none of the children has rebelled outright, their father's refusal to unbend may well have been a factor in the sons' decisions to seek work in Russia, and in the case of the eldest to remain there indefinitely.

Maintaining the Traditions

Holding on to the traditions has not all been negative, however. They have provided a certain cohesion in times of rapid change and have acted as a barrier to social chaos. The result has been that in the 1920s, as in the post-Soviet period, society in Central Asia held together much better than in Russia.

In the latter, the lack of strong traditions has left young people with little in the way of guidance. Females have been particularly affected. In the early postrevolutionary period, male students tried to force their female classmates to have sex by claiming that those who refused did not support the Revolution, thus putting them in a vulnerable position in regard to the new regime. Those who agreed often ended up pregnant, resulting in high rates of female suicide (Fitzpatrick 1978: 256ff).

In the current period, there have been enormous pressures on Russian girls as young as twelve and thirteen to have sex. The result is a growth in infertility rates, owing to a mixture of unsafe abortions and STDs. Street gangs have provided a sense of belonging, but there too girls have been treated as sex objects (Pilkington 1996). Until social controls develop to correspond with the new material situation, this trend is likely to continue. This is the more worrying since Russia is one of the world's fastest-growing regions of AIDS infection (Eberstadt 2004).

In Tajikistan the traditions have so far protected girls from the worst of these pressures. On the other hand, as we have seen, they have also placed them in unhappy marriages, forced them to live as virtual slaves to their mothers-in-law, or kept them in dire poverty through lack of education and proscriptions on taking employment.

Parental insistence on unconditional obedience has encouraged young people secretly to subvert the traditions. This has tended to expose girls to the risk of sexual coercion or to place them in the kind of situation that Ozoda found herself in, with nobody to ask for help or advice. As a result, in the most traditionally minded families, girls may well find themselves in a negative position whether they conform or rebel. The story of Abduvali shows that the position of boys who want to make their own decisions may be only marginally easier.

Collectivism Versus Individualism

As we saw in Chapter 3, collectivism also has both positive and negative consequences in Tajikistan. The pressures towards unconditional obedience can be hard on young people, even in urban areas where parents are finding this less and less possible to enforce. At the same time, the strong sense of the collective has kept many from homelessness and destitution.

Nahdiya's family is a good example of the positive working of collectivism, especially since her abandonment of strict adherence to the traditions. Once she decided not to marry her youngest daughter immediately after graduation from high school, Nahdiya was able to make use of a kind of honorary membership in her late husband's work collective to obtain employment for her.

Owing to her superior skills, Bahorgul earns over three times what her mother does. With some help from Farukh, she has thus become the chief financial support of those living in the family home—her mother, her eldest sister, and the latter's children. This leaves her with almost nothing to spend on herself. However, without her mother's intervention, she would not have an income at all, so the interdependence works in both directions. The strength of this particular collective can be seen from the willingness with which both Bahorgul and Farukh support Tahmina, so as to allow her to remain in the family home.

Similarly, it was the support of her natal family that made it possible for Zebi to leave her husband, and for her elder sister to remain unmarried.

However, collectivism in Tajikistan also shores up (mature) masculine control and supports the concept that family good depends on the public demonstration of such control. This often translates into avoiding shame by forcing daughters back into abusive marital situations.

Collectivism also supports maternal control over children, which has allowed women like Qodil's mother to dictate to her sons. Thus, at the same time as it supported Zebi's return to her parents' home and allowed her to remain there indefinitely, the collectivist ethic was to a large extent responsible for the breach in their marriage by supporting the system that made Qodil feel obliged to bow to his mother's will.

Today collectivism is increasingly strained to its limits by the dire economic situation. The result is that the most vulnerable are starting to fall by the wayside. Tajikistan now has a growing contingent of street children and of young women forced into prostitution. Increasing numbers of destitute women and girls are being trafficked abroad, usually for sexual purposes (IOM 2001).

ISLAM AND IDENTITY

During all these upheavals, and despite being driven underground during Soviet times, the population of Central Asia have remained constant to their religion. This does not mean that most people would wish for the Islamization of the state or that they are fanatical Muslims. My friends and acquaintances do not want to live like people in the most strictly religious regions of Tajikistan, such as Tavildara or Isfara. One reason that the opposition coalition lost the civil war was the general lack of support for the Islamic state they seemed to want to impose.

Almost all Tajiks I have spoken to consider Islam an important part of their identity, something that defines them both to themselves and to the outside world. This is so even for those who neither pray nor fast and whose chief religious practices are limited to the rites of passage.

It is true that Islam is far more in evidence now than in Soviet times, but this is in great part because it no longer has to be practiced in secret. Thus, large numbers of new mosques have been built and serve significant congregations. In Ghamkhori's project villages, young people are studying the Arabic script in order to read the Qur'an, and increasing numbers of people all over the republic are fasting during Ramadan.

Nevertheless, as I explained in the Introduction, it is unclear that there is a serious religious resurgence. Today fewer students apply to the Islamic University than in the 1990s, even though it remains cheaper and easier to enter than the secular schools. In 2003 in Dushanbe beards were uncommon, and it was extremely rare to see Tajik women wearing *hijab*.

There is a small minority of young people who have turned to religion to support them through the difficult times. For some this has meant the adoption of a stricter form of Islam, for others conversion to Christianity. However, the vast majority of people in Tajikistan are experiencing so many socioeconomic problems that they are directing most of their energies towards survival strategies (ICG 2003).

CONCLUSION

Islam, then, remains as ambiguous as other aspects of life in Tajikistan. It is always present, frequently functioning as a mechanism to legitimize control over women and youth, but many of the inhabitants of Dushanbe do not observe its daily practices.

Through their impoverishment of the masses, capitalist influences in Tajikistan are damaging not only the traditions but also the strong sense of collectivism. However, for the moment at least, they both continue to form the accepted basis of social organization in the republic, even though a great deal that is neither traditionalist nor collectivist goes on beneath the surface.

Similarly, discourse around gender norms suggests that women are far more submissive and men considerably more dominant than is actually the case. As I pointed out earlier, while young women in Tajikistan are at a distinct disadvantage, older women may be considerably more powerful than their Western peers. But then young men are also far less powerful than their fathers.

With the republic exposed to the vagaries of nascent capitalism, it is doubtful that the pace of material change will soon slow down or the economy improve to the extent of allowing the growth of a large middle class. The trend towards modernity and individualism will therefore continue to be tempered by young people's dependence on their parents. Unless something happens radically to transform the situation, in all probability there will be an ever-widening gulf between the lifestyles parents wish to impose on their children and the latter's own desires, resulting in increasing problems for young people, and heightened levels of intergenerational tensions.

Notes

Introduction

1. See Chapter 5 for another take on this.

2. While there was general agreement in regard to dress, when we got down to discussing other attributes of modernity there were many arguments, and it was especially noticeable here that there were fundamental disagreements between the girls and the boys, particularly over family-related issues. A discussion of these can be found in the following chapters.

3. National dress is not purchased ready made, but sewn specially.

4. See Chapters 2 and 5 for more discussion on this.

5. The glossary at the back of this book explains the significance of this term as well as of other less well known terminology, and also the meaning of the foreign words used here.

6. See Chapter 2 and Harris (2004) for more detailed discussions of this.

7. In Tajikistan there exists what local people term a women's movement although almost everyone concerned distances themselves from feminism. Members of the women's movement stand up for women in a post-Soviet and antifeminist way that does not allow women agency but determines their needs for it, especially those of poor women. The women in the movement, who are virtually all middle class and urban, commonly suggest that middle-class or educated women don't have "women's problems," only poor, uneducated women do, especially those living in rural areas. Women's NGOs in Tajikistan are largely run by women from the women's movement and are thus very paternalistic.

8. The idea of taking concepts generally considered binary opposites and showing how each position is actually represented by multiple, possibly even overlapping, points along a continuum is addressed by Kane (1995). She suggests that the binary of male and female in relation to sports, whereby men are conventionally considered physically stronger and thus superior in performance to women, is a myth. She points out that many women can outperform many men at any given physical activity, and that at the same time there is as wide a range of sporting abilities and physiques *within* each of the categories of sportsmen and sportswomen as *between* them. This is similar to what I suggest regarding the analytical categories I use in this book.

9. Owing to the Soviet atheistic ideology, Central Asians tend to conceptualize all Russians as nonbelievers, even though quite a few are actually Christians.

10. See Glossary.

11. I should point out that the word *paradise* is very commonly associated with the Soviet period in the minds of the inhabitants of Tajikistan and no doubt of many other Central Asians, showing how little they are in favor of the drive towards capitalism that has produced such high levels of hardship.

12. See Chapters 2 and 3.

13. The best university in Tajikistan (see Chapter 4).

Chapter One

1. Where not otherwise noted the information in this section is summarized from Adshead (1993).

2. Now the capital of Uzbekistan.

3. The word means "Monday," after the market traditionally held there on that day.

4. The most important of these were Rastokhez, the Democratic Party, and the Islamic Renaissance Party of Tajikistan (Akbarzadeh 1999: 163).

5. This was before the introduction of the present currency, the somoni.

6. On December 16, 1998, I exchanged TR in Dushanbe at a rate of 1,200 to US$1.

7. Calculated at the then exchange rate of 1,436 TR to the US$1 (Robertson 2000: 351).

Chapter Two

1. At home they sat on *kurpachas* and ate at a *dastarkhon* (see Figure 2.2).

2. Tajik women do not usually cut their hair. They keep it long and braid it in different ways depending on their marital status.

3. Drinking alcohol is forbidden by Islamic law. Therefore, the Bolsheviks used to try to get local people to drink in order to test the sincerity of their abandonment of their religious principles. Nowadays, drinking has become part of Tajik culture, especially for men, and vodka is sold not just in urban stores but in almost all village kiosks as well.

4. An Uzbek woman of around the same age as Karomat told of similar conditions she worked under during the war in order to support her family and gain a ration card. She was a lathe operator in an ordinance factory, where the workers sometimes stayed working at the factory for weeks at a time without a break (Tokhtakhodjaeva 1995: 119–120).

5. Cotton is still the most important crop in Tajikistan, in fact in the whole of that part of Central Asia. During the war it was especially important, since there were many military usages for it, such as uniforms, parachutes, wadding for cleaning guns, etc. For more details on Karomat's war work, see Harris (1998).

6. Even after the war, the custom of sending everyone who could be spared to the cotton harvest continued (cf. Tokhtakhodjaeva 1995: 113–114). High school and university students would have to spend several months each year picking cotton, to the detriment of their studies. In fact, in December 2003, I found that schoolchildren, students, medical professionals, and other low-level state employees had been forced into picking cotton yet again.

7. See Glossary.

8. According to Nukhrat, when the Bolsheviks started organizing women into clubs and teaching them modern lifestyles, many *mullahs* decided to organize their own clubs for women in which they taught them how to use their traditions to resist Bolshevism. They legitimized this by conflating traditions with religion and insisting that changes to the former were contrary to Islam (1930: 15–16).

9. However, it should be noted that these debates started, in Egypt at least, largely as a result of colonialist discourse decrying oriental societies as backward. Qassim Amin, the leading Egyptian exponent of the importance of raising female status, expressed contempt for his own society in ways that show this to have been heavily influenced by orientalism (Ahmed 1992: 144ff), that is, by a colonialist-inspired racist, sexist, and Eurocentric cultural discourse whereby Easterners, especially Muslims, are seen as the quintessential and always inferior "other." Edward Saïd accused Westerners of using this as a justification for imperialism (1978). The Soviet regime also used orientalist discourse to justify and legitimize its colonization of Central Asia.

10. Evidence to the contrary was presented by the Russian geologist Pavel Nazaroff, who lived for years in Central Asia and thus was able to see the human beings under the veils. According to him, women there had much higher status and better living conditions than Russian peasant women (1993: 83). However, to have suggested such a thing would have been to imply the inferiority of Russian society compared with that of Central Asia, and would have significantly weakened Bolshevik justification for colonizing the region. Bolshevik arguments for "saving" Central Asian women are reminiscent of the way the United States government justified attacking Afghanistan in 2001 to save local women from the *burqa*.

11. See Baştuğ and Hortaçsu (2000) for a discussion of an alternative viewpoint on the significance of brideprice for Central Asian women.

12. It should be noted that, like Nazaroff, visitors to the region before the Bolsheviks started their discourse against the veil had quite different reactions. They saw through the veil to the human being behind it rather than allowing the concept of the veil as evil to dehumanize the person wearing it. See, for instance, Meakin (1903), Meyendorff (1870), and Schuyler (1876).

13. This is explained in greater detail in Chapter 3.

14. An example of this is Qodil's mother in Chapter 6. While she demonstrates submission towards her husband in public, she shows great authority in private.

15. For instance, veiled girls still occasionally managed to have sex. The fear of this was one reason parents were anxious to marry their daughters early (Nalivkin and Nalivkina 1886).

16. See also Chapter 3.

17. Presumably Party members like Karomat's parents were also seen as colluding with the enemy. Perhaps they were able to use their official position to protect themselves. However, their preservation of traditional gender identities would have kept them from being completely socially unacceptable.

18. In other words, it was considered that traditionalism implied such a complete lack of change stretching over a long period of time that there was nothing of any importance to record in history.

19. It is noteworthy that the supposedly religious Iranian girls are wearing miniskirts, something unthinkable in comparatively secular Dushanbe. In Saudi Arabia, too, girls dress far more daringly than in Tajikistan, but in both cases this is because their clothes are not exposed in the street, since they wear black robes called *chadors* or *abayas* respectively over them.

20. Personal communication. I also had the opportunity to read the texts of Kosmarskaya's interviews, where this attitude came out strongly in all but a couple of cases, both of them Russians who had lived in Tajikistan. One of these even suggested that the Tajiks had had a valid culture of their own with which the Russians had interfered without much justification. But this was one opinion out of more than a hundred.

21. Even by the end of the Soviet Union there were fewer than four million people who formally identified as Tajiks in all the republics put together, out of a total Soviet population of almost 280 million (Pollard 1991: 481–485).

22. As a reinforcement of this point, it should be noted that the same phenomenon occurs in (postcolonial) Africa. Generally speaking, members of each tribe claim their own particular customs. However, as soon as issues around gender identities are touched upon, for instance polygyny or male dominance, there is a tendency, especially on the part of men, to say "we are Africans."

23. This study researched over 6,000 men but not a single woman!

24. Moreover, there are different types of modernity, not all of which privilege the emancipation of women. The Islamization currently emanating from Saudi Arabia

and other places is one manifestation of modernity. The push by the Christian right in the United States to force women into a submissive domestic mold is another.

25. Kağıtçıbaşı also uses this term to refer to changes from traditionalism. However, she is critical of the way it is usually applied in the West to signify that the only direction a Southern (see Glossary) society can move from traditionalism is towards modernity (Kağıtçıbaşı 1996: 74).

Chapter Three

1. For more of Sadbarg's story see Harris (2004: 119–122).

2. In Tajikistan polygyny is against the law but it is tacitly sanctioned in practice, as long as it is discreet. Men get around the fact that bigamy is a crime by not registering more than one marriage with the state, any others being celebrated only by a religious ceremony. In this case, the polygynous marriage was celebrated only by *nikâh*.

3. This can be just as constraining as having to conceal oneself in collective societies, if not more so. The problem is that so-called individualist societies prize those who are different from the norm only marginally more than collectivist ones do. The main distinction is that the norms are usually broader and thus leave more room for difference. This leaves true individualists, often termed eccentrics—that is, people who do not conform even to these broader norms—with nowhere to turn. They must either show themselves "authentically" as unacceptable and even at times unintelligible in their own communities or else conceal their real selves in the way collectivists do. (See also note 10).

4. "[T]he substantive effect of gender is performatively produced and compelled by the regulatory practices of gender coherence" (Butler 1990: 24).

5. Of course, gender identities comprise many more characteristics than these. However, I limit myself in this text to those traits that are relevant to the arguments of this book. These characteristics originated in the honor-and-shame syndrome that is still today found in societies on both sides of the Mediterranean in Christian countries, including Greece, Italy, and Spain, as well as in the Muslim countries of North Africa and the Middle East (Gilmore 1987; Peristiany 1966; Wikan 1984). From there it spread over a considerable swathe of the Asian continent (see Harris 2004: 73–89).

6. This is based on the same reasoning as what are known as honor killings in the Middle East, carried out when daughters are found not to be virgins on their wedding night (Bowen and Early 2002: 94). Both are practiced in order to redeem male honor, since this female shame amounts to a public declaration of their fathers' failure to exert adequate control. Such killings are no longer practiced in Tajikistan, due perhaps to Soviet law. However, Tajik men have other ways of regaining their honor should this be besmirched, including casting daughters out of the family.

7. Thus, it does not work for those few who dare openly to deviate from the norms.

8. This is obviously only possible for never-married girls and only vital for never-married boys. Divorce is common in Tajikistan and nobody appears to object to a man who has already passed through this passage to manhood subsequently marrying a widow or divorcée. Only a man who has never been married is required to marry a virgin. This leads me to the conclusion that the most important reason for preserving female virginity is that described here. (See also Harris 2004: 150; Naamane-Guessous 1991: 124.) There are of course other reasons why a man might wish to marry a virgin, including the fact that this was supposed to give especial pleasure (see Harris 2004: 159).

9. Although operations to restore the hymen are carried out in Dushanbe, few girls are in a position to have one, if they even know of the existence of the procedure. It would be too complicated and expensive for most to organize and pay for and girls almost never dare tell their parents they have had sex unless they find themselves pregnant. But it is also expensive for most parents. I have no idea how frequently it is resorted to.

10. Elsewhere I refer to the way people in collectivist societies assume differing personalities as notional masks in order to conceal a lack of conformity behind a surface agreement. These masks permit people to display themselves almost as stock characters in a play (Harris 2004: 21–24). Sadbarg seems to be saying to her parents, "Here you see me, dutiful daughter," while with me she portrays a strong-minded young woman. (See also Geertz 1975). In fact, as Goffman points out, in individualistic societies people can also wear masks. Such masks serve to conceal people's real and inferior selves by representing "our truer self, the self we would like to be" (Goffman 1973: 19). Masks thus function in individualist societies in the opposite way to that in which they do in collectivist societies.

11. Harris (2004) gives a much more detailed analysis of gender identities, including the development of masculinity and the functioning of male control and how it is established and maintained within families through both internal and external pressures. The book also discusses women's part in maintaining this control.

12. The labor migration of young men has not been going on long enough for it to become clear what it will mean for the economic support of parents in old age. However, should this end up as long-term emigration, it may well have serious consequences for the survival of both the collectivist ethic and of older Tajiks. It may even lead to daughter preference.

13. Of course, the fact that she had no way of getting the money to travel was also a major constraining factor in her decision not to follow her inclinations. However, the determining factor was her inability to live independently, since she could have worked her way around the former Soviet Union, for instance.

14. Nor is this limited to Tajikistan. It is unacceptable in societies that prize collectivism, such as Indonesia and Egypt, for young people to move out of the parental home and live independently before marriage. It can even shame parents if young men leave home *after* marriage in those settings where extended families are

the norm (Piercy 1991; Weyland 1994). However, the relatively recent development of what Kağıtçıbaşı (1996: 87–90) terms a family style of emotional interdependence is now encouraging much greater individualism than in the past, and in some settings it has become acceptable for married offspring to live separately, where a few decades ago this would have been unthinkable (cf. Altorki 1986). However, even in these communities it remains unacceptable for young people to leave home before marriage.

15. See Chapter 6 for a detailed discussion of this type of family.

16. Married women do travel to Russia, albeit in far smaller numbers than men. However, it is almost unheard of for an unmarried girl to do so unless she goes there to study. Even so, it is difficult for girls from the most traditionalist households to gain permission to go, as this would remove them from the family control that supposedly guarantees their virginity to their future husbands.

Chapter Four

1. See Glossary. In the Soviet Union this system was used to gain access to a whole array of goods and services as well as promotion. In collectivist societies like Tajikistan such relationships tend to be based on clans, tribes, or regions. Family also plays a major role. The result is that contemporary Tajikistan has inherited both the collectivist and the Soviet ways of using patron-client relations. This may account for their great importance for obtaining positions both at work and in education as well as for gaining access to many services, as the present chapter discusses.

2. This refers to the language of instruction.

3. In the school grading system five is excellent, four good, three pass, and two fail.

4. So called because it is financed and organized from Turkey and the director and other senior teachers are Turks.

5. One hundred somoni were worth about US$33.

6. More about this family can be found in Harris (2004).

7. Another reason was to keep them away from contact with boys (see Chapter 5).

8. Superficially it may appear that Tajiks are more open to outsiders than Russians since they are far more hospitable, welcoming outsiders to their homes with great ease, while Russians take a much more formal attitude towards social interactions. It is only when it comes to introducing newcomers into their families that the boundaries described above come into play.

9. This university, the best in Tajikistan, is run from the Russian Federation, although it does not limit its intake to Russian students. There have been attempts by international entities to establish new Western-standard universities in Dushanbe. However, they have so far not proven successful.

10. This is not peculiar to Tajikistan. The same thing happens in other postcolonial settings. For instance, I was recently informed that several thousand dollars are necessary to purchase a permanent position as a rural schoolteacher in Ecuador.

There, however, even if salaries are low, at least teachers know they have a job for life, with health insurance and a decent pension. In Tajikistan it is mainly the right to take bribes that is on offer. Salaries and medical and retirement benefits are currently worth very little.

11. Since uneducated girls were preferred as *kelins*, families were also willing to pay more *kalym* for them than for more educated ones. This was an additional reason for not educating daughters (Suzi 1989: 179).

Chapter Five

1. Rural students are rarely fluent enough in Russian to get accepted. They usually go to the Tajik State University, where there are courses in their own language.

2. As I said in Chapter 3 (note 6), honor killings no longer occur in Tajikistan.

3. In the beginning, when the Soviet state brought in universal education, there was strong popular resistance even to primary education. Schools were burned and teachers murdered. Gradually, however, parents began to bow to the inevitable and send their children to school (Rakowska-Harmstone 1970: 43–45).

4. Since the cinemas tended to be full of rowdy males, girls could not attend. However, boys often learned about different styles of courtship from movies.

5. Or, to use Soviet parlance, "with a red diploma."

6. *Local* here is used in the sense of region or even village.

7. The series was called "The People's Century, 1900–1999."

8. However, in Tajikistan this appeared to have had little effect. This may in part be due to the fact that movie operators there preferred not to show propaganda films, since these required hard work in helping conduct political agitation afterwards. Instead, they would show popular movies, for which they could get extra income, and which were greatly preferred by their audiences. They would do this without informing the Party organs of the substitution, thus subverting the Soviet media campaigns (Rakowska-Harmstone 1970: 222).

9. See, for instance, Harris (2004) on Tajikistan, Kuehnast (1997, 1998) on Kyrgyzstan, and Mandel (2002) on Kazakhstan.

10. As I suggested in Chapter 2, modernity is not necessarily manifested in greater female emancipation. Contemporary forms of religious conservatism are also manifestations of modernity.

11. *Simplemente Maria* (1989).

12. Owing to their greater complexity and more alien setting, soaps from the United States, such as *Santa Barbara*, incredibly popular over much of the rest of the former Soviet Union (Kuehnast 1997: 273), bored most of the Tajik girls I knew, who found them too difficult to follow.

13. In fact, they are also inconsistent with the general behavior of men in Latin America.

14. These appear to be simplistic versions of the romantic videos produced in other Asian countries, such as Thailand, which have become popular among young people in much of the South. One problem with such videos is that they portray sexual relationships as a kind of romanticized fiction outside the context of community and culture. They show nothing of their dangers.

15. Lenin Park is right in the center of town, used for family recreation on holidays and weekends. It was one of the most frequently used settings for the video clips we were watching.

16. Central Asia is very ethnically diverse. Before the division into republics the two most important historical cities—Bukhara and Samarqand—had at least as many Tajik as Uzbek inhabitants. The present political divisions were created under Stalin's guidance, and they were as artificial in relation to local cultural groupings as those of other parts of Asia and Africa where national boundaries were drawn by the colonial powers (Jahangiri 1997).

17. I knew several young women who only discovered the existence of sex after marriage.

18. I was told this story by one of Ozoda's friends.

19. No doubt it is partly for this reason that suicide rates in Tajikistan are so high (Harris 2005a).

20. However, when we were alone people often mentioned their sexual problems to me. Once the clients of Ghamkhori's Women's Center started to trust the staff, many of them came to ask for help on such matters (Harris 2005c).

21. My own translation.

22. A high school course on family life, set up in the 1980s, dealt largely with moral issues, virtually ignoring sex. In one school when a young teacher tried to give sex education to the girls in her class she was immediately dismissed (Geiges and Sovorova 1989: 39).

23. Sex appears to be rapidly overtaking needle sharing as the main cause of HIV transmission in Central Asia.

24. See Harris (2004, 2005d) for the story of Rustam and his father Malik, in which these issues are discussed in greater detail.

Chapter Six

1. Cow pats, or dung, are used for cooking fuel and to reinforce the clay walls of traditional houses.

2. Middle-class families tend to have higher educational levels than working-class/peasant ones. Since they use their education to gain higher-paying jobs, they also tend to be financially better off.

3. Central Asians would privately sell in Russia, for high prices, fruit and other produce that the state system could not supply.

4. This does not mean she has power over her husband, but rather that he has delegated his power in the household to her.

5. The murder of *kelins* whose families did not pay sufficient dowry for them is a very common phenomenon in India.

6. However, I have known cases where even first cousins were treated with considerable violence.

7. Marital violence is much worse in Uzbekistan, where the government also takes a hand in forcing women to remain in violent marriages. As a result, divorce there remains uncommon (MNAdvocates 2000: 3). In Ghamkori's project villages, parents were very often willing to allow their daughters to learn a trade, as long as they could do this without leaving the village. For instance, they would ask the organization to start a college there. When Ghamkhori staff offered to arrange for the girls to study in the nearby town instead, their parents would generally refuse. The usual reason they gave was that this would be shaming, since they would be unable to control their daughters' movements. Thus, the maintenance of traditional gender identities took precedence over their daughters' welfare.

Chapter Seven

1. It is also possible that they have simply forgotten all these years later what they were thinking of in their youth.

Glossary

English Terms

BBC. British Broadcasting Corporation.

boy. See **girl**.

CBO. Community Based Organization.

dowry. Payment made by a bride's family to the bridegroom or his family (see also *kalym*).

educated. I use this to denote those with tertiary education—virtually everyone in Tajikistan has at least some secondary education.

FSU. Former Soviet Union.

girl. In Tajikistan the word "girl" (*dukhtar*) is employed for unmarried females. It is not age specific but rather implies virginity. Once a girl has had sex she becomes a woman, again irrespective of age. Thus, in theory a forty-year-old never-married female is a girl, while a twelve-year-old married one is a woman. Barring evidence to the contrary, it is assumed that all girls remain virgins until their wedding nights. In this text I use the English word "girl" with the same implications. I also employ the word "boy" to refer to an unmarried male.

grade. In the Soviet Union, most secondary schools had eleven grades. In many rural Tajik schools, however, there are only ten.

Islamism, Islamization. A contemporary political movement centered on Islam. Its adherents (Islamists) wish to put into place judicial systems based on a strict version of the *sharia*. They are much less flexible and peaceable than the average Muslim.

IUD. intrauterine device, or coil. This is a commonly used contraceptive in many Southern countries.

Jadidists. A group of progressive Tatars from the late nineteenth and early twentieth centuries.

local. Synonymous with Central Asian unless otherwise noted.

neolocal. Residence of married couples apart from either set of parents.

patrilineal. Descent through the father's line.

patrilocal. Residence with the family of the husband.

patronymic. Personal name derived from the name of one's father. In Russia such names (*otchestva*) serve a special function similar to that of a surname, although people have both patronymic and surname.

patron-client relations. A patron-client system is one in which relations are formed between important patrons and less important—often younger—clients. Patrons takes their "clients" under their wing and help them in whatever way is appropriate to the system. In the United States, this often happens in business or politics, for instance, whereby experienced senior persons will form patron-client relations with juniors whom they help advance. (See also *blat.*)

South. I use this instead of the terms "developing countries" or "Third World" to avoid chauvinistic implications of inferiority.

telenovela. Latin American form of television drama, very similar to the American/English soap opera.

Soviet Terms

blat. Connections of the kind needed to get something otherwise unobtainable, such as a job or entry to university (*see also* patron-client relations).

Bolsheviks. Lenin's political party. This was the Communist Party that assumed power after the 1917 Russian Revolution. The Bolshevik Party, from the Russian word *bol'she,* "larger," was the majority Communist Party, as opposed to the other Communist Party of the time, the Mensheviks, from the word *men'she,* "smaller."

glasnost'. Period of openness of the press during the late 1980s time of perestroika.

hujum. Literally "attack." It was the word used for the Bolshevik campaign of the late 1920s to push for the abandonment of the veil.

kandidaat's degree. Similar to a Ph.D.

KGB. Committee of State Security, the Soviet agency for internal security.

kolkhoz. Collective farm.

perestroika. Restructuring of institutions of the Soviet Union that took place in the late 1980s under Gorbachev, simultaneously with *glasnost'*.

sovkhoz. State farm.

ZAGS (Zapisy Aktov Grazhdanskogo Sostoyaniya). Civil registry of births, marriages, and deaths.

Tajik/Muslim Terms

burqa. Garment worn by women in Afghanistan and South Asia. It covers the face as well as the head and body, with an area of mesh around the eyes so that its wearer can see out.

chachvan. Thick veil made of horsehair, which covered the entire face and neck. Its lack of eyeholes made it very difficult to see through. It was typical outdoor wear for women of the sedentary ethnic groups living in Northern Tajikistan and some parts of Uzbekistan.

chador. Cloak worn by women in Iran, covering the head and body but not the face

dastarkhon. A cloth placed on the floor used like a tablecloth to put food on. It turns a room into a dining space.

ezor. Floppy trousers always worn under dresses. They both cover the legs and function as underwear.

faranja. A woman's cloak worn with the *chachvan*. It was placed on the head and hung down to the feet, as in photo 1.2. The word was often used as a local way of saying purdah (*q.v.*) or as shorthand to imply the combination of faranja and chachvan. In Russian it was known as *paranja*.

hadith. A collection of sayings, deeds, and stories of the Prophet that are not in the Qur'an.

havli. The traditional Tajik dwelling compound, consisting of one or more separate houses inside a courtyard. All but the most modern are without indoor plumbing. Most have an outdoor pit latrine, and some also have a shower cubicle in the yard. Some have a tap, in the yard. In those that do not, water has to be fetched from a nearby tap or in the countryside more often from another water source, such as a well or irrigation ditch. The urban *havli* may be quite small. However, the peri-urban and rural *havlis* usually have a plot of land used for growing vegetables and fruits. The family may have poultry, small ruminants, and even a few cattle, so that such a *havli* resembles a tiny farm.

hijab. Modest dressing as a religious obligation. While for men wearing clothes that do not tightly outline their bodies is usually considered sufficient, women are often expected to cover their heads, neck, and shoulders as well. In some cultures some kind of loose cloak is also worn, and more rarely the face is covered.

kalym. Bride price paid by the groom or his family to the family of the bride. This marriage custom is common but not followed by all families in Tajikistan. It is different from *mahr,* which is a religiously mandated provision for a divorced or widowed woman, or dowry (*q.v.*).

kelin. Literally "incomer." This word is used to designate a woman who has married into a family and suggests that she belongs to the whole family rather than specifically to her husband. When eventually she becomes a family matriarch, she is no longer referred to as a *kelin.* I use the word in this book rather than *daughter-in-law* because it bears very different connotations.

khalat. A traditional men's dressing gown, also worn as a coat.

kurpacha. Long sitting/sleeping mat stuffed with cotton.

maktab. Local religious school before the Revolution, now also used to refer to secular schools.

medressa. Muslim religious college.

mullah. Male religious leader.

nikâh. Muslim marriage ceremony.

paranja. See **faranja.**

purdah. Literally "curtain." The secluding of women from the outside world, either inside women-only quarters at home or by the wearing of some sort of covering in public.

Qur'an. Muslim holy book roughly equivalent to the Judeo-Christian bible. Along with the *hadith* and other religious writings, it is used to derive prescriptions for daily living, much like the Jewish Talmud. Sometimes spelled Koran.

sharia. Islamic law.

somoni. Tajik currency worth about 33 cents US in 2003. It replaced the ruble.

taloq. Repudiation of a wife by a husband according to Muslim law; the equivalent of a divorce.

Bibliography

Western European Languages

Abdullaev, Kamoludin, and Shahram Akbarzadeh (2002) *Historical Dictionary of Tajikistan.* Lanam, MD, and London: The Scarecrow Press.

Abu-Lughod, Lila (1993) *Writing Women's Worlds: Bedouin Stories.* Berkeley: University of California Press.

———(2002) "Egyptian Melodrama—Technology of the Modern Subject?" in Faye D. Ginsburg, Lila Abu-Lughod, and Brian Larkin (eds.), *Media Worlds: Anthropology on New Terrain.* Berkeley and Los Angeles: University of California Press, 115–133.

Acar, Feride, and Ayşe Ayata (2002) "Discipline, Success and Stability: The Reproduction of Gender and Class in Turkish Secondary Education," in Deniz Kandiyoti and Ayşe *Saktanber* (eds.), *Fragments of Culture: The Everyday of Modern Turkey,* New Brunswick, NJ: Rutgers University Press, 90–111.

Adelkhah, Fariba (2000) *Being Modern in Iran,* translated by Jonathan Derrick. New York: Columbia University Press, in association with the Centre d'Etudes et de Recherches Internationales, Paris.

Adshead, Samuel A. M. (1993) *Central Asia in World History.* London: Macmillan.

Ahmed, Leila (1992) *Women and Gender in Islam.* New Haven and London: Yale University Press.

Akbarzadeh, Shahram (1999) "Islam, Culture and Nationalism: The Post-Soviet Experience of Turkmenistan, Uzbekistan and Tajikistan," in Kortuk A. Ertürk (ed.), *Rethinking Central Asia: Non-Eurocentric Studies in History, Social Structure and Identity.* Reading: Ithaca Press.

Akiner, Shirin (1997) "Between Tradition and Modernity: The Dilemma Facing Contemporary Central Asian Women," in Mary Buckley (ed.), *Post-Soviet Women:
From the Baltic to Central Asia*. Cambridge: Cambridge University Press,
261–304.

_____(2001) *Tajikistan: Disintegration or Reconciliation?* London: Royal Institute of
International Affairs.

Al-Khayyat, Sana (1990) *Honour and Shame: Women in Modern Iraq*. London: Saqi
Books.

Altorki, Soraya (1986) *Women in Saudi Arabia: Ideology and Behavior among the Elite*.
New York: Columbia University Press.

Appadurai, Arjun (1996) *Modernity at Large: Cultural Dimensions of Globalization*.
Minneapolis: University of Minnesota Press.

Attwood, Lynne (1985) "The New Soviet Man and Woman—Soviet Views on Psychological Sex Differences," in Barbara Holland (ed.), *Soviet Sisterhood*. London:
Fourth Estate Books, 54–77.

_____(1990) *The News Soviet Man and Woman*. Basingstoke: Macmillan.

Bacon, Elizabeth E. (1966) *Central Asians under Russian Rule: A Study in Cultural
Change*. Ithaca: Cornell University Press.

Badran, Margot (1995) *Feminists, Islam, and the Nation: Gender and the Making of
Modern Egypt*. Princeton, NJ: Princeton University Press.

Baştuğ, Sharon, and Nuran Hortasçu (2000) "The Price of Value: Kinship, Marriage,
and Metanarratives of Gender in Turkmenistan," in Feride Acar and Ayşe
Günes-Ayata (eds.), *Gender and Identity Construction: Women of Central Asia,
the Caucasus and Turkey*. Leiden: Brill, 117–142.

BBC (n.d.) "Religion and Ethics: Islam, Sunni and Shia," http://www.bbc.co.uk/reli-
gion/religions/islam/subdivisions/sunni_shia (September 26, 2005).

Bell, Diane (1993) "Introduction 1: The Context," in Diane Bell, Pat Caplan, and
Wazir Jahan Karim (eds.), *Gendered Fields: Women, Men and Ethnography*. London and New York: Routledge.

Benjamin, Jessica (1995) *Like Subjects, Love Objects*. New Haven and London: Yale
University Press.

Bouamama, Saïd and Hadjila Sad Saoud (1996) *Familles Maghrébines de France*. Paris:
Desclée de Brouwer.

Bourdon, Marie Ufalvyne (1880) *De Paris à Samarkand. Impressions d'un Voyage
d'une Parisienne*. Paris: Hachette.

Bowen, Donna Lee, and Evelyn A. Early (eds.) (2002) *Everyday Life in the Muslim
Middle East*, second edition. Bloomington and Indianapolis: Indiana University
Press.

Bronfenbrenner, Urie (1970) *Two Worlds of Childhood: U.S. and U.S.S.R.* New York:
Russell Sage Foundation, with the assistance of John C. Condry Jr.

Butler, Judith (1990) *Gender Trouble: Feminism and the Subversion of Identity*. New
York and London: Routledge.

_____(1995) "For a Careful Reading," in Linda Nicholson (ed.), *Feminist Con-
tentions: A Philosophical Exchange*. London: Routledge, 127–144.

_____(1999) "Revisiting Bodies and Pleasures," in Vikki Bell (ed.), *Theory Culture
and Society, Special Issue on Performativity and Belonging*, 16(2): 11–20.

Caroe, Sir Olaf Kirkpatrick (1967) *Soviet Empire: The Turks of Central Asia and Stalinism,* second edition. London: Macmillan.

Conquest, Robert (1986) *The Harvest of Sorrow: Soviet Collectivization and the Terror-Famine.* New York: Oxford University Press.

Constantine, Elizabeth (2001) *Public Discourse and Private Lives: Uzbek Women under Soviet Rule, 1917–1991.* Ph.D. dissertation, University of Indiana.

Davis, Susan Schaefer, and D. A. Davis (1988) *Adolescence in a Moroccan Town: Making Social Sense.* New Brunswick, NJ, and London: Rutgers University Press

De Vries, Marlene (1988) *Ogen in je Rug: Turkse Meisjes en jonge Vrouwen in Nederland.* Alphen aan den Rijn and Brussels: Samsom Uitgeverij.

Drug Control Agency (2003) Report on the Drug Control Situation in the Republic of Tajikistan 2002. Dushanbe: Government of Tajikistan.

Duben, Allan, and Cem Behar (1991) *Istanbul Households: Marriage, Family and Fertility 1880–1940.* Cambridge: Cambridge University Press.

Eberstadt, Nicholas (2004) "The Russian Federation at the Dawn of the Twenty-First Century," *NBR Analysis* (National Bureau of Asian Research) 15(2), http://ww.nbr.org/publications/issue.aspx?ID=04a6faed–989f–4230–b332–7169872d68c3 (August 12, 2005).

Edgar, Adrienne L. (2001) "Identities, Communities, and Nations in Central Asia: A Historical Perspective," presentation for panel discussion "Central Asia and Russia: Responses to the War on Terrorism," held at the University of California, Berkeley, October 29, 2001, http://ist-socrates.berkeley.edu/~bsp/caucasus/articles/edgar_2001–1029.pdf (August 18, 2005).

Edwards, Anne (1988) *Regulation and Repression: The Study of Social Control.* London: Allen and Unwin.

Etherton, Colonel P. T. (1925) *In the Heart of Asia.* London: Constable and Co.

Fathi, Habiba (1997) "Otines: The Unknown Women Clerics of Central Asian Islam," *Central Asian Survey* 16(1): 27–43.

Feijoo, Ammie N. (2001) *Adolescent Sexual Health in Europe and the U.S.—Why the Difference?* Washington, DC: Advocates for Youth, http://www.advocatesforyouth.org/publications/factsheet/fsest.htm (September 26, 2005).

Felski, Rita (1995) *The Gender of Modernity.* Cambridge, MA: Harvard University Press.

Fierman, William (1991a) "The Soviet 'Transformation' of Central Asia," in William Fierman (ed.), *Soviet Central Asia: The Failed Transformation.* Boulder, CO: Westview Press, 11–35.

———(1991b) "Central Asian Youth and Migration," in William Fierman (ed.), *Soviet Central Asia: The Failed Transformation.* Boulder, CO: Westview Press, 255–289.

Fitzpatrick, Sheila (1978) "Sex and Revolution: An Examination of Literary and Statistical Data on the Mores of Soviet Students in the 1920s," *Journal of Modern History* 50(2): 252–278.

Foucault, Michel (1980) *Power/Knowledge: Selected Interviews and Other Writings, 1972–1977,* edited and translated by Colin Gordon. New York: Pantheon Books.

———(1990) *The History of Sexuality, Volume 1, An Introduction,* translated by Robert Hurley. London: Penguin Books.

Geertz, Clifford (1975) "On the Nature of Anthropological Understanding," *American Scientist* 63, 47–53.

Geiges, Adrian, and Tat'iana Suvorova (1989) *Liebe steht nicht auf dem Plan: Sexualität in der Sowjetunion heute.* Frankfurt am Main: Wolfgang Krüger Verlag.

Giddens, Anthony (1990) *The Consequences of Modernity.* Stanford: Stanford University Press.

_____(1991) *Modernity and Self Identity.* Cambridge: Polity Press.

_____(1992) *The Transformation of Intimacy: Sexuality, Love and Eroticism in Modern Societies.* Cambridge: Polity Press.

_____(1994) "Living in a Post-traditional Society," in Ulrich Beck, Anthony Giddens, and Scott Lash (eds.), *Reflexive Modernization: Politics, Tradition and Aesthetics in the Modern Social Order.* Stanford, CA: Stanford University Press, 56–109.

Gilmore, David (1987) "Introduction: The Shame of Dishonor," in David Gilmore (ed.), *Honor and Shame and the Unity of the Mediterranean.* Washington, DC: American Anthropological Association, 2–21.

Ginat, Joseph (1982) *Women in Muslim Rural Society: Status and Role in Family and Community.* New Brunswick: Transaction.

Glenn, John (1999) *The Soviet Legacy in Central Asia.* New York: St. Martin's Press.

Goffman, Erving (1973) *The Presentation of Self in Everyday Life.* Woodstock, NY: The Overlook Press.

Göle, Nilüfer (1996) *The Forbidden Modern: Citizenship and Veiling.* Ann Arbor: University of Michigan Press.

Grotevant, Harold, and Catherine R. Cooper (1998) "Individuality and Connectedness in Adolescent Development: Review and Prospects for Research on Identity, Relationships, and Context," in Eva Skoe and Anna von der Lippe (eds.), *Personality Development in Adolescence: A Cross National and Life Span Perspective.* London and New York: Routledge, 3–37.

Hall, Stuart. (1990) "Cultural Identity and Diaspora," in Jonathan Rutherford (ed.), *Identity, Community, Culture, Difference.* London: Laurence and Wishart, 222–237.

_____(1992) "The Question of Cultural Identity," in Stuart Hall et al. (eds.), *Modernity and Its Futures.* Cambridge: Polity Press, 266–313.

Halle, Fannina W. (1938) *Women of the Soviet East.* New York: E. P. Dutton.

Harris, Colette (1996) "Women of the Sedentary Population of Russian Turkestan through the Eyes of Western Travelers," *Central Asian Survey* 15(1): 75–95.

_____(1998) "Coping with Daily Life in Post-Soviet Tajikistan: The Gharmi Villages of Khatlon Province," *Central Asian Survey* 17(4): 655–672.

_____(1999) "Health Education for Women as Liberatory Process? An Example from Tajikistan," in Haleh Afshar and Stephanie Barrientos (eds.), *Globalisation and Fragmentation,* Basingstoke: Macmillan, 196–214.

_____(2002) "Muslim Views on Population: The Case of Tajikistan," in J. Meuleman (ed.), *Islam in the Era of Globalization: Muslim Attitudes towards Modernity and Identity.* London: Routledge/Curzon, 211–222.

_____(2004) *Control and Subversion: Gender Relations in Tajikistan.* London and Sterling, VA: Pluto Press.

_____(2004a) "Identity Politics: Central Asia," in Suad Joseph (ed.), *The Encyclopedia of Women in Islamic Cultures*, II. Leiden: Brill, 211–2.

_____(2005) "Reproductive Health: Central Asia," in Suad Joseph (ed.), *Encyclopedia of Women in Islamic Cultures*, III. Leiden: Brill, 24–26.

_____(2005a) "Suicide: Central Asia," in Suad Joseph (ed.), *Encyclopedia of Women in Islamic Cultures*, III. Leiden: Brill, 12–14.

_____(2005b) "Drug Use and Addiction: Central Asia," in Suad Joseph (ed.), *Encyclopedia of Women in Islamic Cultures*, III. Leiden: Brill, 17–19.

_____(2005c) "Tackling Sexual Distress: Two Case Studies from the Central Asian Republic of Tajikistan," in Diana Gibson and Anita Hardon (eds.), *Rethinking Masculinities, Violence and AIDS*. Amsterdam: Het Spinhuis, 175–200.

_____(2005d) "Desire versus Horniness: Sexual Relations in the Collectivist Society of Tajikistan," *Social Analysis*, 49(3).

Hénaff, Marcel (1998) *Claude Lévi-Strauss and the Makings of Structural Anthropology*, translated by Mary Baker. Minneapolis and London: University of Minnesota Press.

Henshaw, Stanley K. (2004) "U.S. Teenage Pregnancy Statistics with Comparative Statistics for Women Aged 20–24," Alan Guttmacher Institute, New York, http://www.agi-usa.org/pubs/teen_stats.html (September 26, 2005).

Hobsbawm, Eric (1983) "Introduction: Inventing Traditions," in Eric Hobsbawm and Terence Ranger (eds.), *The Invention of Tradition*. Cambridge: Cambridge University Press, 1–14.

Hoodfar, Homa (1997) *Between Marriage and the Market*. Berkeley: University of California Press.

Hortasçu, Nuran, and Sharon Baştuğ (2000) "Women in Marriage in Ashkabad, Baku, and Ankara," in Feride Acar and Ayşe Günes-Ayata (eds.), *Gender and Identity Construction: Women of Central Asia, the Caucasus and Turkey*. Leiden Brill, 77–100.

_____(1996) "Republic of Tajikistan: Human Development Report," Dushanbe, United Nations Development Program/Government of Tajikistan.

Humphrey, Caroline (1983) *Karl Marx Collective: Economy, Society and Religion in a Siberian Collective Farm*. Cambridge: Cambridge University Press.

ICG (2003) "Youth in Central Asia: Losing the New Generation," International Crisis Group, Asia Report No. 66, Osh/Brussels, October 31, 2003.

Inhorn, Marcia (1996) *Infertility and Patriarchy: The Cultural Politics of Gender and Family Life in Egypt*. Philadelphia: University of Pennsylvania Press.

Inkeles, Alex and David H. Smith (1974) *Becoming Modern: Individual Change in Six Developing Countries*. Cambridge, MA: Harvard University Press.

Inkeles, Alex, David H. Smith, et al. (1983) *Exploring Individual Modernity*. New York: Columbia University Press.

IOM (2001) "Deceived Migrants from Tajikistan: A Study of Trafficking in Women and Children," International Organization for Migration, Capacity Building in Migration Management Programme, Dushanbe.

Islamov, Bakhtior A. (1994) "Post-Soviet Central Asia and the CIS: The Economic Background of Interdependence," in Beatrice Forbes Manz (ed.), *Central Asia in Historical Perspective*. Boulder: Westview Press.

Jahangiri, Guissou (1997) "The Premises for the Construction of a Tajik National Identity, 1920–1930," in Mohammad-Reza Djalili et al. (eds.), *Tajikistan: The Trials of Independence.* New York: St. Martin's Press.

Jacobson, Jessica (1998) *Islam in Transition: Religion and Identity among British Pakistani Youth.* London: Routledge.

Kağıtçıbaşı, Çiğdem (1996) *Family and Human Development Across Cultures: A View from the Other Side.* Mahwah, NJ: Lawrence Erlbaum Associates.

_____(2002) "A Model of Family Change in Cultural Context," in W. J. Lonner et al. (eds.), *Online Readings in Psychology and Culture* (Unit 13, Chapter 1), Center for Cross-Cultural Research, Western Washington University, Bellingham, Washington, http://www.wwu.edu/~culture/kagitcibasi.htm (September 26, 2005).

Kamp, Marianne (1998) "Unveiling Uzbek Women: Liberation, Representation and Discourse, 1906–1929," Ph.D. dissertation, University of Chicago.

Kandiyoti, Deniz (1991) "Islam and Patriarchy: A Comparative Perspective," in Nikki R. Keddie and Beth Baron (eds.), *Women in Middle Eastern History: Shifting Boundaries in Sex and Gender.* New Haven: Yale University Press, 23–42.

_____(1996) "Modernization without the Market? The Case of the 'Soviet East,'" *Economy and Society* 25(4): 529–542.

_____(1997) "Gendering the Modern: On Missing Dimensions in the Study of Turkish Modernity," in Sibel Bozdocan and Reçat Kasaba (eds.), *Rethinking Modernity and National Identity in Turkey.* Seattle and London: University of Seattle Press, 113–132.

Kandiyoti, Deniz, and Ayşe Saktanber (eds.), (2002) *Fragments of Culture: The Everyday of Modern Turkey.* New Brunswick, NJ: Rutgers University Press.

Kane, Mary Jo (1995) "Resistance/Transformation of the Oppositional Binary: Exposing Sport as a Continuum," *Journal of Sport and Social Issues* 19(2), 191–218.

Karam Azza (1998) *Women, Islamisms and the State: Contemporary Feminisms in Egypt.* Basingstoke: Macmillan.

Keddie, Nikkie R. (1981) "Religion, Society and Revolution in Modern Iran," in Michael E. Bonine and Nikki Keddie (eds.), *Modern Iran: The Dialectics of Continuity and Change.* Albany: State University of New York, 21–36.

_____(1992) "Material Culture, Technology, and Geography: Toward a Holistic Comparative Study of the Middle East," in Juan Cole (ed.), *Comparing Muslim Societies: Knowledge and the State in a World Civilisation.* Ann Arbor: University of Michigan Press, 31–62.

Kenyatta, Jomo (1965) *Facing Mount Kenya: The Tribal Life of the Gikuyu.* New York: Vintage Books.

Kisch, Ewin Ergon (1932) "Asien Gründlich Verändert," in Bodo Uhse and Gisela Kisch (eds.), *Gesammelte Werke in Einzelnausgaben,* vol. 3. Berlin and Weimar: Aufbau-Verlag (1980).

Kon, Igor (1995) *The Sexual Revolution in Russia, from the Age of the Czars to Today,* translated by James Riordan. New York and London: The Free Press.

Kondo, Dorinne K. (1990) *Crafting Selves: Power, Gender and Discourses of Identity in a Japanese Workplace.* Chicago and London: University of Chicago Press.

Kuehnast, Kathleen (1997) "Let the Stone Lie Where It Has Fallen: Dilemmas of Gender and Generation in Post-Soviet Kyrgyzstan," Ph.D. dissertation, University of Minnesota.

_____(1998) "From Pioneers to Entrepreneurs: Young Women, Consumerism, and the 'World Picture' in Kyrgyzstan," *Central Asian Survey* 17(4): 639–654.

Kunitz, Joshua (1936) *Dawn over Samarkand*, London: Laurence and Wishart.

Lal, Jayati (1996) "Situating Locations: The Politics of Self, Identity, and 'Other' in Living and Writing the Text," in Diane L. Wolf (ed.), *Feminist Dilemmas in Fieldwork*. Boulder, CO: Westview Press.

Lenin, Vladimir I. (1933) *The State and Revolution*. London: Laurence and Wishart.

_____(1972) *The Emancipation of Women*. New York: International Publishers.

Levine, R. A. (1974) "Parental Goals: A Cross-Cultural View," *Teachers' College Record* 76, 226–239.

_____(1988) "Human Parental Care: Universal Goals, Structural Strategies, Individual Behavior," *New Directions in Child Development* 40: 37–50.

Lewis, Robert A., Richard H. Rowland, and Ralph S. Clem (1976) *Nationality and Population Change in Russia and the USSR: An Evaluation of Census Data, 1897–1970*. New York: Praeger.

Lubin, Nancy (1984) *Labour and Nationality in Soviet Central Asia*. London: Macmillan.

_____(1991) "Implications of Ethnic and Demographic Trends," in William Fierman (ed.), *Soviet Central Asia: The Failed Transformation*. Boulder, CO: Westview Press, 36–61.

Macleod, Arlene E. (1991) *Accommodating Protest: Working Women, the New Veiling, and Change in Cairo*. New York: Columbia University Press.

Maillart, Ella K. (1935) *Turkestan Solo*. London: Putnam.

Makhlouf, Carla (1979) *Changing Veils: Women and Modernisation in North Yemen*. London: Croom Helm.

Mamonova, Tat'yana, ed. (1984) *Women and Russia: Feminist Writings from the Soviet Union*, translated by Rebecca Park and Catherine A. Fitzpatrick. Boston: Beacon Press.

Mandel, Ruth (2002) "A Marshall Plan of the Mind: The Political Economy of a Kazakh Soap Opera," in Faye D. Ginsburg, Lila Abu-Lughod, and Brian Larkin (eds.), *Media Worlds: Anthropology on New Terrain*. Berkeley and Los Angeles: University of California Press, 211–228.

Marcuse, Herbert (1961) *Soviet Marxism*. New York: Vintage Books.

Marx, Karl (1846) *The German Ideology*, edited by C. J. Arthur. New York: International Publishers (reprinted in 1967).

_____(1858) *Grundrisse*, New York: New Left Review (reprinted in 1973).

_____(1867) *Capital: Volume One*. New York: Vintage Books (reprinted in 1977).

Massell, Gregory (1974) *The Surrogate Proletariat: Muslim Women and Revolutionary Strategies in Soviet Central Asia 1919–1929*. Princeton: Princeton University Press.

Meakin, Annette (1903) *In Russian Turkestan*. London: George Allen.

Mernissi, Fatima (1987) *Beyond the Veil: Male-Female Dynamics in Modern Muslim Society*, revised edition. Bloomington: Indiana University Press.

Meyendorff, Baron Georg Von (1870) *A Journey from Orenburg to Bokhara in the Year 1820*. Calcutta: Foreign Department Press.

Mickiewicz, Ellen (1980) *Media and the Russian Public*. New York: Praeger.

Mills, Sara (2003) *Michel Foucault*. London: Routledge.

Minai, Naila (1981) *Women in Islam: Tradition and Transition in the Middle East*. London: John Murray.

MNAdvocates (2000) "Domestic Violence in Uzbekistan," Minneapolis: Minnesota Advocates for Human Rights, http://www.mnadvocates.org/Issues_Affecting_Women.html (608a3887-dd53–4796–8904–997a0131ca54/uploads/Uzbekreport.pdf) (October 8, 2005).

Mukta, Parita (2000) "Gender, Community, Nation: The Myth of Innocence," in Susie Jacobs, Ruth Jacobson, and Jennifer Marchbank (eds.), *States of Conflict: Gender, Violence and Resistance*. London and New York: Zed Books; 163–178.

Naamane-Guessous, Soumaya (1991) *Au-delà de Toute Pudeur*. Casablanca, Morocco: EDDIF.

Naficy, Hamid (1981) "Cinema as a Political Instrument," in Michael E. Bonine and Nikki Keddie (eds.), *Modern Iran: The Dialectics of Continuity and Change*. Albany: State University of New York, 341–360.

Najmabadi, Afsaneh (1991) "Hazards of Modernity and Morality: Women, State and Ideology in Contemporary Iran," in Deniz Kandiyoti (ed.), *Women, Islam and the State*, Philadelphia: Temple University Press, 48–76.

Nandy, Ashis (1983) *The Intimate Enemy: Loss and Recovery of Self under Colonialism*. Delhi: Oxford University Press.

_____(2004) *Bonfire of Creeds: The Essential Ashis Nandy*. Oxford: Oxford University Press.

Nazaroff, Pavel S. (1993) *Hunted Through Central Asia*. Oxford: Oxford University Press.

Nazpary Joma (2002) *Post-Soviet Chaos: Violence and Dispossession in Kazakhstan*. London and Sterling, VA: Pluto Press.

Northrop, Douglas (2001) "Subaltern Dialogues: Subversion and Resistance in Soviet Uzbek Family Law," *Slavic Review* 60(1): 115–139.

_____(2004) *Veiled Empire: Gender and Power in Stalinist Central Asia*. Ithaca: Cornell University Press.

Omran, Abdel R. (1992) *Family Planning in the Legacy of Islam*. London and New York: Routledge.

Pahlen, Count K. K. (1964) *Mission to Turkestan*. London: Oxford University Press.

Park, A. G. (1957) *Bolshevism in Turkestan, 1917–1927*. New York: Columbia University Press.

Pearson, Landon (1990) *Children of Glasnost: Growing Up Soviet*. Seattle: University of Washington Press.

Peristiany, J. G., ed. (1966) *Honour and Shame: The Values of Mediterranean Society*. London: Weidenfeld and Nicholson.

Personal Narratives Group (1989) *Interpreting Women's Lives: Feminist Theory and Personal Narratives*. Bloomington: Indiana University Press.

Piercy, Fred P. (1991) "Of Progress and Palm Trees: Indonesian Families Feel the Strains of Modernization," *Networker,* November/December, 57–62.

Pilkington, Hilary (1996) "Young Women in Provincial Gang Culture: A Case Study of Ul'ianovsk," in Hilary Pilkingon (ed.), *Gender, Generation and Identity in Contemporary Russia.* London: Routledge.

Pollard, Alan P., ed. (1991) *USSR Facts and Figures Annual,* vol. 15. Gulf Breeze, FL: Academic International Press.

Ranger, Terence (1993) "The Invention of Tradition Revisited: The Case of Colonial Africa," in Terence Ranger and Olufemi Vaughan (eds.), *Legitimacy and the State in Twentieth-Century Africa: Essays in Honour of A.H.M. Kirk-Greene.* Houndsmills: Macmillan, 62–109.

Rakowska-Harmstone, Teresa (1970) *Russia and Nationalism in Central Asia: The Case of Tadzhikistan.* Baltimore: Johns Hopkins University Press.

Robertson, Lawrence R., ed. (2000) *USSR Facts and Figures Annual,* vol. 26, II, Central Eurasian States. Gulf Breeze, FL: Academic International Press.

Rogers, Barbara (1980) *The Domestication of Women: Discrimination in Developing Societies.* London: Tavistock.

Rorlich, Azade-Ayse (1991) "Islam and Atheism: Dynamic Tension in Soviet Central Asia," in William Fierman (ed.), *Soviet Central Asia: The Failed Transformation.* Boulder, CO: Westview Press, 186–218.

Rumer, Boris (1991) "Central Asia's Cotton Economy and Its Costs," in William Fierman (ed.), *Soviet Central Asia: The Failed Transformation.* Boulder, CO: Westview Press, 62–89.

Saïd, Edward (1978) *Orientalism.* New York: Pantheon Books.

Schrijvers, Joke (1991) "Dialectics of a Dialogical Ideal: Studying Down, Studying Sideways, and Studying Up," in Lorraine Nencel and Peter Pels (eds.), *Constructing Knowledge: Authority and Critique in Social Science.* London: Sage.

_____(1993) *The Violence of Development.* Amsterdam: Spinhuis.

Schuyler, Eugene (1876) *Turkistan.* New York: Charles Scribner's.

Schwarz, Franz von (1900) *Turkestan, die Wiege der Indogermanischen Völker.* Freiburg in Breisgau: Herder.

Scott, James (1985) *Weapons of the Weak: Everyday Forms of Peasant Resistance.* New Haven and London: Yale University Press.

_____(1990) *Domination and the Arts of Resistance: Hidden Transcripts.* New Haven: Yale University Press.

Singerman, Diane (1995) *Avenues of Participation: Family, Politics and Networks in Urban Quarters of Cairo.* Princeton, NJ: Princeton University Press.

Storey, J. D., et al. (1997) "Perceptions of Family Planning and Reproductive Health Issues: Focus Group Discussions in Kazakhstan, Turkmenistan, Kyrgyzstan, and Uzbekistan," IEC Field Report 10 (August), http://iussp2005.princeton.edu/download.aspx?submissionId=52237(October 8, 2005).

Strong, Anna Louise (1930) *Red Star in Samarkand.* London: Williams and Norgate.

Sunier, Thijl (1998) "Islam and Interest Struggle: Religious Collective Action among Turkish Muslims in the Netherlands," in Steven Vertovec and Alisdair Rogers (eds.), *Muslim European Youth: Reproducing Ethnicity, Religion, Culture.* Aldershot: Ashgate, 39–57.

Tadjbakhsh, Shahrbanou (1998) "Between Lenin and Allah: Women in Ideology in Tajikistan," in Herbert Bodman and Nayereh Tohidi (eds.), *Women in Muslim Societies: Diversity within Unity*. Boulder, CO: Lynne Rienner Publishers, 163–185.

Tett, Gillian (1995) "Ambiguous Alliances: Marriage and Identity in a Muslim Village in Soviet Tajikistan," Ph.D. dissertation, University of Cambridge, UK.

Tohidi, Nayereh (1997) "The Intersection of Gender, Ethnicity and Islam in Soviet and Post-Soviet Azerbaijan," *Nationalities Papers* 25(1): 147–167.

Tokhtakhodjaeva, Marfua (1995) *Between the Slogans of Communism and the Laws of Islam*, translated from the Russian by Sufian Aslam, edited by Cassandra Balchin. Lahore: Shirkat Gah.

Tolmacheva, M. A. (1993) "The Muslim Woman in Soviet Central Asia," *Central Asian Survey* 12(4): 531–548.

Triandis, Harry (1995) *Individualism and Collectivism*. Boulder, CO: Westview Press.

UNDP (1995) "Republic of Tajikistan: Human Development Report," Dushanbe, United Nations Development Program/Government of Tajikistan.

Vaidyanath, R. (1967) *The Formation of the Soviet Central Asian Republics: A Study in Soviet Nationalities Policy 1917–1936*. New Delhi: People's Publishing House.

Vansina, Jan (1990) *Paths in the Rainforests: Towards a History of Political Tradition in Equatorial Africa*. London: James Currey.

Vertovec, Steven, and Alisdair Rogers (1998) "Introduction," in Steven Vertovec and Alisdair Rogers (eds.), *Muslim European Youth: Reproducing Ethnicity, Religion, Culture*. Aldershot: Ashgate, 1–24.

Watson, Helen (1994) "Separation and Reconciliation: Marital Conflict among the Muslim Poor in Cairo," in Camillia Fawzi El-Solh and Judy Mabro (eds.), *Muslim Women's Choices: Religious Belief and Social Reality*. Oxford: Berg Publishers, 32–54.

Weedon, Chris (1999) *Feminism, Theory, and the Politics of Difference*. Oxford and Malden, MA: Blackwell.

Weyland, Petra (1994) *Inside the Third World Village*. London and New York: Routledge.

White, Jenny B. (2002) *Islamist Mobilization in Turkey: A Study in Vernacular Politics*. Seattle and London: University of Washington Press.

WHO (2000) "Violence against Women: WHO 1999 Pilot Survey in Tajikistan—Working Document, Workshop on Violence against Women in Tajikistan, Dushanbe, 29–30 March, 2000." Copenhagen: World Health Organisation, Regional Office for Europe.

Wikan, Unni (1980) *Life among the Poor in Cairo*. London: Tavistock Publications.

———(1984) "Shame and Honour, a Contestable Pair," *Man Quarterly* 19(4): 635–652.

Wixman, Ronald (1991) "Ethnic Attitudes and Relations in Modern Uzbek Cities," in William Fierman (ed.), *Soviet Central Asia: The Failed Transformation*. Boulder, CO: Westview Press, 159–185.

Wolf, Diane L. (1996a) "Situating Feminist Dilemmas in Fieldwork," in Diane L. Wolf (ed.), *Feminist Dilemmas in Fieldwork*. Boulder, CO: Westview Press.

Wolf, Margery (1996b) "Afterwards: Musings from an Old Gray Wolf," in Diane L. Wolf (ed.), *Feminist Dilemmas in Fieldwork*. Boulder, CO: Westview Press.

World Bank (1994) "Tajikistan: A World Bank Country Study," Washington, DC: The World Bank.

Russian Language Books

Bozrikova, Tat'yana (2003) "Tadzhikistan," in *Lyudi i roli: genderny format*. St. Petersburg: Izdatelstvo Zhurnala "Zvezda," 81–106.

Donish, Ahmed (1960) "O pravilakh supruzheskoy zhizni i vrazhde sverkrovi," in *Puteshestvie iz Bukhary v Peterburg*. Dushanbe: Tadzhikgosizdat, 180–202.

Gafarova, M. G. (1969) *Dukhovny oblik zhenshchiny Sovetskogo vostoka*. Dushanbe: Irfon.

Khegai, Margarita (2002) Sovremennye formy brachnykh otnosheniy v Tadzhikistane i prava cheloveka," in *Nekotorye aspekty gendernykh issledovaniy v Tadzhikistane: Sbornik materialov nauchnykh seminarov*. Dushanbe: Open Society Institute, 55–67.

Khushkadamova, Khalimakhon O. (1993)"Otrazhenie sotsial'nogo polozheniya zhenshchin v periodicheskoy pechati Tadzhikistana," kanditat sotsialnikh nauk. Moscow: Rossiskaya Akademiya Nauk, Sotsiologichesky i Sotsial-psikhologichesky Tsentr.

Kislyakov, N. A. (1935) "Izuchenie patriarkhal'noy bol'shoy sem'i v doline r. Vandzh (Tadzhikistan)," *Sovetskaya Etnografiya* 1: 119–121.

_____(1959) *Sem'ya i brak u Tadzhikov. Po materialam kontsa XIX–nachala XX veka*, Moscow and Leningrad: Izdatel'stvo Akademiya Nauk SSSR.

Kislyakov, N. A., and Pisarchik, A. K. (1976) *Tadzhiki Kategina i Darvaza*, III. Dushanbe: Donish.

Lenin, V. I. (1960) *Stat'i i rechi o Sredney Azii i Uzbekistane: Sbornik*. Tashkent: Partizdat TsK.

Monogarova L. F. (1982) "Struktura sovremmennoy gorodskoy sem'i Tadzhikov (po materialam gorodov Ura-Tyube i Isfary)," *Sovetskaya Etnografiya*, 3 volumes.

Nalivkin, V., and Nalivkina, M. (1886) *Ocherk byta zhenshchiny osedlago tuzemnago naseleniya Fergany*. Kazan': Tipografiya Imperatorskago Universitea.

Nukhrat, Antonina Ivanovna (1930) *Bytovaya rabota*. Moscow: Tsentrosoyuz.

Pal'vanova, Bibi (1982) *Emantsipatsiya musulman'ki*. Moscow: Izdatel'stvo Nauka, Glavnaya Redaktsiya Vostochnoy Literatury.

Pechernikova, I. A. (1965) "Vospitanie poslushaniya i trudolyubiya u detei v sem'ye," Moscow: Prosveshchenie.

Raskreposhchenie (1971) *Veliki oktyabr' i raskreposhchenie zhenshchin Sredney Azii i Kazakhstana (1917–1936gg): Sbornik dokumentov*. Moscow: Izdatel'stvo Mysl.

Shishov, A. (1910) *Tadzhiki*. Tashkent: Turkest.

Suzi, Avo (1989) *Tadzhikskaya svad'ba*. Dushanbe: Adib.

Index